PEDALING THE

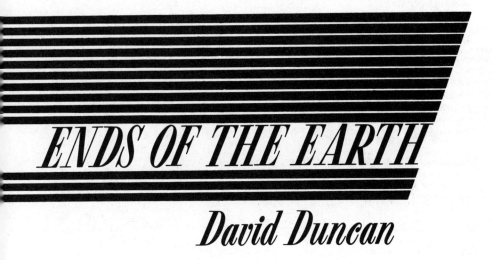

ENDS OF THE EARTH

David Duncan

A Fireside Book
Published by Simon & Schuster, Inc.
New York

This Fireside Edition, 1986
Published by Simon & Schuster, Inc.
Simon & Schuster Building
Rockefeller Center
1230 Avenue of the Americas
New York, New York 10020
FIRESIDE and colophon are registered trademarks
of Simon & Schuster, Inc.

Photo on page 16 © Patricia Duncan.
Photos on pages 40 and 220 © Donald Duncan.
Photos on pages 110 and 168 © David Duncan.

Designed by Levavi & Levavi

Manufactured in the United States of America

10 9 8 7 6 5 4 3 2 1
10 9 8 7 6 5 4 3 2 1 Pbk.

Library of Congress Cataloging in Publication Data

Duncan, David.
  Pedaling the ends of the earth.

  1. Bicycle touring. 2. Duncan, Don. 3. Logan, Jim. 4. Duncan,
David. 5. Cyclists—United States—Biography. 6. Voyages around the
world. I. Title.
GV1044.D86 1985   796.6'092'2 [B]   85-10824
ISBN: 0-671-49289-6
ISBN: 0-671-62805-4 Pbk.

Portions of this book are based on the
following articles:

"Across the Sinai," Kansas City Star,
April 11, 1982, page 1J.

"Day of Rage," Vassar Quarterly,
Winter 1984.

"Smallest of Medical Relief
Organizations," Kansas City Star,
September 5, 1982, page 1F.

"Beyond the Headlines," Bicycling,
January, February 1983.

*To Mom and Dad
and to Laura, my love*

GREENLAND

NORTH
AMERICA

North Atlantic Ocean

SAN FRANCISCO

DALLAS

WASHINGTON

MADRID

Pacific Ocean

SOUTH
AMERICA

South Atlantic Ocean

——— by Bicycle
- - - by Plane, Boat, Train

Arctic Ocean

ASIA

EUROPE

FLORENCE
ATHENS
JERUSALEM
CAIRO
JEDDAH
PORT SUDAN
KHARTOUM
AFRICA

KARACHI

NEW DELHI
KATMANDU

TOKYO

Pacific Ocean

MANILA

SINGAPORE

Indian Ocean

South Pacific Ocean

AUSTRALIA

The World Bike for HOPE
December 1, 1981 – December 16, 1982

Author's Note

I have done my best to provide an accurate depiction of people and places cited in this book based on notes, journal entries, and subsequent research. In a few instances, I was forced to rely on memory. Where possible, I have used actual names. However, on occasion, I have changed names to protect the privacy or safety of individuals.

Contents

I have discovered that the essential difference between me and them is that, for me, hardship is an adventure. For them, it's a way of life.
—Ellen "Gruffy" Clough
American Nurse, Sudan

Introduction: Leaving Home

Just after graduating from college, I decided to take a bicycle trip around the world. My goal was simple. I wanted to immerse myself in the backroads of our planet: to see the colors, breathe the air, and try to understand the world beyond the frontiers of American suburbia. Raised on "The Brady Bunch" and *Star Wars*, I wanted to see if the world out there was real, if it even existed.

Against tremendous statistical odds, I happened to be born in America during the latter stages of the baby boom era. It was a comfortable moment to be born. Growing up in a suburban homestead near Kansas City, I spent my time watching prime-time reruns, eating Stouffer's frozen dinners, and playing astronaut with GI-Joe dolls. In school I was privy to a number of "serious" facts, which were stored in my brain alongside bits of random information ranging from the theme song of "Gilligan's Island" to how many pickles were served on a McDonald's Big Mac.

Yet as I grew up, I sometimes wondered what I had really learned about the world beyond my limited background. I knew words like "poverty" and "overpopulation"—my family frequently talked about these problems over meatloaf and Kool-Aid at dinner. I knew what villages in Egypt looked like from photos in *National Geographic*—full-color shots of neat, mud-dung huts in a lazy grove of eucalyptus trees. I had also seen the severe black-and-white shots of emaciated children on Save the Children posters. I was familiar with concepts like "war" and "violence," having grown up as one of those kids exposed to the Vietnam War in their living rooms. But what did I really know about these things? They were as close and as distant as the bridge of the starship *Enterprise* or the planet Tatooine in *Star Wars*.

In college, I crammed my head full of even more facts about the world. I studied everything from nuclear warfare to Hellenistic sculpture. I watched student productions of Shakespeare, heard speakers discuss starvation in Asia, and attended three Bruce Springsteen concerts. By graduation, my college ascertained that I had learned enough to get the letters "B.A." after my name. I was certified as an educated man, and ready to face the world. My peers in college were likewise certified as a generation on the edge of maturity. We were told it was time for us to begin to assert our influence.

Yet it still troubled me that our basic training was conducted in an atmosphere so far removed from the reality of our planet. We were exposed to more information than any other generation in history, but knowing every fact in the world does not equal understanding.

After graduation, I moved to Washington, D.C., and began playing with the idea of a world bicycle trip. My plan was to take off for several weeks or months and try to reconcile all those confusing facts I had learned with a large dose of reality as observed from the seat of a bicycle. The fact that I was a fledgling journalist in Washington with no money (and no bike) didn't really deter me. I saved my meager salary, bought a bicycle, and began actively talking about my idea with friends over hamburgers and beer.

The project remained stalled in the talk stage for almost a year. I determined that the trip would cost at least $10,000, not counting salary and career momentum lost by checking out of whatever career track I was on. Then came a break. My uncle, a doctor with Project HOPE, the health care foundation, suggested that I organize my trip for charity, like a super bike-a-thon. I could organize sponsors to pay for the trip, and enroll individuals and corporations to contribute "per mile" contributions to HOPE.

It took another difficult year to organize the World Bike for HOPE. It was a time of false starts and dead ends, when it seemed as though everyone in the world was trying to find sponsorship for a trip around the world. At the same time, I was struggling to locate that elusive fast track into a career as a writer and journalist. But finally, with the help of family and friends, I was able to attract corporate sponsors and, with the help of HOPE staffers, organize a worldwide fund-raising and publicity program for Project HOPE. I secured route permissions from foreign embassies, organized international banking and shipping schedules, and began to collect equipment and supplies.

It quickly became apparent that I couldn't safely ride around the world by myself. Searching everywhere for three other fellows who happened to have a year off and were in reasonable physical condition took almost the entire organizational year. My brother Don was the first to enlist. He had just graduated from Bowdoin College in Maine and was anxious to launch a career in photography. Like me, he had done little bicycle touring, but he was in good condition after four years of tromping through the wilderness of Maine with his camera. I thought we would make a good team; he would photograph the expedition and I would write about it.

Next to sign up was Dave French, the thirty-three-year-old Director of the American Youth Hostel's Washington, D.C., chapter, a group active in organizing bicycle tours in the mid-Atlantic states. Dave, a short, balding man with a square chin and quiet demeanor, had been a bicycle commuter for years, and had bicycled across the States and extensively in Europe. As the equipment man for the expedition, he designed special gearing for our eighteen-speed bikes, assembled caches of spare parts, prepared three overseas drop boxes for resupplies, and organized our world itinerary.

Our fourth slot remained open until just three weeks before our departure. Jim Logan, thirty-one, appeared one afternoon in my living room with a dirty beard, a red Afro, and a threadbare army jacket. Outside was a battered Fuji bicycle locked to a street sign. He had been biking north towards New England when word reached him about a world bicycle expedition in need of a cyclist.

Jim was a former legislative aide to U.S. Congressman Thomas Steed, who represented Jim's hometown of Norman, Oklahoma. Steed had just retired from Washington after thirty-two years, which left Jim temporarily without a job. Like Dave, he had been active in the American Youth Hostels, leading some of their organized trips in the Washington area. In the brief time before the expedition left America, he helped Dave assemble equipment and provided a much-needed dose of fussy detail work. He was avid about details. He had a blue notebook with JIM penned in black letters on the front. Inside was a repository of lists of everything from his daily activities to how many birds he had observed in his lifetime (Jim was an avid bird-watcher, and hoped to increase his life list of sightings on the trip).

The World Bike for HOPE began on a cold, drizzly day during the winter of 1981. Just after dawn on December 1, four red, white, and blue bicycles weighing 90 pounds each leaned in a line against the brick wall of the townhouse I lived in, waiting to be taken around the world. Sponsors had donated all the equipment. Fuji provided the bicycles, Suntour and Avocet the gearing, Eddie Bauer the sleeping bags and cold-weather clothing, Northface the tents, and Eclipse the panniers. Inside the bright-red panniers we had packed everything from rabies vaccines to a small library of Berlitz language guides. We had portable stoves, Swiss army knives, a tiny shortwave radio, Project HOPE brochures and contribution forms, traveler's checks, and visas. Our personal gear included Don's cameras, lenses, and film, weighing over 25 pounds. Jim had 10 pounds of bird books and binoculars. I had notebooks and tape recorders for interviews. Dave had only one item: *The Complete Book of Bicycling*, by Eugene A. Sloane (Trident, 1970),* which he called "the bible of bicycling."

We had no idea what we were getting into that morning. Our bikes and panniers were shiny and new, our gears greased and humming. Like Boy Scouts packing off to camp, we were sure

---

* Sloane's book has since been updated and is currently available as *The All New Complete Book of Bicycling* (Fireside, 1983).

the next months would be crammed with adventure and excitement. In retrospect, our lack of preparations were startling. We packed no masks for the dust that pervades the Third World. We packed only one small vial of iodine each for purifying water, and one small jar of dysentery medicine. We laughed over Jim's insistence on taking THREE extra tire tubes and three tire patch kits each, not realizing that each of us would have well over a hundred punctures before the trip was finished.

Our mental preparation was equally unrealistic. We had no comprehension of the difficulties we would face—the choking dust, the steamy, unremitting heat, the fruit and vegetables rotting in the sun, the open sewers and the crowds of filthy, ragged children. Physically, we were prepared for a grueling ride, but we were completely unprepared for the hardships that would slowly break down our bodies and rot away our resolve. Struggling to survive, we would see some of our most cherished notions crushed by the weight of our misery and the misery of those around us. We would confront basic questions about issues of wealth and poverty, war, disease, and privilege. Setting out to immerse ourselves in the "real world," we would get much more than we had bargained for. Racked by dysentery and disease, robbed of some of our basic equipment, far away from home, we would discover the darker edges of our souls, those elements of human nature that drive people to fits of rage and violence. We would also discover unknown strengths and joy, both in ourselves and in the people around us.

The drizzle turned to rain that morning in Washington as we strapped on domed helmets and adjusted little rearview mirrors above our right eyes. Our clothes, like our helmets, were identical—black leg tights, World Bike for HOPE T-shirts, and orange phosphorescent safety vests. Looking like shock troops preparing for a high-powered mission, we climbed onto our bicycles and began pedaling to a send-off ceremony on Capitol Hill. In front of the Capitol my parents, friends, and supporters would bid us farewell as the press recorded our departure. From the Hill, we planned to bike to the National Airport for a flight to Spain, where our journey would begin.

WEST

*Send-off ceremony, U.S.
Capitol, Washington, D.C.
Left to right: David
Duncan, Donald Duncan,
Jim Logan, David French.*

1. Mediterranean Winter

Arriving at the Barajas International Airport outside of Madrid, the four of us wearily packed our bikes and pedaled into a gray, drizzly afternoon toward Old Madrid. Wanting only to find a place to sleep after a long flight from Washington, we took the most direct route into town, a superhighway cutting through concrete neighborhoods of warehouses, factories, and high-rises. Boxy sedans and towering semis rushed past in splashes of muck and clouds of black exhaust. Being unfamiliar with my new bike and my ninety pounds of gear, I struggled to steer a straight course on the superhighway shoulder. It took an extraordinary amount of concentration. One major wobble could have thrown me under the wheels of a speeding car or truck.

About five kilometers * from the airport we eased down a long hill and glided into the black shadow of a highway underpass. As I rode out from under the bridge something heavy crashed to the ground a few inches from my bike. Looking up, I saw

---

* One kilometer equals .6 miles.

two pairs of arms chucking bricks and stones. "Heads up!" screamed one of my companions. "Somebody's throwing stuff off that bridge!" I tensed up and pedaled hard to get out of range as more bricks shattered on the pavement. Then came a loud crash of glass. A tiny sedan, its windshield shattered, swerved toward me. I slammed on my brakes, steering hard to the right, where I slid into a pile of garbage and weeds on the edge of the highway.

On the shoulder, the damaged car stopped near Jim, Don, and Dave. An elderly man stumbled out as the guys dropped their bikes and ran over to help. The old man's clothing and skin were covered with a thin sheen of tiny glass fragments. Blood dribbled from a small cut in his forehead. I pushed my bike back onto the shoulder as Jim pulled gauze pads out of the group first aid kit. Fortunately the brick had crashed through the passenger side of the windshield, so the man was not seriously hurt. But the incident shook us up. In just a few seconds a random act of violence could have ended our journey before it had even begun.

After checking into a budget *pensión* in Madrid, we slept for twenty hours in a whitewashed room smelling of fish and mildew. The room was part of an ancient, dilapidated townhouse on a narrow street in the old city. The proprietor was a fat, toothless man in a sleeveless shirt who charged us an extra five hundred pesetas to allow the bikes into the room.

For two days in Madrid we rested and organized our gear. At night, we drank *cervezas* in brightly lit bars where everyone smoked filterless cigarettes. The young women wore bright red lipstick and pointed, spiked heels. The men had long, curly hair and wore tight blue jeans. One afternoon, we walked through the plazas and narrow streets, using a government tourist map to find statues and famous buildings. We saw the worn stone face of Philip II, who launched the Spanish Armada, and a statue of Isabella, the queen who pawned a jeweled necklace so that Christopher Columbus could afford to discover America.

The morning we left Madrid, a cold mist sprayed over the city. Climbing onto my bike, I pulled a pair of bubble goggles over my face like Christopher George in "Rat Patrol." It was a thrill to push off and tuck my feet into the shiny toe clips attached to my pedals. We were actually beginning the journey! As we bicycled east toward Barcelona and the sea, the ornate, old-world core of Madrid faded into suburbs of dreary concrete high-rises. We passed prefab stores, a huge bullring, and the vast cemetery de la Almudena, where tens of thousands of Spaniards lay buried under iron crosses and groves of bayber-ries and maples. Just beyond the cemetery, the city abruptly ended. We steered off the main highway and onto a two-lane back road. Here we caught a brief, storybook glimpse of rural life in Old Spain. A man in a black beret and a shabby wool coat rode by on a tiny donkey cart loaded with shiny oranges. The cart was decorated with stripes of orange and green paint. Tin bells were strung across the donkey's reins. Don stopped us to take a photograph, but before he could get out his camera, the man and his cart were gone.

In the hills around Madrid, we biked through a half-dozen small towns of neat adobe houses and roadside cafés. Since it was Sunday and close to Christmas, the old churches broadcast Christmas carols over PA systems attached to steeples. The tinny, angelic music echoed through the hills. In one town, where we took a break in a small café, two aged men with yellow teeth bought us shot glasses of cognac to go with our *café con leche* and doughnuts. When we told them about the world trip, the men wagged their hands and grinned, a sign of disbelief in Spain.

Outside the café, kids in heavy sweaters and burr haircuts gathered around to chatter and laugh at our funny clothes. *"Buenos días!"* they shouted, treating us like celebrities. We gave all the kids Project HOPE buttons. While I pinned them on, Don took publicity photographs.

Around noon, the sun popped out of the clouds, tingling our pale winter skin with warmth. Feeling a tremendous relief to be finally on the road, we sang old Beatles songs and shouted out conversations about everything we could think of. We talked about the El Greco paintings on display in Madrid, about Ronald Reagan, and about what it would be like on the Sahara desert.

Each of us had a team job that day. Dave French was the group leader, a position that would rotate each week. He made most of the basic decisions on the road and was in charge of the team purse and keeping expenditure records for HOPE. Jim was the navigator. Riding first, he carried the group maps and kept track of where we were going. Don was in charge of buying and distributing food. I had the unenviable task of cooking and cleaning pots.

That first day we cycled fifty-seven kilometers to Guadalajara, a town built in the foothills of the La Alcarria mountains, one of several ranges stretching across central Spain. We happened to arrive in Guadalajara on a national holiday. It was the fifth anniversary of the new Spanish constitution, the document that restored democracy to Spain after three and a half decades of Fascist rule under General Francisco Franco. Guadalajarans celebrated by shooting off firecrackers and singing patriotic songs. Brass bands played marching tunes, and red and yellow Spanish flags hung from every balcony and doorway in the ancient city. We checked into a small *pensión* with the idea of joining in the celebration, but we were too tired. After a simple dinner of baked chicken, boiled potatoes, and thick red wine, we all went to bed, dropping off into the contented sleep of absolute exhaustion.

From Guadalajara, we turned off the main highway between Madrid and Barcelona to follow a back road marked in yellow on our Michelin maps. Almost immediately we began climbing, steering around switchback after switchback into the dry, rocky La Alcarria range. We planned to use Spain and the rest of Europe as a training leg. It was a time to get into shape and to learn everything we could about bicycle touring and each other. But none of us had expected 10-percent grades and ragged mountain roads. For most of the leg in Spain, we would be climbing up and down mountains or pedaling across wavy stretches of rocky, windswept high country.

Large segments of this land seemed locked away and abandoned by the modern Spain we had seen in the suburbs around Madrid. The roads were narrow and had not been repaired for years. Most of the buildings were either abandoned or in disrepair: ruined farmhouses, shattered sentry posts, and half-abandoned villages. It was an ancient, exotic world to me, full of legends and mystery. I could easily visualize a platoon of conquistadors marching past in glittering armor, or a Don Juan character riding calmly on the back of a donkey. Women along the road were dressed from head to toe in black. Men dressed in simple wool clothing. Some of the villages didn't have running water, and we saw little evidence of automation. Donkey carts outnumbered automobiles in many villages, and most of the hard work in the rocky fields was done by hand.

Dave French, our most experienced biker, devised our daily schedule in central Spain. The routine came straight out of *The Complete Book of Bicycling.* Shortly after dawn we would wake up and begin to break camp. In Spain, this took nearly two hours as we fumbled to disconnect tent poles, fold tarps and sleeping bags, and keep carbon deposits from clogging our MSR stoves. Once on the road we biked steadily, stopping every sixty to ninety minutes (as the book said) for a fifteen- or twenty-minute break. In villages we drank *café con leche* and snacked on doughnuts in local cafés. For roadside breaks, we sipped water from our bike bottles and ate crackers or candy bars. Lunch consisted of bread, cheese, yogurt, and sodas. Afternoon was a repeat of the morning, with breaks and a stop to buy dinner food. About dusk we looked for a flat spot off the road to set up tents. Campsites were easy to find in the sparsely populated high country, although camping in the open made us a little nervous. Every night we completely unpacked the bikes to store the gear inside the tents. The bikes were attached to trees with Kryptonite locks.

One day about noon, we turned off to buy lunch at an ancient village about a half mile from the main road. The village was a small cluster of ancient adobe buildings built on a knoll rising from the floor of a broad valley. Ringing the top of the knoll were the broken walls of a medieval castle, defending several ruined buildings and a tall television antenna held in place by steel guys.

We rode down a dirt path winding through fields of turned soil. Jim and Dave stayed behind to watch the bikes while Don and I walked to the village in search of lunch supplies. Don had his two Nikons and his light meter around his neck. As we got closer I saw that most of the buildings on the upper tier of the village had collapsed. A Catholic church nestled among the ruined buildings on the high street was still intact, although its plaster facade had mostly disappeared. Its squat, Romanesque steeple had a bronze bell weathered as green as the Statue of Liberty. On all four sides of the steeple, under the bell, were large clocks. The one facing us had stopped with both hands aiming at twelve.

Near the village gate we met three old men sunning themselves on a wooden bench. They wore baggy wool clothes and black berets. White stubble grew around wrinkled, sunburned faces. Their lively chatter stopped as we approached.

"Buenos días," I said, taking off my helmet and smiling.

"*Americanos*," I said. They stared at two men in cycling tights and goggles with a dumbfounded look that would become very familiar in the months ahead.

"Dave, do you think they'd mind if I took a photo?" Don whispered.

"I don't know," I said, looking at the confused faces. I sensed that we were intruding. I had a vague sense of violation. It's one thing to see a nameless old man in a *National Geographic* article, but quite another to be facing that nameless old man with a camera. "Why don't you ask them?" I said.

Don held up his camera. The men understood and solemnly shook their heads. They didn't want their photos taken.

"I wish I could talk to them," said Don, "to tell them what we're doing."

Walking under a stone archway, we entered an empty plaza. In the middle, under several shade trees, was a cracked fountain brimming with wet, blackened leaves. The storefronts here were whitewashed. A couple of them had small verandas decorated with curling rails of iron. Painted signs identified the *carnicería* (butcher), *panadería* (baker), a bar, and a vegetable market. But the plaza was empty. It was eerie, as if all of the people had left just a moment before.

"I'm going to get a few photos," said Don, walking toward the fountain.

"I'll get the groceries," I said, heading toward the vegetable store. Our voices sounded hollow against the empty buildings.

As I stepped into the vegetable shop, a damp cool mingled with the sharp odor of pepper, spices, and the softer scent of freshly baked bread. The store was dark and spooky, like a cave. The floor-to-ceiling shelves were stuffed with everything from dried lentils in burlap sacks to cassette tapes of Julio Iglesias and Elvis Presley. The old woman in black behind the counter was almost completely round. She eyed me suspiciously but said nothing. I pointed at a cake of cheese, some bread, a jar of mayonnaise, four oranges, and four Pepsis. The woman charged me 650 pesetas, a gross overcharge. But I was too shy at this point in the trip to argue with a round woman in black. I paid quickly and escaped into the sun illuminating the empty plaza.

Don was nowhere in sight, so I decided to have a look around the village. Turning up a narrow flight of stone steps, I headed for the ruined buildings on the high street. Desolation greeted me: jagged walls, collapsed roofs, and piles of junk. Poking out of the rubble were window frames, decaying shoes, dozens of squashed cans, and pieces of furniture. One of the broken walls was covered with fresh graffiti. It was a surprising sign of life amidst the destruction. It was also a measure of the divergent politics in Spain. I saw the hammer and sickle of the Communist Party, and the initials of the ruling socialist party were slashed out with black X's. The symbol of the right-wing phalangist party, the party of Franco, was circled in black.

I sat on a flat stone and peeled an orange. Across the street was a three-story house whose front wall had collapsed. It was as if a wrecking crew had set a series of explosions designed to rip the wall off neatly so that the interior was suddenly exposed to the street. Inside, the rooms were faintly blue. In one second-floor room, probably a bedroom, sheets of washed-out red wallpaper sagged on the walls like folds of fat stained brown by rain and dust. All of the furniture was gone, except for the bottom half of a steel desk chair. I split my orange into sections, getting the sticky juice on my hands as I popped the slices into my mouth.

A great battle must have occurred here, I thought. I imagined cannonballs arcing in plumes of smoke to shatter these walls. I saw terrified peasants scrambling for cover, and men in bright uniforms shooting muskets from behind the rubble. I assumed that this destruction was caused by war, because I couldn't believe that people would just abandon a whole street. But this guess was almost certainly wrong. Before the trip was over we would see whole cities in Africa and Asia that had been abandoned and then ruined by time almost as thoroughly as if they had been blown up by a squad of crack artillery.

I stood up, tossed the orange peels into my food bag, and walked toward the church. As I opened the door, a cool, musty blast of air blew into my face. Inside was a vision out of an Edgar Allan Poe short story. My skin tingled. The room was nearly obscured by shadows. Medieval flags hung rotting against the walls. Several rows of dark pews led up to the altar, which was covered with clean linens and fresh flowers. The flowers seemed out of place—a freshness and delicacy incongruous with death and decay. Silver candlesticks and other expensive ornaments glinted in faint sunlight falling through tiny windows up near the high ceiling. Taking a step forward, I scraped my cycling shoe against the slate floor. A deafening *squeeeeeeek!* echoed through the musty chamber. I froze, feeling like a criminal caught red-handed as a few dark forms turned from their prayers to stare at this gross violation of their worship. Without looking back, I slipped quietly into the shadows and out the door.

During the first few days of the trip, the four of us got along well, like easygoing strangers assigned to the same hotel room at an Elks convention. We were overly polite, telling jokes and being all-around great guys. We helped each other to excess. A flat tire or loose bolt was immediately surrounded by four sets of tire irons or four wrenches. We spent hours talking in old cafés, on the bikes and around campfires. Jim and I dominated these conversations because we loved to talk, although Don surprised me by having a dry wit (my little brother?) that often kept us amused for hours. Dave remained the quietest of our crew. When he spoke, it was usually about biking or about Vermont, his favorite place in the world. "Jeez," he would say, "you oughta see Vermont in the fall. It's the best biking in the world."

But even in the first few days, arguments began that would dominate the next few months. The obvious arguments over who cleans the pots and who sets up the tents were mostly muted by our system of assigning duties. We also established a number of group rotations: first shower, first up in the morning, first choice of tent or bed, and first choice of meals. This system more or less worked, despite the fact that four people always have four different solutions to every problem.

But our system couldn't cover everything. Within a few days of leaving Madrid, the question of how fast we would pace ourselves became a source of tension. We were torn between a desire to go slow and absorb our environment, and an obligation to follow the World Bike for HOPE schedule. In Washington I had put together a detailed schedule based on pedaling an average of one hundred kilometers (sixty miles) a day. Publicity events, plane flights, our budget, and everything else depended on this schedule. Unfortunately, the schedule was completely unrealistic, failing to compensate for unknown factors like terrain and the availability of food and campsites. We kept to my schedule for exactly one day, the first day, when we pedaled from Madrid to Guadalajara.

The question of pacing was complicated by our individual

personalities. I constantly pushed for speed, encouraging everyone to bike as fast as they could. I tended to push hard and never let up. At the other extreme was Dave French, who favored patience and a steady, measured pace. "The true bicycle tourist is never in a hurry to get anywhere," he would say, citing *The Complete Book of Bicycling*. He called me Rocket Legs, and said it was inevitable that my knees would collapse if I kept going so fast. Between these two extremes were Jim and Don. My brother needed time to get in shape because of an old leg injury, so he began the trip by pedaling slowly. This drove me crazy at first, because I thought he was using the leg as an excuse for not trying hard enough. The truth was that he didn't share my compulsiveness. He was calm and generally took things as they came. Jim, as usual, was complex in his attitude toward speed. Later, it would become obvious that he shared my compulsion to hurry. But in the early days he tried to mediate among everyone's preferences. "I don't think it's worth it to argue about how fast we go," he would say with a smile.

Six days out from Madrid, our ragged back road intersected with a major highway at Molina de Aragón. Above the city a crumbling castle encircled a tall crag, its walls protecting ruined buildings bleached and pocked by the centuries. Modern Molina was an industrial town. The twisting medieval streets in the core had been almost overwhelmed by a thick ring of dusty, steaming complexes of machinery and concrete buildings. Exhausted after the climb through the mountains, we stopped at the first *pensión* we found, the Pedro.

After a shower and short nap, I went to the bar on the first floor of the Pedro. Standing at the counter in my "civilian" clothes of khaki pants and blue oxford-cloth shirt, I sipped an Amstel and watched the bar fill up with truckers and laborers. Under a heavy cloud of smoke, a score of rugged, stubble-faced men drank and played cards at tables made of vinyl and stainless steel. A few men pumped the arms of two slot machines in a back corner. Others blasted aliens on a video machine. Hanging above the bar, a television with the sound turned off was showing *Captain Blood*. I watched Errol Flynn duel with the pirate Levausser and capture the beautiful Olivia de Havilland.

Finishing my beer, I called the bartender for a refill. He was a young man, about thirty-five years old, with a pasty face and oily hair. A broken incisor jutting from his upper row of teeth did not spoil a pleasant smile. He asked if I was an *Americano.*

"*Sí*," I said, adding that I spoke no Spanish.

"You like Ronald Reagan?" he asked in broken English. I shrugged.

"Ronald Reagan very bad," he said, adding something in Spanish. He picked up a bar napkin, smiled, and began scribbling. First, he drew a swastika. "Ronald Reagan," he said. Then he drew a hammer and sickle, and looked up at me. I was supposed to choose between the two. I shrugged again. The bartender, laughing at me, drew a bold slash over the swastika. "Bad," he said. Then he circled the hammer and sickle, which was "good."

Suddenly a man beside me reached across the bar and grabbed the napkin. He had a sunburned face, a rough wool sweater, and tall, black, shiny boots. Scowling, he crumpled it up and muttered something to me in Spanish. Flipping the napkin over his shoulder, he took a long drag from his cigarette and stared at the bartender. Then he pulled out a ballpoint pen, grabbed a new napkin, and redrew the swastika and the hammer and sickle. He looked at me to make sure that I was watching, and then drew three quick X's through the hammer and sickle. He scowled again at the bartender and drew a wide circle around the swastika. Turning to me, he asked, "*Americano?*"

"*Sí*," I said. He smiled and grabbed my hand. His grip was hard as he shook it. "*Viva Reagan!*"

Taking another drag, he pulled a checkbook-sized wallet out of his pants. Opening a zipper section inside the wallet, he slowly withdrew a large peseta coin. Dramatically, he held the coin out for me to see. "*El Caudillo, Generalísimo Francisco Franco*," he announced. On the heads side of the coin was Franco's profile. It had been carefully painted in oils. The background was blue, the face flesh-colored. The uniform was the blue-black of the Guardia Civil, Franco's elite corps of troops who were once the cousins of Hitler's SS and Mussolini's Blackshirts. The man had even brushed in the black, tricornered hat that is the symbol of the Guardia Civil. I carefully studied the coin, hardly believing that I was actually meeting a real Fascist. I had read about Fascists and studied them in school, but I had never expected to meet one.

The bartender, who had leaned over to see what the older

man was showing me, spoke sharply and loudly in Spanish. A half-dozen heads turned toward us. The bartender's face, so passive before, was contorted with anger. He shouted again and pointed toward the door. The Fascist stared at the bartender and put away the coin, like a man might slip his rosary beads into his pocket before swearing. The little group around the bar watched the man to see what he would do as he unleashed a fast, loud barrage of Spanish at the young Communist. He pounded his fist against the bar top. The crowd leaned in as the younger man, his face bright red with rage, shouted back at the older man. They began arguing back and forth and pounding their fists on the counter.

Like an idiot, I looked at one and then at the other, not knowing what to do. How could I stop this? I felt as though it was my fault.

"Hey, wait, you guys," I finally said, raising my hands for them to stop. Two angry faces turned toward me. Now what? Clenching my hands into fists, I aimed a finger at each man and said "Pow." I don't know why I did it, but it worked. Both men stared dumbly at me as I grinned. Then they both laughed, realizing the joke.

It was luck that brought us to Spain for the training leg of the trip. We had originally chosen England as our starting point, before delays forced us southward to avoid the harsh winter in northern Europe. Over the next few months, as we pedaled around the world, it became clear that Spain had been a perfect training ground for what was to come later in the trip. Fate and the Spanish countryside provided us with easy doses of just about everything that would confront us over the next twelve months. We pedaled over ragged roads that tore up our bikes (in two weeks, a dozen tires went flat, two pannier racks cracked, and a rear gear cluster burst apart). Hot sunshine beat down in the daytime, while the temperature fell to near freezing at night. We glimpsed poverty and saw the result of being tied to ancient traditions. We also learned what it means to live in a country that is politically unstable.

By the time we reached Barcelona, we were getting excited about leaving Spain and biking over our first international border into France. Reaching these milestones—the first international border, the first one hundred miles, the first one thousand miles—became very important to us. But even as we pored over our maps of southern France on our last scheduled night in Spain, those forces of fate that had brought us to Spain were conspiring to make our last three days on the Iberian peninsula among the most exciting and frightening of the trip.

One night just north of Barcelona, we sat round our campfire checking maps and drinking cheap wine. Down a steep hill just beyond the tents were a hundred specks of light marking the ships moored off Barcelona to the south. A cold wind blew from the water and clouds obscured the stars. Our big map of western Europe was spread out on the ground as my gloved finger traced a highway curving up into France. It was December 18, our thirteen day out of Madrid.

"We can make it to Perpignan by the day after tomorrow," I said, pointing at a city in southern France. Jim disagreed, noting that the Pyrenees mountains were between us and Perpignan. Don agreed with Jim, adding that the weather looked like it might be "bad news" by morning. Dave didn't say anything as he lifted the top of the little coffeepot to see if the water was boiling.

Our camp was an abandoned trailer court squeezed onto a flat place between two seaside cliffs. Broken trailer stalls, picnic tables, and bullet-riddled trash barrels littered the graveled lot. An old couple in a house nearby had given us permission to camp here. It might have been a nice spot, except that it was in the midst of three major transportation corridors into Barcelona. Over to the west was the Barcelona International Airport. Up the hill was the main coastal highway between Barcelona and France. Directly behind the main row of trailer stalls was a railroad track carrying a primary commuter line into the city. Every forty-five minutes, a roaring diesel pulling ten or twelve cars blasted by only fifty feet from our tents. The train was close enough that we could read the headlines on papers being read by men in gray suits heading home from work.

As the night gathered around us, we stopped talking and finished the wine. Watching the fire burn low into glowing embers, we suddenly heard a sound.

"What's that?" I whispered as the sound moved closer. It was footsteps, and they were coming from the direction of the railroad tracks. I listened hard, trying to see something in the depths of swimming blackness behind the trailer stalls. When we camped out in the open, the thought of thieves was always in the back of our minds. The footsteps stopped.

We waited for a moment, knowing someone was watching us. I was about to shout *buenos noches* or something, when a powerful flashlight beam hit me in the face. Before I could put my hands up to block the light, it was gone. The footsteps trotted quickly down the tracks. We waited for almost an hour, but nothing happened. Exhausted, we stripped the bikes, stacked them, chained them to a tree, and spread an orange plastic tarp over the stack. To scare off intruders, we set empty cans and pots and pans on top of the tarp. If the tarp was moved, everything would come crashing down.

Late that night I was awakened by a frantic whisper. "Dave, hey, wake up!" Dave French was shaking me as I slept deep in my mummy bag. "Somebody's outside going through our stuff!"

I heard the rustle of our plastic tarp outside. Then came the crash of a tin pot. I sat up quickly. A man outside whispered something in Spanish. Footsteps approached our tent. We heard more whispers. I stared into the dark where I knew the door was. Suddenly, someone started struggling with the zippers that opened the tent. Fear shot through me. What the hell was going on? What could I do? Sitting there paralyzed, I saw the darkness abruptly explode into a light that burned into my eyes. A man's head and shoulders pushed into the tent. In his hand was an automatic rifle.

At the same moment, a jet roared overhead, drowning out the man's shouts. It gave me a half second to notice he was wearing a uniform. Some of my fear disappeared. This man was probably a policeman, not a thief. Then I saw the tricornered hat. He was a Guardia Civil! Could he be a Fascist? As the roar faded away, the man seemed to be repeating a question. His tone was harsh.

"*Americanos*," was all I could think to say. Then I added, "*No hablo español*." He stopped talking, growled, and lowered the light out of my eyes. "*Señor in casa donde permission to campo*," I blurted out, grossly mixing up Spanish and English. I pointed in the direction of the old couple's house. The Guardia Civil growled again and pulled out of the tent. He said something to whoever else was outside. There was a short conversation and then nothing. I poked my head outside to see two caped men retreating slowly into the night.

•••

A powerful blast of wind and a loud crash woke us at dawn the next morning. The thin nylon walls of our tents shook and rattled. When I poked my head out a few minutes later, I saw that an old trailer stall had crashed into the gravel. The sky was darkening, and the branches of the trees over the camp were bent over in a strong breeze.

Since leaving Madrid, Dave and Jim, our two most experienced bikers, had marveled at the stillness of the wind. They had constantly warned Don and me that a steady headwind was probably the most frustrating condition imaginable for a cyclist. "Biking into a strong headwind is like climbing a hill that never has a top," Jim liked to say.

Standing in my sweats and stocking cap outside the tent, I wet my finger, raised it in the air, and decided that today I would discover what it was like to ride in a serious headwind. Stray raindrops propelled sideways by the strong wind slapped my face.

We managed to pedal about thirty kilometers by eleven A.M., averaging about half our usual speed of eighteen kilometers an hour. Then the wind really picked up. In the next six hours, we only biked another twenty-four kilometers. Jim guessed that the wind was blowing at least fifty miles per hour. I guessed sixty. It had shifted now to a crosswind, which meant that we were able to pedal forward, but only by leaning into the wind at a forty-five-degree angle. Each of us took at least one spill into the ditch along the highway. Speeding trucks roaring past would suddenly reverse the direction of the wind, causing a suction that threatened to pull us under their tires.

By mid-afternoon, our goal was Figueras, a city about thirty kilometers south of France. But the more we pedaled, the stronger the wind blew. Pebbles, twigs, and a few scattered raindrops pelted our helmets in a constant rush and clatter. Three kilometers from Figueras, Don pulled a muscle in his calf and had to slow down. Jim and Dave broke off and rode ahead (we had to get to a bank in town before closing time to exchange dollars for the coming weekend). As group leader for the week, I stayed back with Don. Two kilometers from town, Don was in pain and had to stop. The traffic on our road was moving slowly in a long line as we started to pull the bikes off the road. Then a gust of wind stronger than anything we had felt all day blasted across the flat sea plain. We braced ourselves, using our bikes as supports. The smaller cars on the road quivered and shook in the gust as a Seat bumped into a Volkswagen bug. Suddenly the bug, jolted by the bump and the wind, flew into the air and flipped over into the ditch.

I dropped my bike, grabbed the group first aid kit, and ran back to the bug as several people from the line of cars gathered around. Inside, a young man tried to move into a sitting position on the ceiling of the car. Blood poured over his shirt. Then someone screamed. Everyone ducked and scattered as another gust of wind picked up the bug's windshield, which had popped out still intact on the road during the accident. The sheet of glass flew toward the crowd, but no one was hit. About a hundred yards up the road, a large billboard advertising Coca-Cola came sailing past, flying across the winter fields like a flattened tumbleweed. Fortunately, the driver was not seriously hurt. His worst injury seemed to be a bloody nose.

By the next morning the windstorm had faded into a cold breeze. Pedaling up the Roc de France pass in the Pyrenees, we went through customs and biked into France. Speeding down the far side of the Pyrenees, we felt a rush of exhilaration at entering a new country. For the first time, we felt like world bikers, even though we had traveled only seven hundred kilometers.

But our excitement faded over the next few days as we cycled around the Mediterranean coast through France, and then across the top of Italy's boot to the Adriatic Sea. Just as Spain gave us a crash course in how exciting biking can be, France and Italy gave us an interminable lesson in how frustrating bicycling can be. The Mediterranean winter threw cold, high winds in our faces, with an almost steady rainstorm from Perpignan to the Adriatic coast. Temperatures ranged from the upper forties during the day to below freezing at night. In the Apennine mountains of central Italy, we woke up one morning to find our campsite covered with snow.

It was miserable biking. Keeping warm was a major problem. Our body temperatures were constantly shifting; we were hot while pedaling and instantly cold when we stopped. Sweat froze to our hair and the cold wind cut through our clothing. Our feet were constantly soaked by icy water kicked up from our tires and chains. Frostbite was a danger. Socks had to be changed three or four times a day.

For twenty-five days we did little more than pedal our bikes, stop in faceless cafés to warm up, and sleep in equally faceless pensions. It took over three weeks to cover the eight hundred kilometers to Ancona, Italy, where we planned to catch a ferry to Greece. The names of the towns and regions resounded with romance—the Riviera, Arles, Cannes, Toulouse, Monte Carlo, Genoa, Pisa, Tuscany, Florence, and the Apennines. But most of the romance was washed out by the cold and gray of winter.

The hours on the bike went agonizingly slow. I had no way to occupy my mind. After the initial flurry of conversation among the four of us, easy topics wore thin. I tried to think about my writing, about books I'd read, about my girlfriend Laura, about anything, but could not keep my mind occupied for long. In the murk and ice of the Mediterranean winter, I was getting bored. I was prepared for blizzards, baking deserts, and harrowing mountain descents, but not for the tedium of those European days. Nothing about my life before the trip had been boring. I was a television child, used to constant stimulation. After a month on the road, I was nearly through training my body, but I was just beginning to grapple with the greatest challenge of the trip—training my mind.

The scenery offered little relief. We often were lost in a haze of gray drizzle that obscured everything but the splashing cars and the roadside strips. Gray dominated this world: gray slime on the road, gray cars and trucks, gray sky, gray buildings, and gray fields of olive groves pruned down to four-foot stumps for the winter. On the French Riviera, the mist obscured all but the vague outlines of the dramatic cliffs and tree-cloaked hills that tourists flock to see in the warmer months. Fog obliterated the turquoise water. The fairy-tale villas and casinos of Monaco were hidden in the mist behind high walls or up steep hills we had no desire to climb. The Italian Riviera was worse. Parts of it reminded me of Highway One in northern New Jersey. Lines of cheap beach houses, some barely shacks, were pressed tight between once grand hotels and canopied beach promenades. Turquoise or bright yellow paint was glopped onto these fading dames of the Riviera in an attempt to disguise eroded facades and broken shutters. Bleached plastic flags on long strings fluttered here and there. The place felt like a used car lot. The long, empty beaches were still littered from the summer season with cups and plates, scattered across the sands like millions of belly-up fish.

The people along the Mediterranean moved across our stage

like shadows. The French generally lived up to their reputation for being cold and unhelpful. They seemed to resent the intrusion of four American cyclists into their deserted towns. On our first night, in a Perpignan youth hostel, the young couple in charge began playing loud rock and roll at one A.M. When we asked them to turn it down, they said "Fuck you" in English and turned up the volume. In the village of Sète, I tried to place a collect call to Laura in New York on a pay phone, but the operator would not connect me to an international operator. "You speak French!" she demanded. When I tried to use our Berlitz French language guide, she grew impatient with my accent and hung up. In Arles, we met a French woman in a café who refused to believe that we were biking around the world. "You fool with me," she said, waving a huge mane of curly hair. "I think Americans are too lazy to bicycle around the world. Drive a car around the world, yes. But never on a bicycle."

It was a relief to pedal into Italy, where the people were vibrant and friendly. They gathered around us at every stop to ask questions and inspect the bikes. They eagerly helped us when we used our Berlitz Italian language guide, laughing with friendly smiles at our atrocious accents. Nearly every afternoon in western Italy, cyclists in one of the many local bicycle clubs escorted us in and out of their towns. Wearing identical sweaters, tights, and stocking caps, these "clubbies" boisterously shouted conversations, asking us about the world trip in broken English.

It was a tough, cold trek over the Apennine mountains to Ancona and the Adriatic coast. In the gray, cold days, the constant company of three other men became tedious and annoying. Speed was still the critical irritant. Don was biking faster as he got in better shape, but Dave continued to keep a slow, deliberate pace. As our frustration increased, we became increasingly intolerant of his slowness. He often kept us out in the bad weather longer than necessary, while forcing us to amend our schedules.

Small aches and pains wore us down. My knees hurt, although I never would have admitted it to Dave. Don was having trouble with his calves, Dave with his back, Jim with his feet. We were becoming homesick for the English language and the American phone system. We missed friends, Mexican food, decent wardrobes, washers and dryers, and good rock and roll. Dave seemed to be afflicted the worst. From the early days in Spain, where breakfast is a roll and coffee, he talked about his craving for an "American breakfast" of bacon, eggs, and toast. He was also becoming less tolerant of people who asked us questions in "foreign" languages. By the time we reached the Adriatic, he was talking all of the time about Vermont, telling the same bike stories over and over again.

In the gloom and grayness of Europe, we even became discouraged about our "world trip." In a couple of attempts to get press coverage, we had attracted almost no attention for the HOPE effort. This was to be expected, since we still had a long way to go before the media or anyone else would be interested in our story. We also knew that more adventure lay ahead in Asia and Africa. But we were of a generation used to immediate satisfaction. We wanted it *now*.

We crossed the Adriatic to Greece on a trucker's ferry and left behind the drizzling winter for the sunshine and warmth of Greece. Sunshine! From the moment our ferry docked in Patras, our spirits soared. Riding out of the port city, we stripped off our shirts and tights and raced along the coast of the Ionian Sea toward Athens. For a while we sang songs. Then Don and I started playing a TV trivia game. One of us would hum a theme song and the other had to guess the name of the show. It took us both back to those long afternoons we spent after school in Kansas City watching the big color set in our family rec room. I hummed the tunes to "Gilligan's Island," "Get Smart," and "The Avengers" before I caught Don on "The Munsters." He caught me on "Father Knows Best."

I broke loose from the group and pedaled as hard as I could, reveling in the warmth and in the strength I had developed over the weeks of biking through Europe. It was gusty over the blue-black sea as we sped east. Foam flaked off the water like a billion doves flapping their wings. Small wooden fishing boats painted red or green or yellow bobbed among the white caps like toys under bright white, triangular sails. Across the narrow sea, orange-brown mountains rose cleanly into the cold, clear sky.

It took five days to pedal from Patras to Athens. The road alternated between high, cliffside runs and narrow, flat spots between the sea and the cliffs. Picture-book villages of whitewashed stucco buildings appeared every few kilometers. Their ancient names were both familiar and magical. We passed Sicyon, where the racially oppressed Doric people revolted against their Ionic masters in the West's first recorded race riots; Corinth, one of the wealthiest cities of the ancient world; and Megara, named after a lover of Heracles. Disappointingly, only a few columns and chips of carved marble remained of the ancient towns. Since I was a small boy, I had been in love with the culture of ancient Greece. In high school, I had wanted to be a classical archeologist. I had often imagined myself as an Athenian warrior or a sailor on the Argo in search of the Golden Fleece. But so little remained of that world that I had a hard time imagining it. My disappointment was magnified when I realized how irrelevant the ruins were to the local farmers and storekeepers along the sleepy highway.

Each village had its Byzantine church, exotic with its multi-domed roofs and high arched windows. Small roadside shrines filled with crosses, lighted candles, fresh flowers, and statues of saints dotted the highways as memorials to Greeks killed in traffic accidents. Occasionally, groves of lemon trees perfumed the air along the road with a ripe citrus scent. Pickers on wooden ladders would wave to us as they clipped the fruits and dropped them into mesh bags around their waists.

But Greece was not completely idyllic. Just a few miles from Patras we were introduced to what would become a major problem over the next few months: The Truck. Not the calm, massive trucks of the West. They roar by anonymously, recognizing bicyclists by no more than a slight deviation from their paths. This new truck was largely a Third World invention combining swaths of bright paint, random chunks of metal and wood, bright decals, and plastic. The drivers of these trucks acted more like cowboys than licensed operators of deadly vehicles. They would swerve over to us, screaming "Hello, mister!" and rev up their engines in great bursts of suffocating smoke. Then they would honk their horns. In Greece we heard horns blasting like freighters, trilling like mezzo-sopranos, tooting disco riffs, whistling, and zapping out electronic noises that mimicked everything from radio static to the beep-o-weeps of R2-D2.

"Truck back," shouted Dave from a few feet behind me.

"Thank you," I shouted back in our usual road banter. A faint roar grew louder as I pumped up a short rise in the road. Slowly, the roar turned into a succession of chugs and grinding gears behind me. I glanced into my rearview mirror as a shrill horn blasted in my ear, *"BEEOOWEEPOOWEEP!"* I grabbed for the whistle around my neck and stuck it in my mouth. *"BEE-OOWEEPOOWEEEEP!"* went the horn. It tore into my head. I wanted to put my hands over my ears but had to hold onto the bike.

In a brown cloud of exhaust and dust, a three-wheeled lorry rumbled up beside me. I was tense, concentrating on keeping my bike steady as I waited for him to pass. But he did not pass. Instead, he slowed down.

"Welcome to Greece!" screamed the driver, waving hysterically and weaving all over the road. "Welcome to Greece!"

Athens rose in a cloud of smog as we biked through the suburb of Eleusis, home of the ancient Eleusinian mysteries. We passed near the port of Piraeus and pedaled along the site of the Long Walls, which the Athenians built to repel invaders after the Persian Wars. But like the rest of the country we had seen, modern Athens bore little resemblance to the Greece I had expected. It presented street after street of row buildings spreading in a huge, sloppy circle around the one major remnant of ancient Greece that still held the magic of the Golden Age—the Acropolis. Standing pearly white on a huge slab of rock, the bare marble of the Parthenon, the Erechtheum, and the Propylaea stood like proud, broken bones above the dingy city below.

We checked into the Apollo House, a discount hotel filled with backpack travelers. Athens was the first of a dozen major cities around the world where we would pause to rest, meet with the press about HOPE, collect mail from the local American Express office, and perform any bike repairs or maintenance necessary. Stopping in these cities also gave me a chance to sit down and write—to catch up on my journal and to start outlining potential newspaper articles about the trip.

For some reason the Greek press loved our story. With the help of the U.S. embassy's press staff, who often help American groups like HOPE, we appeared in Greek newspapers, on Greek radio, and on Greek television. The U.S. press in Athens was less enthusiastic, although we did appear on the Associated Press wire and on NBC radio news.

On our last day in Athens, I telephoned my girlfriend Laura. She was working as an investment banker in New York. Lately, I had been missing her terribly. Her face had started to blur in my mind. I missed her when I was sitting in a Greek café sipping wine or climbing around in ruins below the Acropolis. I missed her at night. I wanted to touch her.

She sounded happy on the phone. "You called at just the right moment!" she said. "I have a surprise for you."

"What?"

"I'm coming to see you in Cairo! I've got some vacation time," she said, "and we aren't too busy here at the firm."

A grin broke out across my face. We would be in Cairo in only three weeks!

On our last night in Athens, I left the Apollo to take a long walk through the city in the direction of the Acropolis. It was a damp, misty night. Streetlamps hung like smudges of light in the sky. Traffic was light, and I met very few people as my shoes clicked on the sidewalk. As I rounded a corner, the Acropolis, lit by spotlights, leaped into view. It stood pristine and delicate in a ball of misty light flaring and pitching like fire as the drizzle blew and shifted against the great rock.

My footsteps slowed as I watched the illuminated mists dancing over the ancient ruins. Caught up in the sorcery of that evening, I saw the mists as spirits swirling over the white spine of the Parthenon. Theseus. Pericles. Plato. Aristotle. Alexander. They had all walked there, all of those legends, back when my ancestors were wearing skins and chucking crude spears at each other on the other end of the European continent. And floating with their spirits were all those of the millions of young men who had journeyed here to gawk and feel inspired.

I walked on in silence, thinking about our journey. It struck me that our route was taking us slowly backward in time as it took us around the world. Already, we had moved from the New World to the Old World, following part of the route that Europeans used to call the Grand Tour, a tour that always ended here in Athens, at the birthplace and symbol of the West. But tomorrow we would go beyond the ancient homeland of the West to journey even further back in time, to lands already ancient when the Greeks built their first primitive temples on the Acropolis. Tomorrow, we were truly leaving home. I wondered what we would find.

MIDDLE EAST

*Jim Logan dressed in
"Sahara suit" near Kassala,
Sudan.*

Black Sea

USSR

GREECE
ATHENS

TURKEY

Mediterranean
Sea

SYRIA

ISRAEL

IRAQ

IRAN

JERUSALEM

JORDAN

CAIRO

LIBYA

EGYPT

Lake Nasser

ASWAN

Red
Sea

JEDDAH

WADI
HALFA

SAUDI ARABIA

PORT
SUDAN

KHARTOUM

NILE

SUDAN

NILE R.

ETHIOPIA

SOMALIA

Middle East
——— by Bicycle
━ ━ ━ by Plane, Boat, Train

2. The Promised Land

"Are you carrying any guns?" The El Al flight attendant snapped off a series of questions as we waited to board our flight to Tel Aviv. "Any plastic explosives? Any weapons of any kind?" Two Greek soldiers armed with automatic weapons guarded the Israeli airline desk at the Athens airport. El Al has long been a target of international terrorism. In fifteen years a dozen of their planes had been blown up, shot at, or otherwise attacked. It was a sobering introduction to the realities of modern Israel.

I'm not sure what I expected to find in Israel. The plight of this tiny country—it's smaller than Massachusetts—has spent more time on front pages and on the seven o'clock news than almost any other story since World War II. *Israel*. The word conjures images of tanks and misery and unshaven men screaming and waving fists. Israel is also the Holy Land, a mythical land of smiling shepherds and good Samaritans that populate Bible pictures in Sunday school. Jerusalem. Bethlehem. Nazareth.

They all mean salvation and conflict; peace and war. This has always been the irony of Israel.

Our plan was to cycle from Jerusalem across the Sinai to Cairo, traversing one of the tensest borders in the world. Camp David was in full bloom, but Israel still held the last third of the Sinai and seemed reluctant to give it up to Egypt. We had no idea if it was possible to bike across the Sinai. The Israeli embassy in Washington had warned us that only army-escorted vehicles could safely cross. The State Department had told us the opposite story, that it was so safe tourist buses were routinely driving the northern route. This contradiction should have warned us to be cautious, but we were completely inexperienced in assessing this type of situation. We chose to believe the State Department, because it supported our plan.

Landing in Tel Aviv, we saw no evidence of conflict on the road between the Ben-Gurion International Airport and Jerusalem. The green flatlands along the Mediterranean coast were peaceful. It could have been rural Kansas, except for the humid, sea-salt air. Long irrigation pipes like steel centipedes spread across quiet fields of soybeans, barley, and wheat. Aluminum-topped grain elevators sparkled in the bright sun.

Steering off the main highway, we followed an ancient route cut by the Romans through the rocky hills surrounding Jerusalem. The peace of the flatlands turned more ominous here; these were the hills where Arabs slaughtered Jewish relief columns in the 1948 War for Independence. The jagged bluffs looked like a Hollywood backdrop for an Apache ambush, although the only movement we saw was the flutter of almond tree blossoms in the light wind. In my excited state of mind, I kept looking up from the pavement to watch for figures lurking in the rocks. At one point, an Israeli army jeep drove past. The soldiers smiled and flashed an American-style thumbs-up.

After a steep climb up the Roman road, we topped out in the sprawling Jewish section of New Jerusalem. The trim, modern streets were empty on a Saturday, the Jewish Sabbath. Our tires buzzed along the asphalt in the silence.

Biking into a wide open space—the pre-1967 border between Jordan and Israel—we passed through a gap in the high stone walls encircling Old Jerusalem. The medieval walls wound like a corset around the crest of a high hill, enclosing a space about the size of Central Park in New York City. Stone, oriental-style domes and television antennas formed the skyline of the Old City. On the far side, across from the Mount of Olives, a large, lapis-covered dome floated above the earth-colored roofs in a haze of sea blue. This was the Dome of the Rock, where Muhammad ascended to heaven. It was also the site of Solomon's temple, and the spot where Jesus turned over the tables of the moneylenders while chiding the Pharisees for disobeying God's law.

Inside the walls, in an open space below David's Tower, the silence of the Jewish Sabbath was broken by the noise and clamor of an Arab market. For Arabs, Saturday is market day. Exotic colors and smells swirled around us. Men wore white djellaba tunics and *kaffiyeh* headgear. Women wore layers of robes and shawls, but few of them were veiled. Children scurried about carrying Turkish coffee on trays suspended like balances by three pieces of rope. Other boys, their arms covered with tin bracelets, tugged on the sleeves of tourists, shouting, "One shekel only, one shekel only."

Streets barely exist in Old Jerusalem. The narrow, twisting alleyways are more like corridors in a great castle. Centuries of housing shortages behind the city's walls have forced Jerusalemites to build up. Streets were long ago roofed over by successive tiers of houses. Bare bulbs illuminate shopping areas lined with makeshift stalls selling everything from baklava and pungent spices to polyester rugs depicting Jesus praying on the Mount of Olives. Occasionally, a shaft of sunlight blasted through sky holes to meander slowly across the street as the day wore on.

"I give you fifty dollars for bicycle," shouted a fat merchant in a trinkets store. We were pushing our bikes along the packed alleyway called David Street. "I give you seventy-five dollars," said a man across the way. I noticed they were bidding in dollars.

"These bikes cost hundreds of dollars," I said, grinning.

"You bargain hard," said the fat man. "One hundred dollars."

I shook my head and kept walking. "One hundred twenty-five!" I heard shouted behind me. "It is robbery!"

Another man tapped my arm and offered to buy my helmet or my watch. I offered him a Project HOPE button, but a boy in a dirty tunic snatched it from my hand and ran.

We embraced Jerusalem. For five days the four of us tramped through its alleyways and sudden open spaces. I kissed the

Wailing Wall and knelt on the doorjamb of the Dome of
the Rock. In the Church of the Holy Sepulchre, I stood on the
ground where Jesus was crucified. At night, we joined other
Westerners in popular cafés to drink Gold Star beers and listen
to American music on cassette players. All of us met women.
Don met an American photographer who had made a fortune
from a postcard photograph of Mount Saint Helens erupting in
Washington State. Jim met a British woman who taught Arabic
studies at the University of London, while Dave and I met a
pair of French nurses at our youth hostel. We could have stayed
in this magical city forever.

In Arab tea shops, I drank spiced *shai* and worked on rewrit-
ing my journal notes from Europe. I outlined a "Letter from
Jerusalem" for the *Kansas City Star,* my hometown newspaper.
I also wrote out our first detailed report to Project HOPE.
These monthly reports contained stories from the road, expen-
diture reports, and publicity summaries. The foreign press
corps in Jerusalem jumped on our story, to our surprise. UPI,
AP, NBC radio, and a half-dozen others interviewed us as the
"first Americans to attempt a crossing of the Sinai by bicycle."
The U.S. consulate helped us coordinate the media coverage.

The consul general was also able to confirm that tourists were
crossing the Sinai. The first buses had traveled to Cairo as part
of the Camp David accords about two weeks before we arrived.
"But you must be careful with the Bedouins," said a deputy
consul. "With the Sinai changing hands, they are taking advan-
tage of the turmoil by raiding villages and attacking travelers."
The Israeli Tourist Bureau disputed that the Bedouins posed a
danger on the Israeli third of the desert. "The Egyptian portion
of the Sinai may be another matter," said a young tourist agent
with a scarred cheek.

It was hard to believe that Old Jerusalem was the center of a
brutal conflict. It seemed more like a giant tourist extravaganza,
combining elements of Disneyland, religious pilgrimages, and
a panorama of history that no other city in the world can match.
But something was not quite right. Jerusalem was a little too
tidy and clean. The ancient walls had been scoured until the
stone shone yellow-gray. Streets were dust-free. Almost none
of the people in exotic robes and *kaffiyehs* were dirty or looked
poor. It was as if some huge organization had hired all of these
people to dress in "native" outfits to give tourists an impression
of Old Jerusalem. It reminded me of Williamsburg, Virginia,

where employees dressed in Colonial garb populate a restored seventeenth-century village. In this holiday atmosphere, we forgot any fears we had about Israel—at least for the moment.

No sign marked the border between Israel and the Occupied West Bank, but it was immediately apparent where one world ended and another began. Only a kilometer out of Jerusalem, the green fields and quiet groves were replaced by dry, flax-colored fields littered with rocks and small boulders. Prickly cacti called sabra grew in long clumps along the highway. Arabs on foot or on donkeys wore dusty tunics and worn *kaffiyehs;* women in black robes balanced everything from bundles of straw to cans of gasoline on their heads. Stone huts and sloppily constructed concrete structures replaced the neat lines of homes and shops in Jewish Israel.

Again, I was surprised by the tranquility of the countryside. In America, the words *West Bank* seldom appeared without modifiers like *violence* or *war* or *tension.* Not long before our arrival, a young Jew was shot dead while waiting for a bus in nearby Hebron. A young Arab died during the resulting rock-throwing skirmishes between Arab mobs and Israeli troops. But we saw no evidence of war. The faces along our route were absorbed in their tasks. No one looked particularly tense or fearful.

Near Bethlehem, about ten kilometers south of Jerusalem, we met two Israeli boys on the only ten-speed bikes we had seen since New Jerusalem. Their Jewishness was advertised by bright blue yarmulkes resting on the crowns of their heads. In yellow raincoats, knapsacks, and track shoes, they stuck out as much as we did among the Arabs on the West Bank.

Introducing themselves as Aaron and Michel, the boys told us that they lived in a new Israeli settlement to the south, near Hebron. They described themselves as *Sabras,* a name for Jews born in Israel.

"Like the sabra cactus, we are tough on the outside but sweet on the inside," Aaron explained.

I asked the boys if they were afraid to be riding alone among all these Arabs on the West Bank.

"Why should we be afraid?" said Aaron. He slipped his knapsack off his shoulder and casually pulled out a small pistol. "You see? I have this gun." His smile was worldly. "We are safe with this gun."

An hour after Aaron pulled out his gun, we were sitting on

low stools in a truck repair shop belonging to a young Arab named Khalil. A boy served us Turkish coffee in tiny demitasse cups while a dozen solemn men stood in the clean garage watching Khalil speak to us. They wore a mishmash of Western and Arab clothing—robes, wool trousers, turbans, and even a New York Yankees sweatshirt. Khalil wore a yellow wind-breaker and a red *kaffiyeh* from Jordan. When I admired it, he took it off and gave it to me as a gift. I gave him a Project HOPE flag in return.

Khalil, a handsome man with a serious face, talked about peace. "You must tell the people in America that we are tired of war," he said. "We are tired of the bombs and the bullets."

He told us that his family had fled from a farm south of Tel Aviv during the 1948 War for Independence. "The Israelis, they robbed us of our land." On the West Bank, Khalil's father bought more land, only to lose it again to the Israelis after the Six-Day War in 1967. "That war was terrible," he said. "Many families had fathers killed. We boys ducked and hid from the bullets and the bombs. Men were fighting here on this street."

"Were you afraid?" I asked him.

"No, Palestine has so long been a battlefield. I am not afraid, just sad, because the fighting never stops."

I asked him if he had any solution to the problem.

"We should throw out the politicians," he said. "They play a big game in Palestine. It is their fault. We are just people. The Israelis are just people. We all want to live in peace. The people would live in peace."

I told Khalil about the Israeli boys with the gun. He shook his head.

"Children copy the adults. It is stupid."

That night, we stayed in a kibbutz dorm with a group of high school seniors on a field trip from Haifa in northern Israel. A guidebook had indicated that the kibbutz, called Ezyon, oper-ated a youth hostel. But the hostel had long ago been converted by the Israeli government into an educational center. High school seniors came from all over the country as part of a pro-gram to familiarize them with every region of Israel. Weekend seminars at Ezyon focused on historic Zionism, the campaign launched by European Jews in the nineteenth century to estab-lish a Jewish homeland. Slick displays in the dorm's lobby fea-tured photos of Theodor Herzl, Zionism's founder, early Jewish settlers in Palestine, and a cracked collage of Nazi death camps. The seminar's instructors were asking the students to ponder the question: "What does it mean to be Jewish?"

The instructor in charge, an American-born Jew from Brooklyn, was reluctant at first to have four muddy cyclists interrupt his program. But two soldiers guarding the barbed wire— enclosed compound convinced him that it was unsafe for us to be biking around on the West Bank after dark. It was also raining heavily, and we were obviously soaked through.

After a cup of hot brewed coffee in the faculty lounge, the head instructor warmed up to us, asking us about the States and slipping into a rusty Brooklyn accent. "I miss some things from America," he said, "like the theater and the movies in New York. But they are unimportant, you know. It is really critical to be here in my country right now. The next twenty-five years will mean life or death for Israel. We need every Jew in the world to help. That's why I left."

After we had showered and changed into "civilian" clothes, Dan, the instructor, introduced us to a seventeen-year-old student named Saer. Because of his excellent English, Saer was to be our guide during our stay. First on the agenda was dinner. In a large, institutional-style cafeteria we ate gooey meat and soggy beans. It reminded me of meals at my own high school in Kansas City. During the meal, we fielded questions in broken English from Saer's friends about everything from Rod Stewart to what the Grand Canyon looks like "in real life." As Americans, we were instant celebrities.

After dinner, the students took part in a mock trial organized by Dan as part of the Ezyon program. The hypothetical case was a familiar one for Israeli Jews: 300,000 Jews, most of them poor and uneducated, are suddenly expelled from an unfriendly Third World nation. Should the three million people of Israel, with already strained resources, a faltering economy, and overcrowded cities, take them all in?

The trial was in Hebrew, so we declined an invitation from Dan to watch it. Back in our dorm room, I was drinking more brewed coffee when Saer showed up. "I found the trial to be boring," he said. "So I have left to come speak with you."

"In America, we call it 'playing hooky,' " I said.

He asked to share my coffee, so I poured some from my paper cup into a white bike cup extracted from a pannier. He said that the instructors wanted him to be the judge in the mock trial because his father was a well-known lawyer in Haifa. "I told him no, I didn't want to. But really, I wanted to speak to you."

Saer planned to be a lawyer like his father and his grandfather. He would go to the University of Jerusalem after he completed his mandatory three years in the army. "I leave for the army in only five months," he said.

"Five months?" It was difficult to imagine this quiet boy and his playful friends as front-line placements in the war. I asked him the same question I had been asking all day: Was he afraid? From Saer, I got my first honest answer.

"Yes, of course," he said. "But it must be done. I do not like war, but everyone must fight for his country. In Israel, it is a constant fight for our survival."

Saer's grandfather had fled from Nazi Germany in the late 1930s, first to America and then to Israel. "Most of my family were killed by the Nazis," he said. "That is why we must survive here in Israel. Here, at this seminar, they ask us what it means to be Jewish," he continued. "But they already have an answer waiting. They say to be Jewish is to remember the past —all that has happened to Jews for 3,000 years. But my answer is different. I want to remember the past, but I am more interested in the future. I think to be Jewish means to believe in the future."

I asked him what he predicted for the future of Israel. Would the fighting ever end? He thought deeply before answering.

"There will be no peace here in my lifetime," he said, "but maybe in the lifetime of my children or grandchildren. I do not know. It may be that the next world war will start here."

Both of us took long drinks of our coffee.

"We have had enough of serious talk," Saer said. He smiled shyly. "Now I must ask you a question for my friends. Will you stay tomorrow and play football? We would be honored to have you play."

I told him that we had to be in Cairo in five days.

"You will cross the Sinai by bicycle? That is very dangerous."

I asked him what he meant.

"The Bedouins will rob you, or attack you." His large eyes showed worry. "They will steal your bicycles. And where will you sleep?"

"We will probably camp," I said.

"You are very brave," he said.

•••

Leaving Ezyon early the next morning, we quickly pedaled the thirty miles to Ashqelon on the coast, passing more peaceful green fields and modern, prefab towns. On the edge of Ashqelon was a tall pole covered with kilometer signs pointing to every major city in the world. One arrow said that Kansas City was 16,828 kilometers away from Ashqelon. Washington, D.C., where we had started the trip seven weeks earlier, was 14,423 kilometers away.

Near the sign, we found a supermarket and bought supplies for lunch and dinner. We planned to camp that night, if we could find a safe spot. Don had been craving Mexican food, so he bought all the ingredients he could find to make nachos. Jalapeño peppers were nowhere in the Western-style store, but we did get some tortilla-like bread and lots of cheese, lettuce, tomatoes, avocados, onions, and Gold Star beer. Our "Mexican sauce" was ketchup mixed with Tabasco.

Outside the supermarket, an old man in a European beret trotted over to show us a Hebrew-language newspaper. On the second page, a blurry photograph showed four cyclists on overloaded bikes pedaling past David's Tower in the Old City. A small crowd had gathered to stare at the photo and then at us.

"You bike on Sinai?" asked an old woman after reading the article. She looked very concerned. "It is so dangerous!" she said. Another man said, "Take many cigarettes."

"Cigarettes?"

"To give Bedouins gift. It is the custom."

I thanked him for the advice.

As we approached the Gaza Strip border, military activity picked up. A troop convoy roared by. Flatbed trucks carried tanks, and troop transports pulled heavy artillery pieces. Fighter planes roared overhead, leaving plumes of smoke like white chalk smears across the blue sky. Further up was a heavily armed fort, encircled by high walls topped by barbed wire and watchtowers with machine gun emplacements and spotlights. Oblivious to these danger signals, we kept biking for a couple more kilometers before stopping to set up camp just a half mile from the Gaza Strip.

In the remaining hour of daylight, we prepared and ate nachos, while drinking enough Gold Star to get a mild buzz. Our campsite was behind a row of trees on the edge of a soybean field. By dusk, we had a small fire burning against an earthen embankment.

About ten o'clock, we heard the first explosions. They were low rumbles, like thunder. Over toward the sea were bright flashes. Quickly dousing the fire, we stood up to look and listen.

"We should go back to that fort," said Don, "and find out what's happening."

"No, not just yet," said Jim. "If something is going on, we'll know soon enough. There'll be troops all over the place."

An hour passed and nothing happened. The peace of the evening settled again over our campsite. It seemed impossible that anything could happen in that heavy quiet. Spreading our mummy bags out under the stars, we quickly fell asleep. But we would not sleep for long.

A blinding light woke me up. Someone was shouting, but I couldn't understand the words. I blinked at the light, struggling to pull my arms out of the bag. The scene came into focus. Guns were pointing in my face. Men, lots of them, rushed through the campsite, shouting at each other. A face with a gun shouted again. I heard a bolt click.

"Americans!" I shouted. "We are Americans! Tourists!"

Confusion. Fear. Who were these men? Were they going to kill us?

"American?" repeated the man, sounding baffled. To my relief, I saw that he wore the olive drab of the Israeli army. He shouted to another man, who seemed to announce a general order. Almost instantly, all guns were slung over shoulders, and the spotlight was turned up to reflect against a tree.

"Why you here?" demanded the man, apparently the officer in command. "You are dangerous." I hoped he meant that we were in danger. "You must leave. We have trouble at Gaza. Terrorists." On cue, another round of flashing lights lit up the western horizon, followed by explosions rumbling across the coastal flatlands.

The officer told us to move immediately to a kibbutz two kilometers back—the fortified enclosure we had thought was some sort of military base. "I come back in fifteen minutes." His voice was hard. "You be gone."

In a flurry of commands, the patrol rushed back to their jeeps and were gone. The darkness and silence came crashing around us. We quickly gathered our gear and loaded the bikes. Back on the road, the half-moon reflected against the pavement. Instinctively, we squeezed into a tight formation, two abreast. Shadows from the moon danced in phantom shapes along the road. The black, quiet fields had shifted from peaceful farmland to something menacing and unknown. What was hiding out there?

It seemed like hours before we arrived at the kibbutz gate. For a few tense moments, we thought the kibbutz's security men were not going to allow us inside, but a man named Ariel finally opened the gate. He led us to a low, concrete building.

"I am sorry, but this is the only place we have for you to sleep," said Ariel. "It is our bomb shelter."

Inside, the shelter looked like our basement rec room back home in Kansas City, with secondhand furniture, a plastic black-and-white television, and piles of beat-up paperbacks and board games. About thirty foam pads were rolled up against a wall. Everything here had been used, and used often.

Ariel invited us to have soup and french fries at the kibbutz's cafeteria, across the street from the bomb shelter. "It is 'midnight snack,' as you say in America," he smiled. "I want to welcome you to our kibbutz. It is the custom of the Middle East to be helpful to travelers." We would hear this frequently over the next several weeks.

Inside a huge, institutional kitchen, Ariel stirred soup that smelled like vegetable beef. French fries sizzled in a deep-fry vat. We asked him about the troops and the explosions.

"I hear on the radio that terrorists try to land from sea tonight." He shrugged and continued casually to stir the soup. "It happens sometimes. We are on the frontier of Israel. Those explosions you hear, they are the navy blowing up the terrorists."

Like the West Bank, the border between Israel and the Gaza Strip suddenly changed from green, estate-sized farms to rocky fields. Closer to the sea, groves of squat date palms began to appear. Poverty was much more evident here. Robes were torn and dirty. Everything was shabby and dusty. Before we had gone five miles, I borrowed a pair of Ray Bans from Jim to keep the dust out of my eyes. Houses and shops were dilapidated. A few were lean-tos constructed out of rocks and scraps of metal or wood. One farm shed was a rusted truck cab with its floor and doors missing. Chickens strutted in and out of the cab, pecking for seeds in the sandy soil.

Heavily armed Israeli troops guarded every intersection and government building. Bushes of barbed wire bristled around each telephone pole. Troops, tanks, and artillery appeared often in the traffic. No one waved at us or even paid attention to four bikers speeding down the battered highway. Our senses were not yet fine-tuned enough to feel the tension in the air, but we did feel uneasy. This was a war zone. We could feel that much.

Khan Yunis, our first Third World city, was a mass of confusion, colors, and an overpowering odor of dung. Flies buzzed in clouds over the people, the animals, the shops, and the open stalls. Thousands of voices haggled over everything from eggplants to cheap cassette players, while dogs yapped and chickens screeched. Dust and smoke from open fires rose in thick clouds, spreading a beige haze over the scene. All of the hand-painted signs were unintelligible to us, written in a script full of curves and dots and slashes. Near the center of the city, a camel turning suddenly into the road almost knocked me off my bike. I veered out of my lane to avoid the beast, only to be grazed by a speeding Mercedes stretch limo loaded with tourists. I barely kept my balance, caught between two worlds.

When we stopped to look for a grocery store, a crowd of boys in tattered tunics pressed around, shouting questions in Arabic and tugging on our sleeves. "Hello mister," they said over and over. The time would come when the words *hello mister* would drive us crazy. But on that first day, we grinned at the attention and at the wild activity and energy in this fantastic world.

With Don and Dave guarding the bikes, Jim and I squeezed into the sprawling open market in the center of Khan Yunis. Wandering among the canvas-topped stalls, with our crowd of kids in tow, I attempted to buy oranges while Jim went to look for Cokes. The oranges were my first purchase in the Third World.

"Hello mister," shouted a stallkeeper crouching on a stool behind a tall pyramid of oranges. An old-fashioned balance scale with lead weights stood beside the pile of fruit. Yellow teeth glimmered inside a rough beard as he smirked. Everyone seemed to be smiling at me and pointing. I felt incredibly foreign with my white skin, blond hair, and Western clothes. With the crowd studying my every move, I fumbled with our Berlitz Arabic language guide, looking up the Arabic phrase for "How much is that?"

"Bikeam haeze," I said.

The stallkeeper's grin broadened as he shrugged dramatically, playing to the crowd.

"Bikeam haeze," I repeated, pointing at the oranges. "Shekels?" I ventured.

"Bikeam haeze!" repeated the man, mocking my accent. The crowd laughed. He loudly announced something. I guessed it was some outrageous amount for the oranges. He held up ten fingers and said "kilo." At seventeen shekels to the dollar, he wanted sixty cents for about two pounds of oranges. In the States, this was a great price, but I sensed I was being cheated, so I held up five fingers. The crowd laughed again; was I *still* paying too much? The man pretended to be outraged at this price. After shouting in Arabic, he held up eight fingers. We haggled like this until I agreed to pay six shekels for a kilo of oranges. By now, the whole city seemed to be watching this spectacle. Later, I found out that a kilo of oranges should have cost three shekels, or about eighteen cents.

Outside of Khan Yunis the small farm plots faded into long stretches of sand. Almond trees and groundnuts replaced wheat and corn. Soon even the almond trees faded into a sea of desolation. Only two colors existed in the desert: the peanut color of the empty sand and the cornflower blue of the sky. This land was the stuff of romance, a place that more than fulfilled my expectations of adventure and excitement. On my bike I could easily imagine myself as Lawrence of Arabia thundering over the dunes with a hundred Arabs on camelback.

Occasionally we would spot glimpses of magic. On a distant dune, a Bedouin warrior would be crouched beside his camel, his white headgear glowing in the sun, and his long, curved sword scratching the sand as he gently rocked back and forth. A few kilometers later a group of women would appear in a small oasis of palms, their gowns decorated with purple and orange and yellow designs. They would drop their veils and wink at us like genies suddenly appearing out of Aladdin's lamp. A moment later, as we biked over the next dune, the Bedouin women would be gone.

Bedouin is a French perversion of the Arabic word *bedawi,* meaning "dwellers in the desert." No one definitely knows where the Sinai Bedouins originated, but they have been feared and respected for their resilience and knowledge of desert ways since Pharaonic Egypt. They have watched some of the greatest armies in history pass across their peninsula, using it as a corridor for conquest or retreat. Ramses, Solomon, Alexander, Caesar, the Arabs, Napoleon, the Imperial armies of Britain, and the modern armies of Israel and Egypt have all coveted this wasteland as a link or a bulkhead between Palestine and the Nile. The trash and litter of many wars lie buried under the shifting sands. Vestiges of the 1967 Six-Day War and the 1973 Yom Kippur War are still scattered across the dunes. The rusted hulks of tanks and trucks are half buried like skeletal mastodons in the sand. Empty foxholes appear frequently on abandoned hills. Occasionally, the current generation of tanks and trucks passed by. As on the West Bank, the soldiers usually waved.

No map gives an accurate kilometer count for the North Sinai road. One map said, "Distances in Sinai are approximate," and then neglected to provide even approximate distances. We guessed that it would take three days to reach the Suez Canal from Khan Yunis, and then another day to make Cairo. We still did not know if the army would let us pedal across the desert. Our plan was to bike to the city of El Arish, on the temporary Israeli-Egyptian border. If we were lucky, no one would stop us.

Our schedule was a critical consideration. In Europe, we had not worried as much about keeping a set pace because we had had no definite events planned for HOPE. But now we did have an obligation. In only five days we were expected in Cairo for the first major promotional program of the trip. Cairo was the only city on our route where a HOPE program was in operation, so we wanted to make the most of it. The HOPE In Egypt staffers were scheduling interviews and photo opportunities all over the city. I also had a personal reason for rushing to Cairo. Laura was arriving in four days. I could hardly think of anything else.

At five-thirty that night the sun abruptly fell in a blaze of golden light. In the darkness, the lights marking the border crossing glowed across the desert. They grew brighter until we could distinguish shapes of boxlike buildings and a tall billboard: Welcome to the Neot Sinai Border. Spotlights illuminated a customs house, several barracks buildings, and a lot filled with jeeps, troop transports, and tanks. A high steel fence topped with barbed wire spread across the sand to the right and left. Red and white turnstile gates blocked both lanes going by a Fotomat-sized guardhouse in the middle of the road. Only two kilometers away was the yellow-white glow of El Arish, where we had hoped to be sleeping. But the Israeli guards had other ideas.

"I am sorry, the border close at five," said a young soldier. "Come back in morning."

We stared at him like he was crazy. "We have no place to spend the night," I said.

"We are on bicycles," added Don. "It has taken all day to come from Gaza."

"You cannot stay on the border!" said the guard. "It is not allowed. This is dangerous place."

"But where will we sleep?"

"I do not know," he said. "I will call my commanding officer."

The commanding officer, a tired-looking man in khaki fatigues, understood our problem, but repeated that it was dangerous for us to sleep on the border. "I have idea for you," he said. "The Neot Sinai kibbutz is up the hill." He pointed into the black night. "Perhaps they will allow you to stay in their compound. I must warn you, though, these people are not friendly. Please follow me."

At the gate to Neot Sinai, two security men from the kibbutz stopped our group. They spoke sharply with the CO. "They tell us no foreigners are allowed inside," translated one of the soldiers escorting us. "Do you know about Camp David?" We nodded. "These people must lose their homes to the Egyptians," he said. "I am sorry they are rude."

As the CO and the security men argued, an intense man with red-rimmed eyes sprinted over from a row of houses across the sand. He carried an Uzi in his right hand. Our translator groaned and said, "This is the leader."

"Go away," screamed the leader in English. Then he let loose a barrage of Hebrew at the soldiers (the same soldiers who would have to move these people under Camp David). "Get away!" he spit out words full of hate. I had never heard such bitter words, full of fear and loathing and violence. "Get away!" His face seethed with rage, but his eyes looked tired.

Back at the border crossing, we were sure that the CO would

send us back. But after a long discussion with someone on a shortwave radio, he guided us to a canvas lean-to across from the customs house.

"This place is a taxi stand in the day," he explained. "You sleep here. Do not move, unless for toilet in customs house. Mines and guns are here. I repeat. Do not move."

The next morning, the customs procedures on the Israeli side were quick and efficient for anyone with a Western demeanor. For a long line of Bedouins waiting to cross the border, customs was a slow process. "They cross here every day," said a customs officer. "They live on Israeli side of the border and work on Egyptian side. Many terrorists try to pass through. We must be careful."

After customs, we pedaled across a wide no-man's-land between the Israeli and Egyptian lines. Full of the excitement of entering a new country, we were eager to get our passports quickly stamped so that we could get moving. But Egyptians seldom do anything quickly. It would be hours before we pedaled away from the shabby, relaxed customs station.

Egyptian customs was a study in contrast with the Israeli side. Hastily built mud-brick buildings on the temporary border were already cracking and their whitewash peeling, but nobody seemed to care. Israeli customs officers had quickly and expertly inspected our papers, changed our shekels to dollars, and said good-bye. Their customs instructions were clean and printed on high-quality paper. Over here, Egyptians in their baggy uniforms smiled lazily and took forever at every small task. Printed materials were smeared and tore easily. It was a frustrating day, a day of waiting in the hot sun for officials to finish tea breaks or long telephone calls. We spent the time sipping warmish Pepsis and eating crackers with a few equally frustrated tourists on the east side of a small café in the middle of the compound. Several dozen Arabs, mostly Bedouins, were sprawled on the south side of the café, laughing and drinking muddy Turkish coffee, happy to be on this side of the border.

The main road through El Arish displayed all the trappings of peace. These were the heady days just after Camp David, when the Sinai celebrated peace after years of warfare. The face of Camp David's hero, Anwar el-Sadat, rose on dozens of billboards and posters. The cartoonlike paintings depicted Sadat in business suits, a general's uniform, and the native *djel-*

laba. In every scene he was smiling or gazing toward the heavens. Sadat was five months in his grave when we entered Egypt, but his presence was still vivid in this land he liberated. Other billboards depicted cartoon doves holding garlands of olive branches that intertwined the Israeli Star of David and the golden eagle of Egypt.

Peace seemed to be bringing prosperity and hope to El Arish and the Sinai as Egypt spent vast sums (most of it provided by Jimmy Carter as part of Camp David) to modernize their new territory. Along the seaside road, beside beautiful white beaches, teams of workers erected new hotels and apartment buildings. Still more billboards featured paintings of houses, oil wells, water pipelines, roads, and television antennas. A Bedouin shopkeeper told us that El Arish was going to be a big resort area, "like Miami Beach."

Just outside El Arish, we encountered our first Bedouin village. Clustered near the highway were thirty dark leather tents surrounded by walls of tightly woven desert scrub bristling with thorns. Camels wandered about with hobbles tied around their front legs. Large barrels of fresh water delivered by truck each morning sat under awnings alongside the road. Two permanent buildings constructed of stone and corrugated tin were stores selling the staples of the desert—canned mackerel, canned peas, tomato paste, Mars bars, mango juice, fresh fruit (oranges and dates were in season), cigarettes, eggs, and Coca-Cola.

Kids in ragged, pajamalike tunics spotted us first. "Hello mister! Hello mister!" they squealed, dashing out from tents to scatter clucking chickens, goats, and dogs. They didn't want to miss four Americans in black tights, orange fluorescent vests, and bug-eyed goggles. "What time is it? What is your name?" they screamed, apparently the only phrases they knew in English.

As the sun set, we began searching for a safe place to camp on the open sands. This proved difficult because of a small Bedouin enclave on top of a distant dune. It commanded a wide view of the entire area. The warnings about Bedouin bandit gangs and murderers had already made us nervous. The possibility that one of those gangs was watching us from atop that dune added another level of fear. Finally, we stopped to scope out the enclave with Jim's bird binoculars.

"We're being watched," he announced. "I see two Bedouins using binoculars." He handed me the glasses.

Focusing, I saw two men in white desert garb. They stood in front of an enclosure of thornbush walls. Peaks of leather tents poked up from behind the walls.

An hour after this first sighting, the Bedouins were still following our progress. We thought about riding at night, but quickly vetoed the idea. The road here had grown thin, and the traffic was faster and more maniacal. It was crucial to find a campsite before dark. Road signs had warned us all afternoon about mines: DANGER: STAY ON MAIN ROAD. MINE FIELDS IN AREA. We weren't eager to be strolling on the sand in the black of night.

Finally, we decided to take our chances. With Don and Dave watching the bikes, Jim and I took a careful walk over a tall dune that blocked the view from the Bedouin camp. Maybe they wouldn't bother us if we were out of sight. By dark, we had the tents up, with the bikes stacked and locked together under our orange plastic tarps. Tin cans and pots were on top to alert us to intruders. Dave rigged a couple of trip wires.

We spread our second tarp on the hard sand as a table cloth for Jim and Dave, that night's cooks. Dinner went quickly and tasted more like sand than noodles and mackerel. Sand got into everything—our hair, our clothes, even our bicycle gears. We would have to clean the bikes in Cairo. As the temperature plunged (deserts are typically hot in the day and cold at night), Jim discovered an effective method to stay warm. We had all bought *kaffiyehs* as jokes in a Jerusalem tourist shop. Jim tried his on and pronounced it warm and comfortable. (The next morning we replaced our helmets with *kaffiyehs*. Not only were they warm at night, they were cool in the heat and kept the blowing sand out of our faces.)

After dinner, when the reassuring hiss of the stoves was shut off, we sat in the hushed darkness under an astounding canopy of stars. No man-made lights diluted the radiance of the starlight. Even without a moon, the sand glowed a cold silver, like snow at night. The utter silence mesmerized me as I stared at the vastness of the desert and the frozen brilliance of the heavens. It seemed appropriate that two of the world's great religions had received inspiration from this desert. Moses received the Ten Commandments here, and Jesus came to fast and gather strength against the temptations of the devil. The Sinai is a perfect place to find God, because its vastness makes a person feel tiny and insignificant while at the same time making him feel the strength and timelessness of the universe, or of God, or of whatever it is that makes one contemplate eternity.

Word spread quickly that foreigners on bicycles were traveling along the Northern Sinai highway. At first, we stayed clear of the Bedouins, remembering the warnings. But it soon became clear that the Bedouins we met along the road were not the bandits and cutthroats we had heard about in Israel. The desert people were actually quite friendly. Despite our fears, we had passed our first night out of El Arish without being bothered. By the second day out of El Arish, the headman of each village was on hand at the edge of the highway to invite us into their tents for tea. We sat cross-legged on wool rugs in large central rooms. Meetings started with a short ceremony of exchanging cigarettes. Jim and Don smoked theirs (they revived old habits on the desert); Dave and I accepted the cigarettes, but kept them hanging unlit from our lips until time to leave.

Questions over tea began solemnly, but soon broke down into good-natured arguments. Bedouins had a habit of waving their hands passionately when they spoke, like Italians. The conversations usually centered on politics. Bedouin leaders were surprisingly knowledgeable about world affairs. "Why does America support Israel?" they asked. "Is it not in the interest of the West to support Arabs?" They universally detested Israel, even though the nation had built the first paved roads on the Sinai and had educated them in new schools.

"They bring guns and bombs and kill our people," said one man. "These roads and schools mean nothing."

One headman spit when I mentioned Israel. A mouthful of coffee and spittle shot from his mouth to splatter across a goat's wool rug. Everyone was sprayed, but no one moved to wipe it off. To do so might have offended the headman.

"Let me speak to you about Israel," he said, licking his lips. "In Israel, five categories exist. One, Jews from Europe. Two, Jews not from Europe. Three, dogs and animals. Four, the dirt on the ground. Five, the Arabs." His voice was low and reverberated with hate. It was almost a growl. He spit again. "It was the best day in my life when Israel moved away."

Before we left, our Bedouin hosts clasped our arms and promised us a safe journey. They didn't *wish* us a safe journey, it was a promise of protection. We heartily thanked them, but we didn't really believe that they could stop some random attack out on the open sands.

It took four days from El Arish to cross the Sinai. I wrote in my journal that we were living some of our most exciting memories, even if they were making us late to Cairo. Everything conspired to slow us down. Besides all of the time spent drinking tea with Bedouins, Don and Dave cracked their pannier racks, which took several hours to repair. We also had to spend a great deal of time cooking food and boiling drinking water. Now that we were out of the West, water had to be considered suspect. We started using iodine tablets brought from home. Iodine would become a major part of our lives for the next few months.

By the third day, I was anxious to reach the Suez so that we could get to Cairo. Laura would be arriving soon, and I was sure that HOPE was wondering if we would make it on time for our press activities. The other guys were less impatient to finish the desert journey. Don was shooting three or four rolls of film a day, and Jim and Dave were enjoying the exhilaration of pedaling across the Sinai.

It was close to dusk on the fourth day when we sighted the city of El Kantara on the Suez Canal. Actually, we sighted the ruins of El Kantara. It was here that Anwar el-Sadat launched a major thrust in the October war of 1973, a surprise attack against Israeli-occupied Sinai. Israel lost dozens of tanks and hundreds of men before throwing the Egyptians back across the canal. In the process El Kantara was decimated and left to rot in the desert sands. We pedaled past jagged, roofless walls and shattered asphalt. Burned-out hulks of tanks littered the streets. It looked like a set for a bombed-out village in a World War II movie, but this was no set. It was real. Real people had died here. We stopped for several minutes to stare, to reflect on the wreckage. It was not hard to imagine the scenes of death and destruction, of children screaming and corpses lying in pools of blood. I caught sight of a sun-bleached rag wrapped in a pile of rubble. Was this a piece of clothing? Who had it belonged to? Several rotting shoes were scattered about. It struck me that in photos and TV clips of war in civilian areas shoes are always plentiful among the debris. Why do the dead always leave behind their shoes?

El Kantara was a poignant conclusion to our journey from Jerusalem. It seemed to tie together the random events and meetings of the past few days, to put into perspective this land of conflict and suffering. I thought of the explosions we had heard near Gaza and shuddered at the thought of men blown to bits. I thought of Khalil and his stories of dodging bullets as a boy. I thought of Saer and his young friends killing or being killed in the Israeli army. I thought of the Israeli boys with their gun and of the other instruments of destruction we had seen. Out on the desert, I had felt close to God. But what God could allow the suffering that had occurred in El Kantara to take place? In silence, we pedaled through the destruction toward the canal.

The Suez Canal as it flows by El Kantara is a crack of water barely a kilometer wide. Huge tankers tower above the shore, sometimes clearing the banks on either side by just a few meters. Day and night the ships float by in a relentless stream of commerce. We crossed the canal on a tiny ferry shaped like an alligator. Egyptians and Bedouins crowded on board carrying everything from canvas bags of lentils to live goats. One boy in a bright green sweater and gray slacks played twangy Middle Eastern music on a large cassette player.

The skipper of the ferry delighted in stopping at the dock for only a few seconds, forcing the passengers to leap and scramble frantically off and on the boat. In a whirl of confusion, hands reached out to help us pull the bikes onto the snout of the boat. I grabbed onto a winch in the stern and held my bike tight as the boat lurched and pitched in the wake of the big ships. Slipping between a Russian freighter and a Kuwaiti tanker, we arrived on the opposite bank, where hands again grabbed my bike and started pitching it toward the dock. This time, it almost fell into the canal. I grabbed my rear wheel just before my livelihood slid into the water.

Then, suddenly, we were on the dock and the ferry was gone. Pushing the bikes into the clamor and dust of the darkening city, I sensed that we were embarking on a new phase of our journey. Part of it was the fact that we were on a new continent, Africa. But the feeling was deeper. For the past two months, we had been more or less living an adventure. Spain and Israel had been thrilling, intoxicating experiences for a romantic like me. Coming from a world of television, books, and movies, I had viewed these places in terms of stories and images, as realms of make-believe, of magic and fantasy.

Then came El Kantara. It brought into sharp focus this region of conflict, where death and suffering were not only real, they were ugly and disgusting, reflecting a barbaric streak in the nature of people. This was a shock for me. I had always been taught that people were basically good. Yet I was seeing that evil, real evil, exists in the world. It was a frightening revelation, one of those startling instances where a deep truth begins to take hold.

From the dock, we pushed the bikes into a wide, turbulent avenue congested with donkeys, camels, people, smoke, and dust. The odor of burning kerosene and manure blew strong in my nostrils. Overhead, bats swooped through the darkness as the low moaning of a muezzin atop a minaret called the faithful to evening prayers.

3. Five Thousand Years Up the Nile

I stroked Laura's hair, lying beside her at Cairo's Shepheard's Hotel, a restoration of the great colonial hotel burned by Nasser's revolutionaries in 1951. Eight floors below our room the gray-brown waters of the Nile swirled through the heart of El Qahira the Triumphant, the jewel of the Nile, the city of a thousand minarets. A thin sliver of afternoon sunlight blazed between drawn drapes. Laura's winter skin glowed against the pale light. I studied her face as she slept. When I lightly brushed my lips over hers, she stirred and smiled dreamily. After a sixteen-hour flight from New York, she was in a deep sleep, trying to catch up to a time zone ten thousand miles away.

Jim, Don, Dave, and I had arrived in Cairo just after noon, after a morning ride from El Kantara. The guys were asleep down the hall. The next day, they planned to move in with Project HOPE families living in Cairo, while Laura and I stayed on in the old-world luxury of the Shepheard's. Laura was giving me ten days at the hotel as a present for my twenty-fourth birthday, which was five weeks away.

•••

Project HOPE's Egyptian office had been in operation for six years when we arrived in Cairo. Its aim was to improve the education of doctors, nurses, and health care workers in Egypt. The core of the program was several courses taught by HOPE professionals at the Cairo University medical school. A HOPE nurse was also organizing an effort to train nurses in the southern city of Asyut.

HOPE's administrative office was located in a tidy suburb across the Nile from the Shepheard. A vivacious woman named Melvina ran the office with a dour Egyptian colonel assigned by the government as a sort of troubleshooter. "He's here to cut through the bull of Egyptian bureaucracy," Melvina told us. The latest problem for the colonel was the sudden and mysterious cancellation of HOPE's duty-free status for overseas supplies. "One day we had the privilege, and the next day *puff!*, it was gone," Melvina said.

I was disappointed in the HOPE office. It was just a few rooms in a house filled with stainless steel desks, file cabinets, and several posters of American HOPE doctors helping foreign-looking children. It did not come close to my vision of a charity operation in a Third World country. I had imagined a big white building sitting like a miracle in the midst of poverty. "*Everybody* is disappointed when they first come," Melvina told me. "It's a major misconception in the States that charity money is instantly transformed into medicine for dying kids. It just isn't like that. It takes a hell of a lot of money just to get the stuff over here. In our case, we're getting doctors over here to teach. That's expensive, not to mention the constant headache of dealing with a foreign government."

"You sound frustrated," I said.

"Oh, not really," she smiled, "it's just a lot of hassles. We have reports to file with the Egyptian government, with the U.S. government, and with HOPE. I mean, look at all this paperwork!" She waved dramatically at several sloppy stacks on her desk. "I hate to tell you this, but charity work these days is mostly a bunch of papers getting shuffled all over the place. It's sad, because there is so much work to be done. You'll see it when you bicycle. You'll see garbage all over the place and kids drinking right out of the Nile. It makes you want to scream sometimes, because nothing seems to be getting done. But you gotta do what you can, and you gotta do it despite all the stupid hassles. That's my idea of charity. Doing what you can, 'cause it's all you can do."

Our publicity program in Cairo was less extensive than I had hoped. Melvina had contacted most of the Western news agencies and the major Egyptian newspapers, but no one had coordinated a central press conference or publicity schedule. Consequently, we ran pell-mell around Cairo, stopping at NBC radio one day and Cairo's *El Ahram* newspaper the next day. Only one major publication refused to interview us. *Time* magazine's bureau chief said we would have to be kidnapped by terrorists before they would cover the story. While working on publicity, Jim, Don, Dave, and I also prepared for the African phase of our journey. Jim had several pages of his list book filled with items "to be done immediately," things like getting visas for Sudan, overhauling the bikes, and buying necessities like iodine, Chapstick, and sunglasses.

One afternoon we had a session with the colonel and some HOPE staffers about food and water problems in Egypt and places to sleep at night. We already had learned that all water should be boiled and food washed with soap and boiled water. "We spend half our time here scrubbing veggies," said Melvina. She said that coffee and tea were okay, because the water was boiled. Cokes and other soft drinks were all right too, because the water used was supposedly purified by the bottlers in Egypt. All other drinks—milk, fruit juice, homemade sodas—were forbidden. So were salad greens and raw vegetables.

"Use common sense," said one HOPE staffer. "If something looks bad, don't eat it."

HOPE field people told us that we would be able to buy all the food we needed in village markets, but they were leery about camping. "It will be hard to find campsites where you won't be bothered," a HOPE nurse told Jim. "You've got a strip of land five miles wide packed with thirty-five million people. There just isn't much free space left."

HOPE doctors warned us to avoid the Nile at all costs. Everything from typhoid to diphtheria swirled through its brown waters. Even worse was a microscopic organism called schistosomiasis, carried by the larvae of a tiny snail. Small enough to pass through human skin, these microorganisms clamp onto one's capillaries and then multiply by the thousands. Eventually, they block the flow of blood enough to first debilitate and then kill a victim. Eighty percent of all Egyptians suffer from schistosomiasis.

Laura managed to tolerate the activity in Cairo, although it wasn't exactly her idea of a vacation. But we enjoyed being together after two months apart. At the end of a workday, we would go back to the hotel, have a nice dinner, a bottle of awful Egyptian wine, and a quiet evening together. We also found time to stroll through the cavernous, dusty rooms of the Cairo National Museum, climb the Citadel built by the Khedive Muhammad Ali, and steer through legions of hawkers and beggars selling bogus artifacts in the city's tourist bazaars.

In our moments alone, Laura told me about New York, about dancing at Studio 54 and Danceteria, about going out for late-night cappuccinos or a Häagen-Dazs cone with friends. At her investment bank she was putting together a public stock offering for a computer software company. She was thinking about business school and was going to volunteer to work for Planned Parenthood if she could find the time. I listened intently, but her world seemed far away.

The night she left, which was our last night in Cairo, we both cried as the taxi waited to take her to the airport. It seemed like our ten days had gone by in a flash of time. "Are we really going to be apart for eight more months?" she said. "That's such a long time!" I clung to her, wanting to tell her I was sorry for putting her though this, and that I would make it up to her. But all I could blurt out was, "I love you."

Riding south from the HOPE office, we pedaled in a tight line along the wide Sharia al Giza avenue toward the Great Pyramids. Our helmets were strapped tight, our goggles in place, and our road whistles hanging from our lips to tweet at cars that came too close. The rear man called out what was approaching from behind. The front man warned about problems ahead. We envied the native cyclists riding blithely side by side, carrying on conversations as cars and trucks and buses narrowly missed crushing them from a thousand different angles.

The bikes were tuned and working smoothly. I touched my right gearshift lever and watched the chain flip effortlessly across scrubbed-clean cogs. The brakes were trigger sensitive. Both wheels shimmered in the sun rising over the Nile. My new Cycle Pro tires were not even dusty. In our panniers were three-week supplies of everything from Quaker Oats oatmeal to HOPE buttons and flags. A *Time* magazine was clipped onto my rear load for easy access during water breaks. From a box of equipment sent from the States, we had new water bags for the desert, insect repellent, malaria pills, mosquito netting for our heads, and a multitude of spare parts. I had a crisp, new copy of *The White Nile* and a book of Scott Fitzgerald short stories. Jim had new bird books and *The Blue Nile.* Don had a copy of *The Innocents Abroad,* and Dave had purchased a copy of a best-selling spy novel called *KGB.*

We were traveling lighter than at any time in Europe or Israel. Gone were wool sweaters, sweats, and leg tights. Anything that wasn't essential had been pruned away. Unread books, spare parts that we were unlikely to use, and other assorted items had been sent home. This cleaning process became a regular ritual every couple of months on the trip. It was like cleaning out the drawers in my desk back home.

The frenzy of Cairo engulfed us as we steered among three streams of traffic: the kamikaze trucks and cars in the middle of the avenue, the donkey carts and bicycles moving along the edge of the road, and the flow of people, dressed in everything from suits to ragged djellabas, pushing and shoving on the sidewalk. In the lead, I squeezed my brakes and screamed "Slowing" as a bicycle vendor loaded with tomatoes jerked out in front of us, forcing me to veer left, where an old Austin-Healy was roaring down the wrong side of the road. I squeezed hard on my brakes, blowing a loud peal from my whistle at the tomato man. I fought an urge to close my eyes and scream as the Austin-Healy narrowly missed squashing me.

South of the Great Pyramids, on the edge of the city, the shabby blocks of two-storied commercial buildings began thinning out into an occasional outdoor stall or coffee shop and then stopped altogether, replaced by strips of tall elephant grass and coconut palms. Rats scurried into the thick grass as our tires buzzed across the roughly textured asphalt. This was a minor road mostly used by tourists heading for the ancient city of the dead at Saqqara. To our left was a black canal, part of the nation's intricate system of irrigation. Across the canal in the direction of the river grew a thin band of tobacco and a distant line of trees. To the east was the Sahara desert, marked by a long string of pyramids marching south toward Memphis, the capital of Lower Egypt during the Old Kingdom.

This world was silent and still after the chaos of Cairo and modern Egypt. The panorama of palms, tobacco, and pyramids flowed with the steadiness and serenity of the great river beyond the trees. In some ways, the landscape was like the desert in its timelessness. I had a sense that nothing had changed for centuries, that the ancestors of the people we saw had performed identical tasks thousands of years ago. The same small girls had guided water buffalos hitched to wooden wheels that lifted canal water into irrigation ditches. The same men on miniature donkeys had carried greens in baskets, and the same farmers had studied their crops while squinting in the sun and chewing on sweet shucks of sugarcane.

Near Saqqara, we passed a squalid row of dried mud and concrete huts across the canal. Festering piles of garbage and excrement stood between the huts, drawing clouds of flies. Chickens, dogs, and children played in the garbage piles, while their mothers knelt beside the polluted canal to wash tin kettles and clothing. On one level, I was shocked and disturbed by seeing open sewers, earth huts, and the pocked, wrinkled faces of men who at age twenty-five looked fifty. I felt the blend of embarrassment and outrage that Americans typically feel when confronted with the inequities of the world. Fresh from the West, I thought of how absurdly lucky I had been to be born an American in the late twentieth century.

Yet on another level, the poverty in Egypt was not nearly as bad as I had expected. My image of poverty in the Third World was a montage of distended stomachs, open sores, and half-dead men begging desperately for food. Poverty to me was black-and-white glossies of starving children and primitive shacks on Project HOPE and Save the Children posters. The people I saw in the villages south of Cairo were not really destitute. Many of the villagers lived in concrete, government-issue huts, and a few had electricity. Food seemed to be no problem. Several communities had radios, cassette players, and motorized irrigation pumps. These people were poor, but not in the desperate sense I had always equated with the term *Third World.*

At dusk the quiet, pastoral road intersected with the modern insanity of the Egyptian National Highway, the "red road" on our map that follows the Nile for a thousand kilometers between Cairo and Aswan. Trucks rushed past at blinding speeds, their horns squealing like air raid sirens, their lights blurring in a rush of color. On the edges of the road the air was heavy with the scent of burning metal and gasoline from smoky repair garages. Men in greasy tunics worked as fantails of steel-blue welding sparks splashed off battered fenders, illuminating faces with mustaches and blue-tinted goggles. The dust was thick. It stuck in a gooey film on our sweaty skin and choked us so much we resorted to wrapping bandanas around our mouths like outlaws in the Wild West.

Our Egyptian guidebook called this stretch of road, about forty kilometers south of Cairo, the "industrial heartland of Egypt." The thick haze of truck yards seemed to go on forever. High smokestacks hovered like phantoms in the distance, emitting billows of smoke and steam in swaths of Dickensian grays and blacks. As night fell, we looked for a hotel or campsite, but none existed. Donning reflector vests and attaching flashlights to our handlebar bags, we kept biking through the eerie industrial glow. It was a frightening ride as speeding trucks careened past, rushing south from Cairo. Gradually the truck yards began to thin out into more plots of elephant grass and fields of wheat and corn.

"We're going to have to find a spot to camp," Dave announced when we stopped to assess the situation.

"It's too dangerous," said Don. "We're too close to people, and we can't see anything." He was peering into the black nothingness just off the road.

"Unless you know of a hotel nearby, camping's our only choice," said Dave.

We eventually found a spot across a narrow canal, behind a thick entanglement of sabra cactus bushes. It was flat enough for two tents and out of sight of the road. But we were apprehensive. The colonel at HOPE had warned against camping in the open. "It is dangerous and illegal," he said. "But if you must camp, find a secluded spot out of sight."

We quietly raised the tents, stripped the bikes, stacked them, and locked them to a tree. Crickets and less familiar bugs buzzed in the humid air. I jumped when the stove was lit. It sounded like an explosion that could be heard miles away. We quickly diced several tomatoes, onions and okra, adding them to a pot of boiling bouillon. This "gruel" would become disgustingly familiar over the next several months. The HOPE people had warned us to boil vegetables in Egypt for twenty minutes, to kill all amoebas and viruses. Twenty minutes seemed to take hours. I timed it with my Casio digital watch.

That night we slept with our whistles in our hands, ready to blow if we heard an intruder. Every breath of wind rattling the palms woke us up, until the exhaustion of the day's ride finally put us into a deep sleep sometime after midnight.

In the morning, voices woke me. Poking my head out of the tent, I saw three boys in rough-spun robes staring at our two green domed tents and stack of eighteen-speed bikes sitting on the edge of their sugarcane field. It must have been as strange as my waking up in Kansas City to find a Martian flying saucer in my backyard. When the muezzin's call came wailing over a distant loudspeaker, the boys scampered away, down a corridor cut into the tall, green canes.

In the light of day, the world seemed much safer than it had in the darkness. I thought about waking up the guys but saw on my watch that we still had seventeen more minutes to sleep before the alarm went off at six A.M. Exhausted and stiff from the hard ground, I slid back into my sleeping bag and fell back to sleep.

For the next several days, we biked through the schizophrenic blend of ancient, pastoral Egypt and frenetic twentieth-century Egypt. Our pace was leisurely, about seventy kilometers a day. Jim, Don, and Dave insisted that we not repeat the quick pace of Europe and Israel. Jim wanted time to see the scenery, Don wanted time for photographs, and Dave just liked going slow. I still wanted to keep a faster pace, but I was outvoted.

We quickly established a daily routine. Waking to the muezzin's call, we fixed our breakfast of oatmeal and jam, carefully boiling water for cooking and adding doses of iodine to drinking water. We struck camp while listening to the Voice of America's "Breakfast Show" over our little shortwave. As the morning mists cleared and the egrets flew over the canals, we donned dust masks, goggles, and helmets and began pedaling slowly south, pausing every hour to down a cold Coke in roadside huts selling tea, biscuits, Mars bars, and cassette tapes featuring twangy Arab songs. We sometimes played tourist in the mornings, stopping at some of the abundant tombs, ruined temples, and Coptic churches.

At noon we ate a light meal of mackerel on pita bread and took a short nap. About two-thirty we stopped in one of the frequent villages to haggle with stallkeepers over groceries for dinner. Late in the afternoon we began searching for a campsite, a spot flat, secluded, far enough from a canal to avoid mosquitoes, and far enough from a village to avoid the curious kids that popped up everywhere. At night, after eating a meal of gruel, we discussed routes, our maps spread out in the dust. Later we turned on the shortwave for the nightly rounds of "radio wars" broadcast to Egypt from America, Russia, Israel, South Africa, Britain and—to our surprise—Cuba. Speaking to "African comrades," Radio Havana claimed one night that Canada was on the brink of economic collapse, and that a Communist "liberation" was imminent. On a later broadcast, Radio Moscow claimed that President Reagan was planning a first strike against Eastern Europe that could occur "at any moment." The VOA also broadcast propaganda, but it was much more subtle, featuring slick programs on pop music, movie stars, and America's technological achievements.

By eight we retired to the tents to write postcards and read a few pages from our books before falling into a deep, exhausted sleep. Some nights I fell asleep listening to the cascading rhythms of Vivaldi's *Four Seasons* on my Aiwa tape player. Vivaldi always reminded me of Laura. As I drifted into sleep, I could see her and almost touch her.

From the beginning Egypt was fascinating. I spent hours on the bike observing the scenery: the green landscape set flush against the bleakness of the desert; the myriad of architectural styles ranging from decaying Ottoman gingerbread to the domed, pueblo-like churches of the Coptic Christians; and the constantly shifting waters of the Nile. Stallkeepers in quiet villages often gave us gifts of tea and biscuits. When farmers found us camped on the edge of their fields, they shyly approached us, accepting our invitations to have coffee. One evening we sat around a smoky fire of dried palm branches and taught two young farmers who spoke no English how to sing "When the Saints Come Marching In."

Unfortunately, not all Egyptians we met were this calm. The kids were the worst. Like crazed maniacs, they would appear out of nowhere when we stopped, grabbing at our bags and clothes and throwing rocks if we failed to wave or smile. Like mice behind the Pied Piper, dozens of them followed us everywhere, even when we ducked behind palm trees to relieve ourselves. "Hello mister, hello mister," they shouted incessantly. Their shrill voices became as annoying as the truck horns on the highway. Many older Egyptians were not much better. Stallkeepers in larger towns always made a special effort to haggle vigorously with us, amused by our lack of experience. They seemed to make a point of trying to grossly overcharge us every time we bought something. Sometimes they asked for as much as fifty times the usual price even though it was obvious we knew the going rate. Eight or nine times a day, *shai* stand owners would ask as much as seven dollars for a Coke (the actual price we paid was about fifteen cents). Everyone we met wanted something out of four young Americans. In the larger towns, students in Western clothes speaking broken English asked us repeatedly for help in obtaining visas to America. Others wanted to sell Egyptian pounds for dollars so they could buy motorcycles and tape players on the dollars-only black market. "Change dollars," whispered young men on street corners.

We attracted attention simply by existing. We were a curiosity for children and a symbol of potential profit for adults used to seeing tourists unload vast sums of money on trifles. Eventually the constant hassles, day after day, began to wear us down. A week out of Cairo, we met two American cyclists heading north toward the capital. After several months of biking and travel through the Third World, they were exhausted and sick of what they called "the hassle factor."

"I can't wait to get the hell out of this country," said one of the cyclists, a man who called himself Louisiana Bill. He had wide shoulders, long hair tied back in a ponytail, and a thick walrus mustache. His companion was a woman named Julie. For some reason, she was wearing at least four layers of sweatshirts and T-shirts despite the eighty-five-degree sun. "This place is a fucking pesthole," Louisiana Bill continued. "It gets to you after a while. The water's bad, the food tastes like shit, and there are always little urchins grabbing at you. Can you believe these kids?"

"Yeah, they're bad news," we agreed.

"You know why Julie has on all those clothes?" Bill asked. " 'Cause the maggots along the road keep grabbing at her tits. They think since she's traveling with a man she's not married to, she's a whore. It's all because they see these damn ads for Coke with titty blonds holding the soda bottles like pricks. Then they go and watch Farrah Fawcett jumping from bed to bed on television. Goddamned maggots." He asked us how long we had been biking in Egypt. When we told him, he shook his head. "You guys are in for a real swell time," he said sarcastically. "You'll see what I'm talkin' about."

Bill told us that he had been traveling in Asia and Africa for almost two years, some by bike, some by freighter, and some by train. In America, he had been an electrician on an oil rig in the Gulf of Mexico. "I'm goin' back to the States as soon as I can," he said. "I've been across Europe, Turkey, a little in India, and now in Africa. This stuff just isn't that fresh anymore."

As we talked, several kids popped out of sugarcane fields along the road and started running and screaming in our direction. "Here they come again," muttered Bill. Flipping open his handlebar bag, he drew out an eight-foot whip and casually cracked it toward the kids. They stopped so fast that one of them ran into the other and fell onto the road. Bill nonchalantly recoiled the whip and slipped it back in his bag.

"Damn whip works every time," he said, grinning.

As we pedaled down the road that day, I thought about Louisiana Bill cracking his whip. It seemed a remarkably callous act, an Ugly American tactic showing a gross lack of sensitivity. Yet deep down, it did not bother me as much as it might have a few days earlier. In the States, I would have deplored such an act. But somewhere in the darker corners of my mind, I was beginning to feel just a twinge of the resentment that compelled Louisiana Bill to snap a whip at Egyptian kids. I would never have admitted it then, but the "hassle factor" was starting to get to me.

The day after meeting Louisiana Bill, we were robbed by a group of kids during a sudden sandstorm blowing off the Sahara. One moment the sky was blue and the air clear, the next it was dark as twilight as the wind flung dirt and pebbles hard against our skin. Finding shelter behind a road embankment, we quickly set up the tents to get out of the storm. Fighting to slip the poles into the tent sleeves, we were surprised to see the usual gang of kids come running toward us shouting "Hello mister" and "baksheesh." Scarves were wrapped around their heads. Otherwise, they seemed unconcerned about the storm. We ignored them as we grabbed our essential bike bags and dove into the tents. Inside, I lay down, suddenly feeling tired. Despite the storm, I drifted off to sleep. A few minutes later, I woke up to a chorus of more "Hello misters" outside the tent Dave and I were sharing. My head ached from being suddenly awakened from a deep sleep. Then I heard something pop off the tent.

"Those urchins are throwing rocks at us again," said Dave. "Get out of here, you fucking urchins!" he screamed at the kids. The rocks stopped for a moment and then started again. We both lay back fuming as the kids shouted "Hello mister" and sprayed our tents with pebbles. "I'm getting sick of these damn urchins," Dave muttered.

"Why don't they leave us alone," I said quietly, feeling tired and irritated.

"I'll get them to leave us alone," Dave said, sitting up. He unzipped the tent door and ran at the kids, screaming like a maniac. They scrambled away into the storm, squealing with fear and delight. When Dave came back inside, he was smiling smugly. "I showed the little bastards," he said.

After napping for another thirty minutes, we emerged from the tents to a still, blue sky. It was as if the sandstorm had never happened. I started to collect our tent stakes when Jim discovered we had been robbed. Against the retaining wall, our bike panniers had been rifled, and most of our gear scattered across the dust.

"They got one of the stoves," said Jim. "It's the good stove, the one with the cleaning kit."

"They got my tools," said Don.

"We're lucky they didn't take the bikes," I said as we sat back against the wall, feeling a mixture of exhaustion and frustration.

"It was those fucking urchins," said Dave. "I could strangle them."

After nine days on the road, we checked into a clean, inexpensive hotel in Asyut with basic amenities like beds and running water. Rooms at the Cleopatra were only three pounds ($2.50) apiece. When we pushed our bikes into the hotel lounge, several Western "hippies" in makeshift caftans and baggy *baruka* trousers were watching "Dallas" on an old black-and-white television. J. R. Ewing drawled invective at some woman with fluffy, curly hair. "I get what I want, sweetheart," he said. Arabic subtitles floated at the bottom of the screen.

Early that afternoon, an Egyptian boy named Sherif took us

to a restaurant near our hotel. The building was a crumbling Ottoman-style house. We were led upstairs to a private room that had once been the dining room. A door carved in a lattice pattern led to a veranda that overlooked the frenetic street below. Almost immediately after sitting down, we discovered what Sherif wanted from us. "Can you help me get visa?" he asked. "If only I could go to your country!"

"Why do you want to go to America?" I asked.

He rolled his wide, brown eyes and told me that America was the best country in the world. "I can make money and buy a car and a television," he said. Then he leaned closer and whispered, "I also know there is free sex in America."

"Free sex?"

"I have a friend who writes me from New York. My friend, he says that he fucks a different girl every day."

As we talked, a waiter served Egyptian *foule,* a bean, flour and spice dish served with okra and greens. Since the greens were probably contaminated, we carefully picked them out of the *foule.*

"You are not eating the greens!" said Sherif. "They are very good! You must try them." He was looking at me anxiously, waiting for me to eat. I didn't want to be impolite. Hoping the stuff had been cooked, I ate a bite.

"That's very good!" I said, trying to smile.

Two hours later, I woke up from a nap in my room at the hotel with a sharp pain in my stomach. It was as if someone had knifed me. I struggled to stand up, feeling my stomach muscles vibrating wildly. Rushing down the hall, I made it to the Turkish-style toilet just in time to vomit. For ten minutes I retched. Sweat dripped from my head, and my stomach quivered in pain.

I was too sick to get up from bed for two days. I immediately tried Lomotil, an opiate drug provided by the doctors at Project HOPE. Lomotil was supposed to be the toughest medicine in existence for dealing with stomach bugs. If it helped, I didn't notice. The guys set up a stove somewhere in the Cleopatra and fixed me meals of oatmeal, chicken bouillon, and tea. I didn't keep any of it down. Don found some fat bananas in an Asyut market. He hung an entire bunch on the wall above my bed. Bananas are good for replacing the potassium lost during dysentery. The guys also found a canned goods store with bottled mineral water from Italy, which I drank by the liter.

I spent those two days sleeping, getting sick, listening to radio wars on the shortwave, and writing letters. I didn't have the strength to work on any articles. One of the hippies staying at the hotel told me that the longer we stayed in Egypt, the sicker we would be. "I am leaving as soon as I am well. I have been here six weeks, and have been sick for the last three."

I was still weak when we pedaled out of Asyut, but we couldn't afford to wait any longer. My stomach was stable, yet as delicate as glass. Every pothole or ragged patch of road caused a nauseating ripple effect. Just north of the city, we crossed the Asyut Barrage, a bridge that led to a newly paved, smooth road on the opposite bank, away from the frenzy of the Egyptian National Highway. Small tanks and machine gun nests guarded each side of the bridge. (As we headed south, military activity seemed to be picking up, although we never found out why.) Louisiana Bill had suggested this route. It was marked in yellow for "partially improved" on our Michelin map, but Bill had sworn that it was the most beautiful road in Egypt. "It'll get you away from those pissant trucks," he had said.

The Nile's east bank rolled by in a steady progression of fields and small, pueblo-like villages surrounded by eucalyptus and palms. It was a pleasant ride. Only a dozen trucks passed in fifty kilometers. The air was clear of the gagging dust and exhaust that canopied the National Highway. Spooky, bare white bluffs rose off to the left, marking the edge of the desert. Occasionally, caves with lotus-topped columns were cut into the cliffs. Our guidebook said they were used to store grain in the New Kingdom twenty-five hundred years ago. Jim stopped us to watch great blue herons, egrets, and bee-eaters.

Just after lunch, we discovered why we were alone on the east bank road. Abruptly, the smooth, black asphalt stopped, replaced by hard dirt. In the afternoon heat, we shed everything but T-shirts and shorts. Two kilometers from where the pavement ended, a Bedford lorry came tearing along the road, blowing a plume of dust into our faces. We donned dust masks, goggles, and helmets. As the ragged road buffeted my stomach, I had a short attack of dysentery. After gulping several sips of Kaopectate, I kept biking.

Three kilometers later, the road abruptly changed again, this time to a deep sand path. Pedaling fast, I hit the sand without warning. It was like hitting a beach at the end of a boardwalk.

The sand stopped my bike, but I kept going, flying off the seat to hit the sand as my machine fell on top of me. Like a glass crashing down from a great height, my stomach shattered and I cried out. Sand filled my mouth and eyes and stuck to the sweat on my skin.

"You okay?" shouted my brother, running over. I moaned and didn't speak. He gently unstrapped my helmet and wiped the sand from my face. He and Jim helped me to a shade tree on the side of the road. Dave came over with our last bottle of Italian water from Asyut. The cool, fresh water tasted good.

"Can you go on?" asked Don. As we sat under the tree, a gang of kids gathered to laugh and yell and point at us.

"I'm afraid he's going to have to go on," said Jim. "There's no place to camp here, especially with these kids everywhere."

The guys each took part of my gear to lighten my load, but when we tried to bike, the sand was too deep. With the kids in tow, we started pushing the bikes through the heavy sand. My stomach was a throb of pain. Time became surreal as I kept pushing and pushing. The road, the dust, the palms, the flies, even the pain became distant sensations. Cold beads of sweat dripped from under my helmet. I was aware that the crowd was growing. This stretch of road was a nonstop series of villages. At each town, the people dropped their work to join in the procession and gawk at the Americans slogging eighteen-speed bikes down their road. Over a hundred people had gathered by the time the road hardened enough to bike. I tried to shake off my lethargy. The crowd pressed in all around me, smelly, hot, and sticky. Hands grabbed at me. Voices shouted and laughed. I wanted to escape, to run away. "Let's get the hell out of here," Dave shouted from somewhere nearby.

Slinging a leg over my bike, I started to climb into the saddle. At the precise moment I was balancing myself, a hand from the mob grabbed my wrist and pulled. Another hand grabbed a mesh bag full of food dangling from my front rack. Abruptly, I was rushing through the air. For the second time that day, I came crashing to the ground. But this time I immediately sprang up, strengthened by a burst of intense anger. I grabbed a kid on the edge of the crowd. The frustrations and hassles of the past few days welled up inside. Jim, who was next to me, leaped off his bike to tackle the kid who had stolen the food. The four of us crashed in a heap to the ground. Like a ripple in that tightly packed mob, people fell down in a cloud of dust, cursing and screaming in Arabic. I held my boy for a few seconds before he squirmed away. I jumped up to run after him, but my stomach could take no more. I doubled over, feeling the knife of dysentery cutting into my abdomen.

When we finally got to Sohag, a town across the river, I was sicker than ever. The guys decided that I needed to be taken to a city with a good doctor and medical facilities. The next morning they put me and my bike on a train to Luxor, 250 kilometers to the south. Dave, who was also feeling sick, went along as my escort.

For two days in Luxor, we slept in clean sheets with an AC blowing cool, filtered air into a room at the four-star Luxor Hotel. I hated the idea of being so sick that I had to take a train and check into a luxury hotel, but I had no choice if I wanted to get well. Dave slept in the bed next to me. A hotel doctor loaded us up with blue-and-white capsules, and poured tablespoons of concentrated potassium down our throats. Convinced that my blood pressure was too low, he gave me a clear liquid that was supposed to boost my heartbeat. I tried to explain that I had been a runner in the States, which lowers one's heartbeat, but he didn't understand. In Egypt, nobody runs for fun.

On our third day in Luxor, Dave and I felt well enough to leave the Luxor Hotel and walk to the nicest hotel in town, the Etap, where we were told a coffee shop served hamburgers and french fries. In my khakis and oxford-cloth shirt, I felt refreshingly normal among the pale tourists strolling along the riverside corniche. Without our cycling tights, helmets, and bicycles, we were anonymous. No kids screamed and no people stared.

My first stop at the Etap was the newsstand, where I bought every English-language magazine they sold. I bought *Time, Newsweek, The Economist, The International Herald Tribune,* and six other magazines. I bought about sixty postcards to send to friends at home. In the coffee shop, we bit into soggy hamburgers and french fries brought by an unsmiling man in a maroon suit. With two watery Stella beers and ice cream, the bill came to eighteen dollars—the equivalent of two full days on the road for all four of us. With our hotel and doctor bills, Dave and I spent in two days of convalescence what had taken ten days for our whole group to spend on the road.

Jim and Don surprised us by pedaling past the Etap just as we emerged from lunch. At our usual 70 kilometers a day, they should have taken almost four days to bike the 250 kilometers between Sohag and Luxor. But they had managed to average a hundred kilometers a day, covering the distance in two and a half days. This feat put Jim and Don firmly on my side on the speed question, and reopened our arguments with Dave about pacing. For the rest of our stay in Luxor, we worked to get Dave to agree to up our daily average to at least 90 kilometers. He shrugged and said little, knowing it was in his best interest not to quote *The Complete Book of Bicycling*.

That afternoon, the four of us checked into a budget hotel in the hippie colony near the train station, where cheap hotels accommodated long-haired men and women in caftans and sandals. Dusty cafés sold omelets, Nescafé, and balls of gooey tobacco for rented hookahs. Disco and heavy metal music blew out of the speakers.

Luxor, the site of ancient Thebes, is an amalgam of a lazy tropical resort, a dusty Moslem village, and the Egyptian wing of a major museum. Along the corniche, the scrubbed ruins of the Luxor temple, dedicated to Lord Amon-Ra, are flanked by a half-dozen Western-style hotels. Moored to docks along the river are more hotels—floating resorts shaped like giant shoeboxes with windows. Senior citizens on cruise trips from Cairo stroll up and down gangplanks to haggle with hawkers over soapstone scarabs and strings of glass beads. In the shade of red-blossomed *kerkede* trees, horse-drawn tonga carriages glittering with bronze medallions and trinkets waited to carry tourists to the great temple complex at Karnak or to one of the ferry landings running across the river to the Valley of the Kings. Behind the corniche was Moslem Egypt. Its domes and neon-lined minarets rose in a confusing skyline against ancient pylons and modern hotels. Along the back side of the hotels and temples was an Arab bazaar, a dusty street where Luxorites sold everything from dried lentils and eggplants to djellabas embroidered with I Visited Egypt.

We spent two days touring every temple and museum and tomb on both sides of the river. Actually, only Jim, Don, and I toured the sights of Luxor. Dave, who had never shown much interest in the ruins we saw along the Nile, spent most of his time in the Etap eating hamburgers and reading *KGB*. It seemed incredible that he never once crossed the river to see the Valley of the Kings, but this was only the latest manifestation of Dave's growing distance from the group. Jim, Don, and I spent hours discussing this problem over spiced coffee in the hippie cafés. It was obvious that Dave was not fitting in. The three of us were growing closer because we shared many of the same likes and dislikes. We had all been raised in the Midwest, we were ambitious, we loved to have long discourses on every topic imaginable, and we spent as much time as possible studying what was going on around us. Jim had his birds, Don had his photography, and I had my writing. All Dave had was biking, and he was a near fanatic about it among companions who were mostly using bicycling as a vehicle for travel, not as an end in itself. We didn't share his rigidity about pacing, bike maintenance, rest stop strategies, and most other aspects of bicycle touring. Dave also hated Egypt. It was not his idea of a place to take a bicycle tour. He was talking all of the time now about biking in Vermont. He missed what he called "normal bicycle touring."

South of Luxor, Egypt's thin band of green narrows until the sand almost reaches the thin, blue river. Villages are farther apart and populated by a different race of people, the Nubians, with skin the color of polished mahogany. Their villages are small, walled compounds of squat, rectangular buildings. In the center of each village a domed, whitewashed mosque shines like a daisy against the desert and the distant bluffs. The dust is sparser here, and the heat much drier. The temperature was over a hundred degrees, but there was so little humidity we hardly sweated. Dave rode far behind us for the entire 235 kilometers between Luxor and Aswan. We told him that we were shooting for 90 kilometers a day, hoping that he would keep up. But he was stubborn as usual. We ended up spending at least an extra hour a day waiting for him.

After nearly three weeks of kid attacks and manic crowds, our original politeness had deteriorated into a barely disguised dislike. At one point, some kids ran up, but before they started screaming at us for baksheesh, we shouted "Baksheesh!" and "Hello mister!" at them. Holding our hands out like beggars, we continued to scream "baksheesh" until the baffled kids stepped back. Later, a man offered me a bundle of greens. I think it was a gift, but I angrily threw it back in his face. Another time, when all of us were riding together, two kids accidentally kicked a ball into the road in front of Dave. He threw down his bike, chased and grabbed the kid, and held him up by his collar as he screamed in fear. Then Dave turned to us. "How long do you think I ought to hold onto this urchin?" The boy was petrified by now and had stopped kicking.

"I'd hold him another minute," said Don, grinning like a little boy who is about to pull the wings off a captured fly.

Dave held him for another few seconds and then asked, "Should I let him down now?"

"Why not," I said. "Maybe he'll run all the way down the Nile and tell every urchin along the road to leave us alone."

We arrived in Aswan on my birthday, March 8, in time for lunch at a café on a street that looked like a shabby corner of Paris or Rome. Tables and chairs constructed of greasy planks were filled with hippies laughing, playing backgammon, drinking spiced coffee, and smoking hookahs. Young Egyptian imitators sat on the fringes, dressed in the same ragged caftans, baggy pants, and beards as the paler originals from Berlin, New York, London, and Paris.

A tall, long-haired Egyptian waiter in one of the cafés brought us chicken sandwiches and Cokes. A Western woman in a sari-like outfit and hair dyed red sat down uninvited at our table and asked where we had come from. She called herself Diva and said she had just come up from Sudan, where she claimed to have been the mistress of the U.S. ambassador. We tried to ask her questions about Sudan, but her mind was moving too fast. "I'm speeding," she said, laughing nervously. "They hang you for that here."

Diva told us to go to the train station to find cheap hotels. "Stay at a place called the Sukker," she said. "But don't touch the cats. I think they're diseased."

From Aswan we planned to take a steamer down Lake Nasser to Sudan. When the Aswan High Dam was finished in 1971, the lake obliterated all roads leading into Sudan, leaving the steamer as the only means of transportation south. We waited two days in Aswan for the weekly boat to set sail. I spent the time in the cafés of Aswan writing an article for the *Kansas City Star* and a short story called "Lucy" about a girlfriend I once had at Vassar. The story took place in the forests of New Hampshire, a place that seemed impossibly far away. When I wasn't writing, Don beat me in sixty-six straight games of backgammon. On our last night an emergency shipment arrived on the train. Jim had ordered the stuff from the States through the HOPE office in Cairo. The most important item was a new MSR stove to replace the stolen one. There were also large caches of insect repellent, iodine tabs, new bungees, brake cables, and water bags. These were all items that we would need for crossing the deserts of Sudan.

"God, that stuff must weigh a ton," I said when it was all laid out in our hotel room.

"It does," Jim said. "But when we get out in the middle of the Sahara desert, we'll be happy we've got it."

On our last night in Aswan I got a call through to my parents. My mother had good news. The *Kansas City Star* had published an article I wrote about our Sinai crossing, and the press from Cairo on the trip was "spectacular." "I'm so proud of you," she said. "You were in the papers, on TV, and on the radio. You're famous!"

4. Nubian Tales

Once a week, a rickety steamer named the Seventh of Ramadan shoves off from a dock below the High Dam at Aswan. It plods slowly through the hazy blue waters of Lake Nasser, past empty shores of desert rock and sand toward the Sudanese outpost village of Wadi Halfa 565 kilometers away. Since the lake buried the roads and train tracks connecting Egypt and Sudan, the Seventh of Ramadan—named for a special day in the Moslem holy month—has been the only "land" link between the two countries.

Actually, the Seventh of Ramadan was two boats lashed together with hemp rope as thick as my arm. Both boats were rectangular, like oversized buses with no sides. Large Mississippi riverboat paddles on the back. Thick billows of sooty steam blew out of lean stacks topped with Egyptian and Sudanese flags bleached by the sun. The starboard boat housed a small room with throttles and a wheel. Behind it was the kitchen, a greasy room that produced steamy kettles of tea and dirty bowls of goopy beans. Near the kitchen were eight first-class cabins. For sixteen dollars, a first-class passenger got a doorless room with two plywood bunks and an electric light at night. The other classes paid two-fifty for a spot on the open, empty deck below the bridge or on the two open decks on the portside boat. Almost three hundred passengers had claimed territory on these decks, spreading out colorful blankets, mats, caged chickens, and plastic suitcases on the wooden floor. Wives and children remained ensconced among their bundles for the entire voyage, cooking their families' meals on tiny kerosene stoves. The other inhabitable areas of the boat were the roofs. Several Sudanese men and a small group of Western hippies scrambled up a pole ladder to get away from the mayhem on the decks below. After securing the bikes and setting up a guard rotation, we carried sleeping bags, stoves, and food sacks to the roof.

With a groan and cackle of ancient motors, the Seventh of Ramadan lurched backward, pulling out of the dock below the High Dam. A battered temple built by Ramses II guarded the small harbor as we steamed south. For the first few miles, a thin veneer of life clung to the shores: wild reeds, a few huts, and primitive wooden fishing boats. This quickly faded into endless stretches of tawny-brown sand spreading east and west beyond a line of jagged limestone bluffs. Mile after mile, the shore was completely empty, an absolute nothing, a moonscape.

After our dinner of gruel cooked on the roof, the sun dropped in a blaze of gold over the Sahara desert. The Arabs on the roof laid out mats and began dipping in prayer toward Mecca in the east. I almost tripped over the steamer's captain as I slung myself up the ladder in front of the bridge. He completely ignored me, although another crew hand glared at me as if I were an infidel. After prayers, the men gathered on the roof in small groups to smoke, drink *shai*, and laugh over games of dominoes. On the lower decks their wives prepared meals. Someone began playing a low, minor tune on a small flute. Someone else hummed along. One of the hippies, an Italian with a huge, curly mane and a purple waistcoat, started softly strumming a battered guitar. After a while, the Arab men headed down to eat dinner and the boat quieted as an astounding array of stars popped out in the darkness gathering over the lake.

Just after dark, Jim and Don moved their sleeping bags down by the bikes for that night's guard duty. Dave and I stayed topside. It would be our turn to guard the bikes on the next night. For at least two hours, I lay on my back inside my bag, staring at the stars. With no lights anywhere on the horizon, and no dust or pollution, it was like floating in space. Shooting stars blazed every few minutes. At about eight-thirty a bright shock of light poured onto the water as a full moon emerged between two jagged bluffs. It began as a distended yellow ball over the ridge, slowly straightening out to a button-sized circle of white. Like a spotlight it illuminated the quiet deck of the Seventh of Ramadan, where almost everyone was already asleep.

For the next two days, life on the Seventh of Ramadan was a festival of Arabic songs hummed by black Nubians in white tunics and turbans, long domino bouts, daring leaps across the gap separating the roofs of the two boats, and slow discussions over *shai* or warm Pepsis as gulls cackled in our wake. I worked on a piece called "Cycler's Chronicles," a collection of trip incidents ranging from the night the Guardia Civil "visited" us in Spain to our robbery during the sandstorm in Egypt. I also wrote long letters to Laura and several friends and prepared our February report to HOPE. But I could only write in the early morning. By ten A.M., when the heat reached 115 degrees Fahrenheit, it was too hot to write, or even to think. These were times of indescribable peace. For a few brief hours, I lived completely in the present, enjoying the sensation of the wind, the sky, and the desolate beauty of the lake.

At first, we approached the Sudanese on the boat as if they were Egyptians. We closely guarded the bikes and established our sleep area as far away as possible from anyone else. But the Sudanese were not Egyptians. "Why do you bother to guard those bicycles?" asked a young, easygoing man named Monsder. "Everyone on this boat is from Sudan. We do not steal anything. Sudanese have a reputation for being friendly." With his black face, plastic shades, and scarred cheek (three long scars were the mark of the Dagu tribe in Sudan), Monsder looked like a dangerous man, but he was really quite gentle. We spent several hours exchanging information on our countries. I asked him what it would be like to bicycle in Sudan.

"You are very brave to try it," he said. "Sudan is such a harsh country. We are the biggest country in Africa. We have one and a half million square kilometers of land, but only nineteen million people. Almost everywhere is uninhabitable desert. We are a very poor country. It is difficult to survive in Sudan."

I asked him about the roads in Sudan, telling him that we

hoped to bike from Wadi Halfa, where the boat was to drop us off, to Khartoum. From Khartoum, we planned to bike to Port Sudan on the Red Sea.

"The road from Wadi Halfa to Khartoum is very bad," he said, "but the road from Khartoum to Port Sudan is excellent. It is a new road." He suggested we take the train to Khartoum. "It is a bad train," he said, "but it is better than the road."

"How long does the train take to get to Khartoum?" I asked.

"It may take twenty-four hours or it may take five days," said Monsder, "depending on the condition of the engine. It is a steam engine and very unreliable."

The Westerners on board were part of a steady trickle of hippies who come to Egypt and head south into Africa. They follow the Nile into Uganda or Kenya and keep going until they reach Capetown, run out of money, or disappear in the jungle. Those we met were akin to the young expatriates we had been meeting since Europe, except they were older (in their thirties) and hardened by years of travel. They were also more serious about escaping from the West. This is what separated them from the usual summer vacation hippie we had seen in Egypt. These people were lifetime drifters, part of the long tradition of escapees who have fled the West since the first sailing ships left European ports for exotic lands.

Each of them had a story of disillusionment. A Swede on board claimed he had once owned an engineering firm in Stockholm. "I go bankrupt," he said, "because of the government always interfering. They taxed me to death." A German man talked about the "fucking clowns" running the world. "How can I stay in Germany when it is run by men as bad as Nazis?" he asked. An Italian woman recounted her life in suburban Milan. "It was like prison," she said. "I was told when to eat, when to drink, when to marry."

I asked another Italian, the one with the guitar, why he was traveling south. "Don't know," he said, smiling. "My life in Italy was no good." He strummed a few chords. "I go to Sudan, and south to as far as I get." He strummed another chord. "I have nothing else to do."

Wadi Halfa was a tiny outpost of three dozen one-story buildings lined up at the edge of the desert like toy blocks in a sand pile. Before Lake Nasser it had been just one of a hundred villages barely surviving along the baked Nubian shores of the Nile. Now it had a new train station, several dry goods stores, and a pair of huge microwave dishes attached to the top of a nearby bluff. Monsder told me those were for the army.

After being fumigated by soldiers in crisp blue uniforms, we left the Seventh of Ramadan, pushing the bikes down gangplanks and into Sudan. Everyone was briefly delayed when it was disclosed that the guitar player and the woman from Milan had copulated on the roof of the boat. Monsder said this could be grounds for denying the couple entry into Moslem Sudan. Still detaining the Italians, they let us go.

In town we discovered that the road to Khartoum was just a path in the sand alongside the railroad tracks. Only the presence of stone kilometer markers gave any indication that a road existed at all. The sand was so deep that we decided to buy third-class tickets and take the train until the road became bikeable.

While waiting for the train to leave, we had lunch in a mudbrick building in town. The only item served was a type of *foule* that had beans, rings of some strange meat, and a gooey sauce with the consistency and look of mucus. The stuff was eaten with one's hands or by scooping it up with charred pita bread. After a couple of bites, we saw what the meat was. In the back of the room was a man dicing goat's intestines soaked in water.

Third-class tickets on the train bought us slatted wood seats in a dirty car packed from floor to ceiling with Sudanese, their bundles, their chickens, and a couple of goats. Before we pulled out from Wadi Halfa, several armed soldiers provided the Westerners with an exclusive claim over several seats at one end of the car. But as soon as the soldiers left and the train lurched out of the station, our section was overrun by Sudanese.

From Wadi Halfa the Nile runs south and then swerves north and south again in a huge S shape. Our train cut across four hundred kilometers of open desert to close the top half of the S. As we moved away from the river, the Nubian desert spread out in a vast emptiness all around us. Limestone outcrops appeared in the yellow sand like tepees of stone. Every fifty kilometers or so, we passed a water station, where water was held in conical mud-brick containers (apparently, the cones help deflect the sun and discourage evaporation). A few domed tents made of tanned camelskins appeared near some of the water stations. Nomads on camels watched the train chug past.

As the train struggled toward Khartoum, I began a series of

conversations with Dave about his unhappiness with the expedition. Since Luxor he had been talking more and more about his dissatisfaction with the trip. He hated the hassles of Third World biking and was tired of the arguments about pacing and touring styles. He had also come to realize that he didn't really fit into the group. We didn't talk much about this, but it was obviously a prime concern to Dave and to all of us.

"I have not really enjoyed the biking since the Sinai," he said as the train rumbled through the desert. "I'm tired of the asshole Egyptians, the dust, and all the other bullshit." Toward the end of the ride, he announced that he was going to quit the trip in Khartoum. "If I can get a flight, I'm gonna fly back to D.C.," he said.

"Is there anything I can say to change your mind?" I asked.

"I'm still thinking about it," he said, "but I'm pretty sure."

We arrived in Khartoum at dusk on March 13, pushing the bikes onto a paved street covered with at least an inch of blowing sand. Most of the hippies from the boat, including the copulating Italians (they had been allowed to stay after all), accompanied us to the Khartoum student house. Run by Khartoum University, the student house was in a small compound walled in by thick, thorny *kitar* bushes. Inside was a rectangular concrete building with room for several bunks and lots of storage. More space was available for sleeping outside on a deck and on the grass. It was like a small summer camp. For thirty piasters (about twenty-two cents) we got five-inch foam pads, a patch of grass, padlocked storage space, and use of a large bronze spigot in the middle of the lawn. A man about thirty-five years old in a knit beanie and white tunic ran the place with a fat, combative wife and several well-behaved children.

The clientele was almost exclusively Westerners living on the cheap. These young drifters included two Americans writhing and sweating in the throes of malaria on their foam pads. Like Greg Allman clones, they had goatees, long blond hair, and light vests fringed with leather.

"Hey, man, you guys got any chloroquine?" one of them asked. "We gotta get some chloroquine." Chloroquine is an antimalarial drug we had been taking once a week since Jerusalem.

"Why don't you guys go to a hospital?" we asked, giving them a few of our precious chloroquine tabs.

"Our visas have run out, man," said one of them. "They'll deport us."

Harriet was another American, a twenty-two-year-old English major from the University of Virginia. Under several layers of dirt and tangled hair, she had a tough beauty, like a young Katharine Hepburn in need of a shower. She never stopped smoking hashish during the five days we stayed in Khartoum. "I'm traveling south," she said, echoing what the hippies had told me on the boat. "Why not? I don't have anything else to do."

As we pulled out our foam pads and locked up the bikes, a filthy Irishman suddenly accosted us, pulling at Don's sleeve and begging for benzene, the local low-grade fuel. With a stringy beard and ragged coat, he looked like Fagin in *Oliver Twist*. "I gots this stove," he said in a deep brogue, "but they 'aven't got nothin' in the way of petrol in this stinkin' country. Can't yah give a fellow some petrol?"

Khartoum is a hot, lazy city built where the Blue and White Niles join into one river flowing north. Since the time of the Pharaohs, Khartoum and its sister city of Omdurman have been distant outposts of civilization. Like Timbuktu, the name Khartoum is synonymous with mysterious, faraway lands. It was a major focal point for the famous African explorers of the last century. Samuel Baker, Sir Richard Burton, John Speke, Dr. David Livingstone, and Henry Stanley all spent time in Khartoum. It was the city of Chinese Gordon's last stand, where an army of Moslem dervishes led by a strange holy man called the Mahdi rose out of the desert to keep the most powerful empire in the world at bay for over a decade. It was near the site of the last major cavalry charge before mechanization made horses obsolete—a charge led, in part, by a young lieutenant named Winston Churchill. In ancient times, it was the sight of a great city of the Nubian Empire, whose black-skinned Pharaohs conquered and ruled Egypt almost three thousand years ago.

Modern Khartoum is a poor desert city composed of flat-topped, boxy buildings baked a uniform beige color by the intense heat. It has an unfinished feel to it, like a frontier town in cowboy movies about the American West. Electricity, plumbing, and communications are haphazard and primitive. We never got a single call or telex out of the country. With scarce benzene strictly rationed, Khartoum's streets were almost empty of cars and trucks. People got around on foot, walking in the intense heat from one shaded soda stand to another, pausing to chat and sip a cold Coke.

It is the heat that defines life in Khartoum. We arrived during the hottest time of the year, when daytime temperatures in the city are routinely 115 to 120 degrees Fahrenheit. But the heat was very dry. With 40 percent humidity, no one sweated (or smelled), and any garbage left in the streets was immediately flash-dried into dust. This lack of moisture kept the city clean with a sort of sand-blasted sterility. Because of the heat, most people started their day in the cool of dawn, moving slowly along the broad, sandy streets under the British-style arcades covering many of the sidewalks. As the sun arced to the top of the sky and the heat became unbearable, shops and offices closed for the afternoon. At noon, the city shut down. The well-off retreated to their clubs to relax and chat with friends in cool gardens. Khartoum is dotted with clubs—the Engineers Club, the Staff Club, the Press Club, the American Club, and dozens more. The less affluent sat under canvas awnings in the city's *suqs* to sleep or to chew on peanuts and watermelon (both were in season). At five work resumed. Government offices and stores reopened until eight, when Khartoumites went home or returned to their clubs for dinner and a game of snooker or billiards.

The people of Khartoum were remarkably friendly after the frenetic crowds in Egypt. When we stopped at a soda stand, three or four of them would insist on paying for our sodas and would look forlorn or even depressed if we didn't enthusiastically accept their offer. When I went to see a movie one night at Khartoum's Friendship Hall, a man in a wool suit befriended me and bought me coffee and pound cake at intermission. He refused to let me pay. When I insisted, he looked hurt. I had to order two cakes before he smiled again.

Jim's list book was filled with things to do in Khartoum. We had to research desert conditions, buy food, repair and lube the bikes, secure visas to Saudi Arabia, Pakistan, and India, and figure out how to get Dave back to the States. We were surprised when the embassy provided a car, a driver, and a Sudanese aide named Gasseme to take us to press functions and to run errands. He took us to register as foreigners at the Sudanese Foreign Ministry, helped us secure press and photographic credentials, and took Dave to British Air to buy a ticket from Khartoum to Washington. Gasseme also took us sightseeing to the Khartoum Museum, a huge, dusty camel market, and the ruins of a dervish fort in Omdurman. Near the Sudan TV station, he introduced us to Sudan's only movie star. The country had so far produced only one movie, a farce about love and marriage.

We had one major disappointment on our rounds with Gasseme. At the Saudi Arabian embassy, the Saudis would not grant us travel visas to bike across their country. This was not completely unexpected. In Washington, the Saudis had rejected our plan, telling us Saudi Arabia only grants visas for two groups: those invited to work in their country and Muslims on a hajj to Mecca. We did, however, get a twenty-four-hour transit visa since our plane from Port Sudan was scheduled to land in Jeddah on the way to Pakistan (we were bypassing Iran and Afghanistan). Our last chance of biking in Saudi Arabia was to use the twenty-four-hour visa to dash into Jeddah and try to get the U.S. consulate to help us obtain longer visas. The U.S. embassy in Khartoum wired the Jeddah consulate to expect us in about three weeks.

When we met with the U.S. consul in Khartoum, a former marine named Clarence, he eyed us sternly and warned us not to bike across Sudan. "Do you guys realize that this is one of the harshest climates on earth? Without food or water you'll die in a matter of hours." He warned about wild animals; lions and wild dogs had been known to kill people. Scorpions were also a danger. Antidotes for scorpion poison existed, but we would be hundreds of kilometers from any hospitals or medical facilities.

"You've also got thieves," said Clarence. "The highway between here and Port Sudan is a wild road. The government has little control over desert people who attack cars and trucks. Are you carrying any weapons?"

"No," Jim answered, telling him that we considered it more dangerous to carry than not to carry guns.

"How are you carrying food and water?" he asked. I told him we could carry up to eight gallons of water each, and four or five days' worth of food. Jim pulled out a list and ticked off the survival gear we were taking with us—medical supplies, space blankets, emergency rations (bouillon cubes and dried beef), flares, and special white suits that would cover our arms and legs in the hot sun. We showed him a detailed map of our route. Truck stops and water stations were marked in red.

"I'm impressed by your preparations," Clarence said, "but I want to repeat again that I would prefer you didn't bicycle in Sudan." He looked at us like a parent admonishing his sons. "It is one of the most unpleasant duties of a United States consul to be responsible for sending the remains of deceased American citizens back to the States."

In another session with Clarence, he warned us about terrorists. "This may seem like a quiet country full of friendly people," he said, "but don't let that fool you. There are terrorists out there, and you should be aware of that. We have terrorists from Libya, from revolutionary groups in the south, and God knows where else. I don't want to scare you, but you guys will be wonderful targets for these terrorists. You're in the news, and, if you'll pardon my frankness, you'll be sitting ducks out there."

As we had moved about Khartoum, we had picked up information about the political realities of Sudan. The country occupies an extremely volatile corner of the world. Out of the eight countries bordering Sudan, two were embroiled in civil wars, two were enduring dictatorships less than a year old, one was a chaotic mess called Uganda, and one was the domain of an Islamic fanatic named Muammar al-Qaddafi. Sudan itself had just ended a seventeen-year civil war in 1973; its government was a military dictatorship.

To give us a feeling for the volatile atmosphere in Sudan, Clarence gave us a rundown of what had happened since the first of the year. In January, food riots in central Khartoum had caused two deaths and dozens of injuries. In February, terrorists had tried to blow up the American Club by planting plastic explosives in new stereo speakers. Also in February, a fresh outbreak of violence in civil war–torn Ethiopia had forced tens of thousands of refugees across the border into Sudan. They joined a population of almost two million refugees driven into Sudan by the turmoil and chaos of neighboring countries.

"The politics in this region of the world can be as dangerous as wild lions and the heat of the desert," Clarence said. "Be careful!"

On our last night in Khartoum, Jim, Don, and I helped Dave load up his bike and escorted him to the small international airport for his flight back to Washington. He was happier than I had seen him since Europe. "I'm gonna have a Big Mac for each of you guys when I get back," he told us as we said good-bye at the airplane gate. A British Air 737 was taking him to Cairo, London, and then Washington. As I shook Dave's hand, he said he had a parting gift for me. Fishing around in his bag, he pulled out his dog-eared copy of *The Complete Book of Bicycling.* "I want you to have this," he said, flashing an ironic smile. I handed the book back to him.

"I appreciate the gift," I said. "But you need this more than I do." He laughed and slipped the book back into his bag. A minute later Dave was gone, and our group was down to three.

Long before sunrise the next morning, I lit a match and fired up the new MSR stove to heat water for oatmeal. By four o'clock, we were testing brake alignments, chain lubrication, handlebars and everything else, silently running through the checklist that Dave French had taught us long ago in Washington. At four-twenty, with the icy blue light of dawn coloring the sky, we quietly slipped out of the student house, past the sleeping forms of the two Americans with malaria, the English major from Virginia, and the wild Irishman. Outside we mounted our bikes, shifted into low gears, and began pedaling toward the Red Sea, eleven hundred kilometers to the east. It was March 16.

We were grossly overloaded that morning. Our bikes weighed over 120 pounds, including 24 pounds of water apiece. The water bags were wrapped in damp towels to keep them cool; our bike bottles were wrapped in damp pieces of denim from a pair of jeans Don had turned into cut-offs. Food accounted for an extra 15 pounds, including bouillon, canned goods, powdered soups, Nescafé, candy bars, and dried meat tasting like beef jerky. Divided among us was the group gear Dave had been carrying, including a tent, a stove, and about 8 pounds of spare parts. One final item was four Heinekens each "for the road." The beers were divided up and wrapped in damp towels.

Khartoum slowly petered out as we passed a wealthy area of houses with tall walls topped with broken glass, several cotton mills, and a Shell petrol station on the edge of town. About 350 vehicles were queued up in a mile-long line at the pumps waiting for their rations of benzene. Past the Shell station, the desert spread out in all directions. The earth was colored cocoa brown, indicating a slight degree of fertility in comparison with the yellow sands to the north. Here on the edge of the desert, a thin, struggling layer of tangly shrubs and a few stalks of adust grass spread out toward the horizon, resembling thin, sickly hairs on the scalp of a balding man. A handful of thick-skinned trees with tiny, pebblelike leaves were scattered across the desolation, about ten per square kilometer. To the east we could see a bluish hue hanging over the horizon, marking the Blue Nile. Only a thin band of vegetation, mostly cotton and sugarcane, grew along its banks. Sudan had few of the intricate canal systems that Egypt had built over the centuries.

In the midst of this desolation, it seemed incredible that our highway was so good. It had been built for Sudan by a curious consortium of foreign partners. Britain, the People's Republic of China, Yugoslavia, and Italy had each sent engineers and money to construct segments of the highway to Port Sudan. As a poor, strategically placed country, Sudan took help from anyone who offered it. With the benzene shortage, the road was almost empty. The few trucks coming from Port Sudan were filled with consumer goods. Trucks heading toward Port Sudan were loaded with raw goods like cotton, sorghum, peanuts, tobacco, and chunks of gum arabic.

A few kilometers south of Khartoum, we started passing dead animals and junked cars half buried in the sand. Most of the dead camels, goats, and donkeys had dried in the sun so quickly that circling vultures often had no time to eat their remains. Inside bright white rib cages were the shrunken, mummified internal organs. The hides had shrunk to sheets of leather so brittle that they cracked apart when touched. The cars had all been stripped. Only the bare bodies remained. Seeing this casual death was very disconcerting as the sun arced higher and the temperature climbed.

By ten, my legs felt rubbery and weak as the temperature hit 125 degrees. Even under our white desert suits, the heat burned through us. The desert was lost in waves of vaporous mirages. We drank water almost continually, keeping it cool by dampening the covers wrapping the bike bottles. Each of us drank close to a gallon of water in just four or five hours. At ten-thirty we sighted a lone shade tree about two hundred meters off the road. "That's lunch," I said wearily.

Leaning the bikes against the tree, we spread a tarp in the

shade. Moving slowly, we cut up half-squashed tomatoes and eggplants, opened a can of beef resembling Spam, and started a pot of water and bouillon boiling. Then we broke out the Heinekens, which were still passably cool. About this time the branches above us filled with bright green birds chirping noisily. Jim hurriedly looked them up in his *Birds of Northeast Africa* and announced that they were Carmen bee-eaters.

After eating, Jim and Don fell right to sleep, but I stayed up to scratch a few things into my journal and then to read a few pages of a Hemingway short story while I drank the last warm, frothy sips of beer. When the birds abruptly stopped chattering, I looked up and saw a column of dust swirling in our direction. The Sudanese call these cyclones dervishes. "Hey guys, wake up!" I shook Jim and Don. But before they could open their eyes, the dervish struck. It was like having an air cannon blow dust in your face. It went up my nose, in my eyes, in my mouth. Then it was gone, moving like a raging phantom across the wasteland.

That night, after a late afternoon ride across the cooling desert, we slept at a school of the Koran in a small village called Aeti. When we stopped to ask for water at the cluster of dried brick huts, several boys in white robes invited us to stay the night. "It would be a great honor for you to stay," said a serious boy in excellent English.

The boy led us to a low, adobe building with a turquoise blue roof of corrugated tin. This building, which the boys referred to as a clubhouse, contained two rooms—a classroom filled with placards quoting passages from the Koran and a recreation room taken up by a large, battered Ping-Pong table. In the classroom, we stashed our bikes and prepared our evening meal. As we sliced juicy red onions and tomatoes for a soup, the older boys at the school set up tables and chairs outside to play dominoes. The younger boys played Ping-Pong. We never saw a single female in Aeti. When a couple of the little ones got too close to us, an assistant master used a very effective disciplinary technique. He swatted the kids with a whip made out of old fan belts.

After dinner we moved outside, where three large light bulbs lit up the yard. Blackness spread out into the desert beyond the yard as two small boys struggled with a giant black-and-white television. This was a surprise. As the boys sat down on the benches, a master turned on the set. It crackled and whirred. Soon we were watching an American cops and robbers series that I had never seen before. The boys sat transfixed as beautiful women in slinky clothes and blond men in tuxedos chased each other around in fast sports cars. Lost in the program, I momentarily forgot that I was in the middle of an African desert.

From Aeti we began a two-week journey across the eastern Sahara desert. The Sudanese National Highway took us south another one hundred kilometers along the right bank of the Blue Nile to the city of Wad Medani, where the road left the river to make a gradual swerve east and then north along the border of Ethiopia to Port Sudan on the Red Sea coast. We would pass through the far eastern wastelands of the Sahara, with the dry edge of the savannah grasslands to the south and the rugged mountains of the Bedja tribal region to the northeast.

Because of the intense heat, we were forced to divide our days in half, biking from four A.M. until ten or eleven, when the heat became unbearable. Then we would fix our main meal of the day and sleep for three or four hours under a shade tree or under one of the grass-roofed lean-tos scattered along the highway. At three or three-thirty we would resume biking. An hour or two after dusk, when no trucks were in sight, we would slip off the road and walk back onto the desert to find a secluded place behind tangles of *kitar* bushes. Remembering Clarence's warnings, we set up camps like those we'd made in Egypt— tents close together, bikes piled under a tarp, and cans and tripwires set to discourage intruders. We were also careful to keep the tents zipped at all times to keep scorpions from crawling inside. Before leaving Khartoum, I had heard a grisly tale about scorpions. Once on Lake Nasser, a small boat carrying about twenty-five people sank after the fuel tanks caught fire. Everyone on board survived to swim ashore, only to be attacked and killed on the desert by swarms of poisonous black scorpions.

Riding through the harsh, beautiful land of central Sudan was a refreshing change after the long, frustrating days in Egypt. It was exciting to be surviving in such a rugged environment. As on the Sinai, I felt that this was a true adventure, a challenge that pitted our guile and planning against the dangers of the desert. On the Sahara the difference between life and death was no more than the amount of water we could carry on our bicycles. Death was everywhere. The flash-dried carcasses of camels and goats continued to litter the highway. Several times we saw vultures tearing at the bloody remains of some unfortunate beast. A few times, we saw dead camels that had been slit open by their riders for the water they held in their stomachs.

We seldom saw people, but those we did see were a curious counterpoint to the inhospitable landscape. As on the boat and in Khartoum, the people were friendly. No one hassled us. Stallkeepers in village markets sold us food at fair prices; children were curious but usually kept a respectful distance. Lorry drivers frequently stopped to offer us cold Cokes and tell us stories in broken English. One morning early in the journey, as we cooked gruel under a shade tree, two young Sudanese men approached in a Datsun pickup truck. My mind still full of the warnings from Khartoum, I was sure they wanted to rob us. When they pulled out a small pistol, I was ready to give them anything they wanted. But they turned out to be friends, not thieves. The gun was a gift. "Please, you need protection," said one of the men. "All men have guns on desert. Many thieves and crazy men here." I almost accepted the gun but could not quite overcome an ingrained fear of weapons. When I was at home growing up, guns were depicted as evil instruments used by maniacs and fascists. I have never been able to shake off this deeply rooted prejudice.

Most of our food and water came from truck stops. They usually appeared every sixty or seventy kilometers (a few were over a hundred kilometers apart). The makeshift *shai* stands and lean-tos consisted of woven straw mats laid over wooden frames. Water was trucked in each day to be stored in high clay pots under thatched awnings. Villages appeared infrequently on the desert. With names like El Kamlin, El Hasiheisa and Hufeira, they were clusters of mud-brick and cinder-block buildings. In the center of most villages were remarkably ornate mosques rising above the adobe huts like cathedrals out of medieval hamlets in Europe. The other standard feature was the village *suq* selling everything from peanuts and straw chicken cages to camel saddles and Western-made oil filters. Peppers and sliced okra were laid out on mats to dry in the sun. The curved swords worn by nomads on the desert were laid out according to size on blankets in the dust. Silversmiths sold good luck charms filled with passages from the Koran. In the deeper deserts, the nomads believed these charms would protect them from bullets and sword blades.

On the fourth day out of Khartoum, we began passing patches of desert cultivated with rows of sorghum and millet. Round grass huts with conical tops called *tukus* began replacing mud-brick structures. Approaching the city of Gedaref, 410 kilometers southeast of Khartoum, we began skirting the border between Arab Africa and Black Africa. Tribal scars appeared on the dark black faces along the road. Women were much more in evidence, wearing bright-colored robes and pounds of beads and jewelry. Gedaref itself had an Arab core of mud-brick and concrete buildings, a large *suq*, and three or four mosques. Surrounding this core were successive rings of *tuku* huts spreading out by the thousands in a panorama that looked to our eyes so African it could have been a painted backdrop to a Tarzan movie.

Gedaref, situated about eighty kilometers from Ethiopia, was the home of nearly fifty thousand refugees fleeing from two tragedies afflicting their homeland: civil war and famine. Gedaref is a district headquarters of the United Nations High Commission on Refugees, which attempts to coordinate several dozen international relief groups operating in Sudan. As we biked through the edge of the city, we passed neat rows of *tuku* compounds provided for the refugees. Huts were divided into "neighborhoods" according to tribe and the relief group responsible for their support. Refugee women were everywhere, carrying water in earthen jars, grinding sorghum in bowls, and tending their children. The refugee men were either in the vast sorghum fields working for two Sudanese pounds a day ($1.60) or were back home fighting in the civil war.

We ate lunch with a refugee named Gideon at a restaurant with long, cafeteria-style tables and ceiling fans with wooden blades. Gideon was a gaunt man with sensitive eyes who seemed ready to wince if anyone raised his voice. He wore a red rugby shirt. He had owned a bar in Assab, an Ethiopian port city, before the Marxist government took over in 1973. "I served American navy men in my bar," he said. "The Americans were good people. I hate to see them go away when the Communists kick them out." He spoke with a chronic look of worry on his face.

•••

North of Gedaref the villages were filled with refugees and the relief workers servicing them. Two days out of Gedaref, we spent a layover day in Abudah, another camp of neat, orderly *tukus* lined up in the desert near the Atbara River. Like the camps in Gedaref, Abudah was not what I had expected a refugee camp to look like. In America the word *refugee* automatically conjures up an image of ragged, starving people living in squalid, makeshift huts. Abudah had none of these things. It was cleaner than many of the villages we had seen in Egypt. The people were dressed in decent clothes and appeared to be adequately fed. But these were surface impressions.

A small American relief group called Lalamba coordinated the aid sent to the five thousand refugees in Abudah. To our surprise, we discovered that Lalamba was based in Kansas City. A Kansas Citian named Hugh Downey had started the program in the early 1960s while stationed in Ethiopia as a sergeant in the U.S. army. Concerned by the poverty and lack of medical facilities, Hugh and his father, a lawyer in Kansas City, raised money to buy a mobile clinic complete with examination rooms, X-ray equipment, and a pharmacy. They shipped the clinic to a small village on the Gash River in northern Ethiopia, under a mountain called Lalamba. In 1979, the civil war forced the villagers to flee into Sudan. The project's small staff of doctors and nurses, with the help of the villagers, dragged the clinic trailer two hundred kilometers across mountains and desert to the town of Showak, a few kilometers west of Abudah.

Lalamba called itself the "smallest relief organization in the world." The staff at Abudah consisted of one doctor, two nurses, and a physical therapist. Only the nurses were in camp when we arrived. Ellen "Gruffy" Clough, thirty-two, was a lean, strong woman who had been an Outward Bound instructor in Colorado before coming to Sudan. Megan Burns, twenty-three, had just graduated from nursing school in Los Angeles. Lalamba's doctor was in Gedaref recovering from hepatitis, and the therapist, Gruffy's husband, was in Saudi Arabia raising money.

Lalamba's clinic was an enclave of whitewashed huts and canvas tents in the middle of the camp. Our layover day was the weekly "feeding day" for malnourished children at the camp. "We give the kids food packets to supplement their meals," explained Gruffy as we traveled from the Lalamba living quarters to the clinic. "These kids aren't starving," she said, "they're just not getting anywhere near the right amount of nutrition. A common cold, something that might make you or me a little sick, can kill one of these little ones."

When we arrived at the clinic, a large tent was already filled with Ethiopian women in brightly dyed muslin gowns, scarves, and rubber thongs. Gold jewelry dangled from their noses and ears. Their tiny babies, many naked, laughed and played on woven floor mats. The kids looked surprisingly healthy. "They aren't on their deathbeds," said Gruffy, "at least not yet."

"But they're laughing and playing," I said.

"Of course they are," she said, smiling. "They're kids, aren't they?"

As we spoke, Ethiopian helpers began serving a high-protein drink to the children and to mothers still nursing babies. Gruffy told us that the drink was made from a powder sold as a dieters' supplement in America.

"Do you get most of your food from the States?" I asked.

"Yeah," said Gruffy, "although it's usually donated through different groups here in Sudan. Unfortunately, we don't have much money to buy our own supplies." She pointed to a pile of plastic bags filled with grains and sugar. "The Catholic Relief people provided the rice for today's feeding day," she explained. "The World Food program gave us the durum. We bought the lentils. And, let's see, the Sudanese government allocates the sugar. We're constantly hassling about finding supplies," she added. "It's one big frustration trying to keep everything running." I remembered that Melvina had said the same thing about running Project HOPE in Egypt.

As Gruffy got busier with the feeding program, she asked an Ethiopian aide named Tweldeberhum Elazar to show us the camp. Tweldeberhum, forty-seven years old, was one of the men who had helped drag the Lalamba trailer across the desert from his village of Kalluka. He was thin, with red-rimmed eyes and a troubled expression. As we walked around, he told his story. When the civil war erupted in 1973, Tweldeberhum had been training to be a priest in the Ethiopian Orthodox Church. He fled his country and his seminary because both the rebels and the national army were threatening to conscript him into their ranks. "I do not believe in this war," he said. "It is fought for no reason at all. I hate to fight, so I don't fight. But I must be away from home. It is such a tragedy." He left behind an aging mother, his wife, and seven children.

"I am bitter about leaving my family," he said. "I do not see my mother since 1973. She is only two hundred kilometers away, in that direction." He pointed east. "She might be dead, because I don't often get information." Tweldeberhum's job in Abudah, besides working for Lalamba, was assisting the camp's priest in services. He also worked as a religious counselor for those of his faith in the camp.

"What is the worst problem facing your people here?" I asked.

"This is so unhappy," he said. "Our life is so unhappy. The people have no joy. Home is far away, and we cannot return. Everything here is unfamiliar. We live in mountains at home. This is desert. We are Christians. Here they are Muslims. The Muslims do not like us. They treat us badly."

"Is there anyone to complain to?"

"We have no person to complain to," answered Tweldeberhum. "If a man causes trouble, the soldiers come move him. We can go to another place. Some are not so cruel, I think. They pay enough for our work. But my friends and my church are here."

That night we slept outdoors on cots in the Lalamba compound. Watching the brilliance of the desert stars, I tried to imagine what it would be like to be excluded forever from Kansas City or from America because soldiers were shooting at each other in my backyard or because I didn't have enough to eat. I thought of the green forests around my home and the great fertile prairies stretching west from Kansas City. It is a place of peace and prosperity, where the fear of war and famine have been largely eliminated. It was impossible to conceive of an event short of nuclear war that could exile me from my home. Yet for most of the world, war and economic disaster are constant fears. Over eight million people are listed as refugees by the United Nations, most of them displaced by war. *Eight million people* just like Gideon and Tweldeberhum. It was absurd! How could the world allow it to happen?

The next morning, I asked Gruffy if she ever got overwhelmed working at Abudah. "Sure," she said in her straightforward manner. "The job is a big one, and there is so much pain here. I mean, look at the people's faces. They are faces full of sadness and despair. We're talking about real suffering— people with no homes, with little food, with no future. You just don't see this sort of thing in the States. Sometimes I wonder if it's all worth it. Other times I get angry at the unfairness of it all." She looked hard at me. "But then I'll see the look on a kid's face when I know I've helped him. At that moment, it's me and him. It's one person helping another who has a problem. This is an important lesson to learn out here. You can freak out over the immensity of the problem, or you can pick a little corner and try to help where you can."

"It must be tough to keep going sometimes," I said. "Do you ever have days when you wish it would all go away?"

"Yeah, definitely," she said. "I've had days when I lock myself in my hut, turn on some rock music, and try to shut everything out. I mean, it really gets to me. The hassles, the heat, and the plight of these people. I start to think about home and wonder what I'm doing here."

It was critical, she said, to keep things in perspective. "Life out here is one hardship after another, for us and for them. It's easy to let it get to you. I mean, the desert is not the easiest place to live. But look at what's really happening here. First of all, I'm here by choice. I can leave anytime. If I want, I can drive to Khartoum, check into the Intercontinental, and pig out. The people in Abudah are stuck here. They can't go anywhere. Second, and most important, you have to look at what hardship really means. I have discovered that the essential difference between me and them is that, for me, hardship is an adventure. For them, it's a way of life."

From Showak we continued to pedal steadily north, beginning a five-hundred-kilometer leg through the desert to Port Sudan. During these long, hot days we kept our routine of waking up at three A.M., riding until ten, sleeping until four, and then riding again until dusk. Only a few villages, railroad water stations, and truck stops appeared in this isolated stretch of desert along the Ethiopian border. Occasionally we saw bands of nomads on camels or living in small clusters of lean-to huts. The nomads, members of the Bedja tribe, wore long swords and let their hair grow in huge Afros decorated with colorful bits of cloth and bone combs. Bedja men are famous in Africa for raising excellent camels. Their herds often appeared along the highway in great, puffy clouds of dust. One afternoon, we watched several Bedjas racing camels as if they were horses. One morning, a band of nomads joined us for tea. They were tough, sinewy men who never smiled, although they did marvel at our stoves and bicycles.

It was on the stretch between Abudah and the Red Sea that the heat began to seriously damage some of our equipment. Every substance with the least amount of moisture was shrinking. Our leather gloves were almost too small to wear, and our shoes—they were vinyl and leather—were becoming uncomfortably small. The nylon tents had shrunk so much that it was almost impossible to fit the poles into the prefitted grooves. Worst of all was the heat's effect on rubber. Our tires were crumbling away. If the roads had been at all bumpy, the tires would have disintegrated. We also had problems with the plastic grooves that attached our panniers to their racks. They buckled and broke in the heat or melted into useless shapes. Jim had to tie his panniers on with rope one morning to save the one intact groove he had left. Somehow, this equipment had to last until New Delhi, where our next spare parts shipment was being sent by HOPE.

Our other problem on this difficult stretch was the wind. Every morning, when the hot sun cut into the cool evening air, headwinds would start whipping across the sands. At about eight o'clock we would start to feel a strong push against our faces. By eight-thirty we were downshifting, as if we had suddenly hit a steep hill. By nine we were moving into 20 or 25 mph winds at about half our usual cruising speed. Occasionally the wind gusted up to 40 or 50 mph. The wind was unpredictable, always appearing without warning to slow us down and frustrate our plans. Two or three times we came close to running out of food and water because the wind kept us from reaching resupply villages. Eventually we developed a method of drafting the wind. Like bicycle racing teams, we rotated the lead man riding directly into the wind. For ten-minute intervals, each of us rode lead while the others rested.

Except for brief spats on the bikes, the three of us got along well in Sudan. We were now moving at a decent speed, even with the wind. By Showak, we had formally abolished the group leader system. The three of us worked so well together that we didn't need a formal way of assigning tasks.

We pedaled into Port Sudan on the Red Sea on April Fool's Day. The city was a sleepy, sprawling town of functional British architecture and a few modern concrete colonnades. Two or three giant ships were berthed against long piers with cranes and hoists poking into the sky. We checked into a hotel called the Olympia Park, an aging mansion facing a sloppy city park

filled with camels ambling about like stray dogs. It was a relief
to check into a room with real beds and sheets. After long naps,
we rummaged through our bags and found our civilian clothes.
We asked the owner of the Olympia Park, a Greek, where we
should eat dinner. He suggested the British Club. "It's the only
decent place to eat in the city," he said. "They've even got
Heineken beer."

The British Club was guarded by a pair of toy cannons and a
Sudanese maître d' who refused to let us in because we were
not members. Jim explained to him that we had just bicycled to
Port Sudan from Khartoum and we really needed a beer. The
maître d' was still being obstinate when a boisterous group of
Brits shouted, "Let 'em in. If they really bicycled 'ere from
bloody Khartoum, they deserve a beer." We walked inside and
sat down at the Brits' table.

"Bring these boys each a beer," shouted a barrel-chested
man with muttonchop sideburns and a Scottish accent.

"You boys really bicycled across from Khartoum?" asked a
large man with short blond hair. He looked like Rod Steiger.
"You ain't pullin' no April Fool's joke on us now, are yah?" We
told the men about our trip, but when they asked for proof, we
realized that we had none with us.

"We'll make yah a deal," said the Scotsman. "We'll buy yah
dinner and all the beer yah can drink, assumin' what you're
sayin' is the truth. But if y'are pullin' our petunias, you'll pay
for yours and ours tomorrow."

"Tomorrow we'll bring proof," I said as a tray full of Heinekens arrived at our table. The Brits raised their cans and toasted
the "fool Americans" who had "pulled their petunias" about
biking across from Khartoum.

When we rode our battered, dusty bikes over the next day
they bought us lunch and another round of beers.

Two days later at the tiny Port Sudan airport, we were almost
barred from boarding our flight to Jeddah. "My friends, you
have been in Israel," said an Air Sudan agent. He pointed at
our wrinkled airline tickets, which listed all of our flights since
Washington, D.C., including the flight from Athens to Tel Aviv.
"You will not be allowed in Jeddah if you have traveled to
Israel."

"Saudi Arabia will not let us in with Tel Aviv on our tickets?"
I asked. We had already had a long argument with the Air

Sudan people over the bikes. At first they had refused to put them on the plane.

"I have a solution to this problem," said Jim. He pulled out a black Bic and scratched out the *Tel Aviv* on his ticket. "Now we have never been to Israel," he said, "and you can let us on the airplane."

From the air the lights of Jeddah glowed in neat yellow rows as our little jet circled the runway and landed. We were the only Westerners on board. Everyone else was a Muslim on a hajj to Mecca. They each carried empty suitcases and empty plastic containers to fill with souvenirs and holy water from the sacred city. As we stood to get off the plane, the Sudan Air flight attendant told us we were to wait for a special bus. A few minutes later, a large bus stopped and lifted itself up to the level of the fuselage door. We stepped into the empty, brand-new bus and sat down in air-conditioned comfort as it lowered itself down.

The Jeddah International Airport had just been completed by a consortium of Western companies led by Bechtel, the American multinational. It was supposed to be the largest airport in the world. Saudi Arabian Airlines planes were arrayed in long rows on the tarmac. Every other major world airline had 747s parked in flanking rows. The main terminal itself was a giant nomad tent done in concrete and plaster. The bus dropped us off in front of a grand glass entryway.

Inside was a high-tech extravaganza. Television monitors listed flights, news items, and daily activities. Philippine and Pakistani custodians in neat uniforms scooped up errant pieces of trash or cigarette butts, while American technicians ran about with identification badges and walkie-talkies. Slick signs on the restrooms showed a man with a beard and *kaffiyeh* for the men's room and a woman in a veil for the women's room.

At the check-in area marked Non-Muslim Foreigners, we presented our twenty-four-hour transit visas to a uniformed customs guard. Pale white Westerners in Bermuda shorts and business suits stood in other lines. Most of them had on nametags identifying their companies—Caterpillar, Bechtel, or Aramco.

"When is your flight out?" asked a crisp Saudi soldier. We showed him our Air Pakistan tickets. Our flight was scheduled to leave in twenty-three hours. "You will have to wait in the transit area," said the guard.

"But wait," I said. "We wanted to go into town."

"I am sorry, but transit passengers are not allowed to leave the airport. You do not have the proper visa." We told him that the Saudi embassy in Khartoum had assured us we could move freely in the country for up to twenty-four hours. "They were incorrect," he said.

"May we place a call to the U.S. consulate?" asked Jim. The soldier looked us over and asked why we wanted to go into town. We told him briefly about our trip, the arrangements we had made with the consulate, and our hope to bike in Saudi Arabia. "Please follow me," said the guard.

"I'm sorry, but it is impossible to grant your request," said an officer in the customs office. "You cannot leave the airport. Therefore, it is pointless for you to call the consulate."

"You are not going to let us call the consulate?"

"You do not have the proper visa." The man's face was impassive, bureaucratic. He spoke to two guards in Arabic. They took us to a special wing of the terminal, which was padlocked shut by a tall iron gate. We were furious. Throughout the trip, the combination of our being Americans and members of a special trip had meant that we had always received preferential treatment. Now we were being shut out in what we considered a summary, illegal fashion. They wouldn't even let us call the consulate!

For the next twenty-three hours, we rested and ate plastic fast food in the high-tech transit area, while bemoaning the state of the world. Not only were we unable to bike in Saudi Arabia, we were having to skip Iran and Afghanistan as well. Pulling out Jim's big map of the world, we saw all of the land that we were being forced to skip over. It was upsetting that so many countries were either inaccessible because of politics, bureaucracy, or war. At the end of the twenty-three hours, we were escorted out of our locked wing by Saudi soldiers, who made sure we got on our flight to Karachi in Pakistan. Whether we liked it or not, we were beginning a new phase of the expedition.

SOUTH ASIA

Donald Duncan in crowd,
northern India.

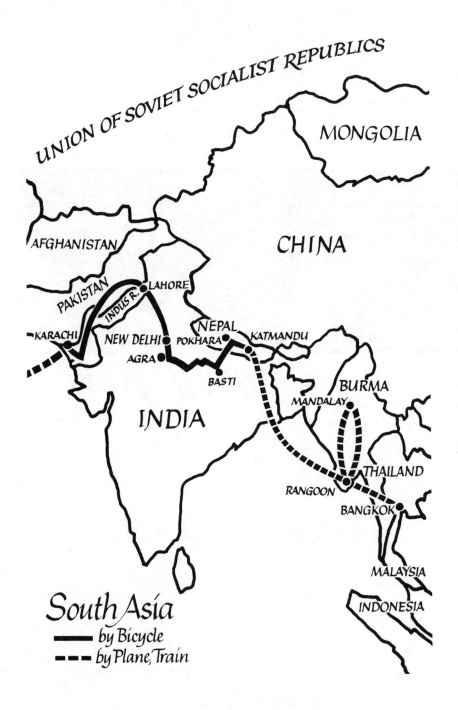

UNION OF SOVIET SOCIALIST REPUBLICS

MONGOLIA

AFGHANISTAN

CHINA

PAKISTAN

LAHORE

INDUS R.

KARACHI

NEW DELHI

POKHARA

NEPAL

KATMANDU

AGRA

BASTI

BURMA

MANDALAY

INDIA

THAILAND

RANGOON

BANGKOK

MALAYSIA

INDONESIA

South Asia
——— by Bicycle
- - - by Plane, Train

5. Among the Believers

The small terminal at Karachi International Airport was like a poor man's shanty compared to the grandiose complex at Jeddah. Dust swirled in fine layers across the wooden floors, animated by blowing ceiling fans vibrating noisily with every turn. But the fans did little to drive away the moist heat soaking every armpit in the terminal, whether they belonged to Pakistanis in Western business suits or to pilgrims in baggy *chalwar* pants and cloaks returning from a hajj to Mecca. The crowd was almost exclusively male. A dour young woman in a gray dress held the hands of two tiny boys with slick hair and British-style prep school suits with short pants.

When we stepped out of the airport door, the heat was even worse. It felt like the hot blast of an oven opening up in my face. We were used to heat, coming from Sudan, but the heat in Pakistan introduced a new element—humidity. Our World Bike for HOPE T-shirts were drenched within minutes. Sweat poured in thin streams down my face. Flies buzzed around us, a bird of prey cackled overhead, and I could smell a faint odor of rotten garbage.

•••

Karachi is the third largest Muslim city in the world after Ja-
karta and Cairo, but at first glance it looked more like an outpost
of British India than a haven of Muhammad. The English language was everywhere—on signs above shops, on posters and
billboards advertising 555 cigarettes and Coca-Cola, and in
bookstores selling Penguin paperbacks. The architecture was
ponderously British. Biking into Karachi from the airport, we
passed huge, Victorian-style government buildings, a couple of
Gothic revival cathedrals, and several sprawling parks filled
with European trees and flowers. But beneath this aging,
shabby veneer of empire, it was clear that the dominant influence in Karachi had little to do with the British and everything
to do with Islam.

Hundreds of compact, brightly painted mosques lined the
sidestreets behind the imperial avenues. The call to prayer bellowed over the dusty streets five times a day, and street vendors
sold the Koran and Islamic texts as briskly as vendors in the
States sell *TV Guides.* A new set of Islamic laws propagated
under martial law banned Western music and dancing and out-
lawed alcohol, except for wealthy foreigners who could procure
a rare "non-Muslim drinking permit." The new laws banned
women from holding many jobs, censored the media according
to Islamic (and military) guidelines, and provided for floggings,
mutilations, and hangings according to ancient Islamic law.

Most of these laws had been introduced during the resur-
gence of fundamentalist Islam that rocked the Middle East during the late seventies. A divisive debate was still raging among
Pakistanis over the role of Islam in their country. On one side
were the moderates who generally advocated the Western no-
tion of separating church and state. These moderates had run
the country as a Western-style democracy until 1977, when the
last elected prime minister of Pakistan, Zulfikar Ali Bhutto, was
overthrown by the military. On the other side was a coalition of
military leaders and conservative fundamentalists who advocated strict adherence to Islamic law. This group, led by
Pakistan's dictator, General Mohammad Zia ul-Haq, was responsible for most of the Islamic "reforms."

"This used to be a very different city," an old man told me
one afternoon in a downtown restaurant near our rooms at the
Karachi YMCA. His face was grizzled. His hands were pocked
with scars. He claimed the police in prison had beat his hands.

"I was a jazz pianist," he explained in excellent English. "I played once with Count Basie, in London."

I asked him why he had been put in jail.

"I used to play in the clubs here," he said, "and I was involved in politics. When Zia took power, he shut down the clubs, because he said they were anti-Islam. During this time, I was arrested, like many others."

"You must be bitter about going to jail," I said.

"Of course," he said. "But you should understand. It was a chaotic time, with religious fanatics in every place. In the streets, we had riots and violence. Bhutto, he did not stop the violence, so Zia took over with the army. I do not like the army, but we do have order restored now, so it was not a complete disaster."

I asked the man if he still played the piano.

He answered me by holding up his scarred hands. "I cannot play now," he said. "It is too painful."

It took four days to complete our business in Karachi. At the YMCA we overhauled the bikes, mended clothes, and scrubbed off the last traces of Sahara sand. At the Pakistani National Bank we picked up two thousand dollars wired by HOPE. In the modern shopping areas near the YMCA, we browsed through English-language bookstores and bought basic food supplies. With the help of the U.S. consulate in Karachi, we met with a half-dozen Pakistani reporters who wrote long stories about our project in their heavily censored papers. On April 8 the *Pakistan Times* ran an article titled "Carrying the Message of HOPE." After introducing us, a reporter named Shahid Mahmood wrote in Pakistan's curious English:

> Braving many adventurous hardships, the expeditioners have traveled from place to place and people to people telling them about Project HOPE. The better moments have been the most since they reached Pakistan. They have found the people of this country most hospitable and friendly, and ever so helpful. They set out to see different cultures on their dream-come-true expedition and so far have found their experience fascinating.

One afternoon, we visited the U.S. consul's office to get information about such things as roads and the availability of good food. We also wanted to find out if the political situation would affect us in Pakistan.

"Pakistan is an explosive country," the consul said. "You've got religious fanatics running about. You've also got a large element of the people who don't like Zia. Things have been calm lately, but I want you to be extremely careful." Like Clarence in Khartoum, he worried that our high visibility might make us targets of anti-American fanatics. He was also worried about thieves. "In the rural areas, thieves are a big problem," he said, suggesting that we avoid sleeping in roadside hotels and truckstops. He told us flatly not to risk camping. "You will be safe enough bicycling in the daylight," he said, "but I would look for a police compound or a government guest house at night. They should let you set up tents in their compounds."

At the American Express office, large packets of mail had collected for us over the past several weeks (our last American Express mail stop had been in Cairo). My packet was filled with weekly letters and cards from Laura covering the period between her trip to Egypt and our arrival in Karachi. In the first few letters, she sounded happy. Then came a series of more discouraged letters. Apparently the few letters I was able to send from Sudan had not reached her. "Why don't you write me?" she demanded. "The mail can't be *that* bad that *all* of your letters are lost. I love you too much to wait patiently for another month to go by with no word." I immediately went to the Karachi telephone and telegraph office but was unable to get a call through to the States.

Besides letters from Laura, I got a *Playboy* magazine from a friend (it somehow got past the Pakistani censors), several packages from my parents, and a letter from *People* magazine. "We have assigned a reporter in *Time*'s New Delhi bureau to write a story on your extraordinary effort," wrote a *People* editor. He asked us to contact *Time*'s office in New Delhi as soon as possible. My mother wrote that Eddie Bauer, one of our sponsors, was printing a poster of us to distribute in stores. We had already received a telex from Scott Patton at HOPE reporting that articles were pouring in from all over the world about our trip. "Apparently you guys are hitting the big time," Scott wrote. "We're all proud of you here."

On April 9 a fast tail wind blew us east out of Karachi toward the Indus River 200 kilometers away. From the British heart of the city we passed a series of gradually deteriorating neighbor-hoods until reaching the outer slums. The poverty here was equal to the worst we had seen in Egypt. Through a haze of dust and smoke from kerosene-fired braziers stood rows of huts constructed of skinny saplings, greasy scraps of wood, and can-vas. Chickens clucked and lazy dogs scratched at flies buzzing in swarms alongside the highway. A stench of sewage lapped at the road. Open trenches in front of the huts were choked with excrement and refuse.

By the time we stopped for a break, the temperature was already blistering. The humidity, hovering at 85 percent or more, permeated the air, picking up the dust and turning the world a sloppy brown color. Shades of brown stuck to our sweaty skin, creasing into thin lines of dirt as elbows and knees worked up and down. Our T-shirts and shorts and helmets quickly turned mucky. Wet dirt collected in greasy clumps on our oiled chains and gears. Eventually the heat and drenching humidity would combine with the poverty of rural Pakistan to wear us down; life for us would become much more miserable than it had ever been in Africa. But on the first few days we were still high from the adventure of Sudan and excited about the growing success of the project.

Sometimes the brown hues of outer Karachi were broken by flashes of color. A red piece of cloth was tied to a corner of the tin awning at our first Coke stand. Bits of shiny foil and bright decals—stuck here and there on wooden shelves stuffed with cartons of Red and White brand cigarettes, jars of hard candy, biscuits, and hard-boiled eggs—glinted against the earthy col-ors. Pakistani bicycle wheels were laced with bright ribbons. Fuzzy plastic foxtails hung from their handlebars. Pakistanis also wore some of the most colorful hats I had ever seen. Every fourth man we saw wore a flat-topped hat embroidered with glittering threads that swirled in patterns of circles and abstract shapes. These hats were the mark of a Sindhi (we were in the ancient land of Sind). Later we would see the white puggarees of the Punjab, the yellow and blue turbans of the northwest frontier, the curled cotton hats of the Pathan tribesmen, and the colorful, beanie-like hats of Afghanistan. In Asia you can usu-ally tell where a man is from by his hat.

But hats and foxtails were nothing compared to the trucks and buses. Decorating running boards, hoods, ceilings, cabs, hubcaps, and windows is a highly refined art in Pakistan. Braids carved into wooden side panels and doors frame intricate processions of painted images, ranging from boats and land-scapes and animals to depictions of revered Islamic sites like the Dome of the Rock in Jerusalem and the Great Black Shrine in Mecca. Geometric designs and Arabic calligraphy swirl around the images, connecting each of them into a whole re-sembling a cross between a Persian rug and a Barnum and Bailey circus cart. Politics blended with art on some of the trucks. A few side panels were devoted to huge, cartoonlike portrayals of General Zia in full dress uniform.

Despite their beauty, Pakistani trucks and buses made our lives miserable. They were much worse than in Egypt. The drivers were like cowboys as they roared from city to city, rul-ing the roads in a reign of terror. With an absolute disregard for smaller sedans, ox carts, bicyclists, or pedestrians, they often raced side by side in twos or threes, hardly slowing down even for crowded village streets. "Catch me if you can," said the back panel of one bus. Not surprisingly, the edges of most vil-lages were littered with stripped wrecks, off to one side so the spirits of the dead will not haunt the living in the village.

For two days we biked due east from Karachi, following the Arabian Sea toward the Indus River and the city of Hyderabad. From Hyderabad we planned to follow the river twelve hundred kilometers north to Lahore, where we would cross into India. Our first night out, we camped near a field of ancient Muslim tombs called Chaomoi. The elaborately carved tomb-stones were shaped like a series of single-load toasters with bread sticking out of their tops. Underneath them slept a couple of dozen sultans who had ruled Sind in the name of the early Muslim caliphs. A lone, tiny man tended the tombs. He told us to beware of ghosts, especially "in the time just before the rising of the sun," when a murdered sultan sometimes roamed the cemetery. "He looks for his brother, who murdered him and took his wives," the little man told us.

The next day we saw more tombs, this time at the village of Tatta. But here the tombs were no mere toasters. Some of them were small-scale palaces. The sultans who built these monsters lived in the golden age of independent Islamic Sind, just before Moghul invaders mowed them down on their way to India. In the middle of the cemetery was the tomb of Bin Qasim, the young general who conquered the Sind for Islam in the eighth century. He died at age nineteen when the caliph falsely accused him of sleeping with a royal concubine. The execution was accomplished by pouring water onto a dry leather suit that slowly suffocated the young man. When the caliph later discovered the general's innocence, he built the lavish tomb at Tatta. Brightly painted tiny minarets decorated an entrance that looked like a Muslim version of the Magic Castle in Disneyworld. Again the colors broke out of the drab brownness like a rainbow in a dark sky. Pilgrims intent on throwing *rabel* blossoms on the hero's sarcophagus filled a small courtyard. We brought a string of blossoms to pay our respects, but an aged imam—an Islamic teacher—stopped us by letting loose an angry barrage of Urdu. Then he slapped a walking stick across my right thigh.

"You are naked," explained a nearby pilgrim, a man in a pajamalike outfit called a *shalwar* chemise.

"Naked?" I said, looking confused. The imam glowered at us, holding his stick up in the air.

"Yes, I am sorry, but you must have coverings," said the pilgrim, pointing at my legs. "This is a very religious place in Pakistan."

Steering north along the flat gray waters of the Indus, we began a journey up a river that seemed a cousin to the Nile. Both rivers cut through otherwise uninhabitable deserts, and both are banked by a thin belt of fertile land replenished annually by silt-bearing floods. The Indus River Valley, like the Nile, was also a cradle of civilization, although no pyramids or lotus-topped pillars survive. The ancients who lived on these shores built their monuments from perishable materials like clay bricks and wood—the same materials that their descendants now use to build their huts along Pakistan's Highway 5.

Like the Egyptians, the Indus River people live as one with the steady seasons of the river. I sensed the same timelessness here, as if these people and their predecessors had been working at the same tasks for centuries. The same children guided the same water buffalos in endless circles around the same grinding stones. The same fishermen in white loincloths dragged nets through the same black sewer estuaries. The same wheat and sugarcane, irrigated by the same sort of primitive windmill pumps, grew in ragged rows right up to the edge of the Great Thar Desert.

But the lower Indus River Valley is much poorer and less

developed than the Nile valley in Egypt. Only 25 percent of all Pakistanis live alongside the river's main channel. The majority of the nearly ninety million Pakistanis inhabit the more fertile plains of western Punjab, a land stretching from Lahore north to Kashmir, and west to the foothills of the Hindu Kush. We saw few factories in Sind outside of Karachi, and little evidence of mechanization in the dry fields of wheat, tobacco, and corn stretching out on either side of the road. It was unusual to find dependable electricity or any sort of running water in the small, chaotic villages. Sodas were plentiful but almost never cold, unless we happened on a *shai* stand where ice had just been delivered. Pharmacies, which had been plentiful in Egypt, were rare; canned goods stores did not really exist. This excluded items from our menu that we had considered basics in Egypt and Sudan—things like Tang, canned vegetables, canned meats, noodles, and evaporated milk. Green herbs were nowhere to be found. When our last bottle of oregano was finished, we had to flavor our boiled, tasteless gruel with the fiery local spices: cumin, peppers, and hot mustards.

Sanitary conditions in rural Sind were appalling. A typical hand pump well, our major source of water, was often planted in the same community area where open sewer troughs ran, or where rotting garbage was dumped into sloppy piles. Children defecated and women washed their clothes right at the pumps. The Indus itself was light gray and smelled like a sewer. To combat the filth, we tried doubling and tripling our iodine ration and boiling everything we ate to a consistency of mush. But it did little good, because the room for error was enormous. Just one drop of unpurified water on the lip of a bike bottle had the potential to infect us with any of a dozen different diseases.

Our daily routine in Pakistan was a modified version of our Sudan routine. Rising at dawn, we biked until noon, when the heat and humidity became unbearable. Stopping under a roadside tree, we cooked our main meal and napped. In mid-afternoon, we resumed our journey until late afternoon, when we looked for a place to sleep. We never rode after dark, heeding the U.S. consul's warning about thieves. Usually we spent the night in a village police compound. The alternative was to camp or to pay a few cents for a cot in a roadside inn. Just about everyone who spoke English echoed the consul's warnings about camping. As for the inns, they were infamous as targets for thieves. Truck drivers often slept with loaded pistols under their pillows while innkeepers sometimes stood guard with shotguns. Tales of criminal gangs abounded. One afternoon we were delayed at a police roadblock while teams of uniformed soldiers and police combed a field for a particularly nasty criminal. Each constable was heavily armed with a rifle, pistol, and chains. In the distance, hounds bayed and men shouted.

As in many Third World countries, Pakistani police play an exalted role that would never be tolerated in the States. They are powerful figures in the community, often acting under martial law as arbiter, judge, and, if they deem it necessary, executioner. Wearing trim olive green uniforms and red berets, they patrol the villages and countryside with the pride and swagger of elites. Slung over their shoulders were old British Lee Enfields, like those we had seen in Egypt. But unlike their Egyptian counterparts, these policemen wore neat, pressed uniforms and shiny boots. Their mustaches were trimmed into perfect curves over their upper lips. Trained in the British style of military discipline, they crisply saluted superiors and seldom smiled. Their compounds were islands of discipline and order amidst the bedlam of the roadside villages. Typically, the compounds contained a jailhouse, a row of barracks, a radio room, and a small home for the district's commander, called the Station House Officer (SHO).

One afternoon in a small village we met Achmed, a SHO who introduced himself by saluting briskly from a jeep he was standing in as it roared into the village police compound. His men jumped up and saluted as their leader sprung lightly out of the jeep. With his dark goggles, jodhpurs, riding crop, and holstered sidearm, he looked like George C. Scott in *Patton*.

Achmed shook our hands with bone-crunching grips. He was a large, swarthy man with shrewd eyes and heavy cheeks. The constable who had greeted us at the compound gate gave the SHO our newspaper clippings from Karachi. "Ah, you are famous cyclists," he said. "You are honored guests." His accent was upper-crust British. "I will expect you at dinner, at seven o'clock. Please make yourselves comfortable." He spoke a sharp command in Urdu to two constables. "These men will show you where to erect your tents."

Crossing the compound, we passed the jailhouse. Outside a corner cell stood a small, nervous, well-dressed man conversing in whispers with an equally well-dressed prisoner. The small man came over to speak with us as soon as the constables had left. Introducing himself as a local doctor, he said he had read about us in the newspapers. "One of you is a journalist?" he asked. "Please, I want to tell you a story of corruption and evil." He whispered the words *corruption* and *evil*, as if someone were listening. "You should go back and tell all Americans that there is no justice in Pakistan. The martial law is evil. The police are corrupt. They take money from the people and steal everything." He paused to look around, making us all feel nervous. He was obviously frightened that he would be overheard. "It is no good to talk here," he whispered. "Please, would you join me for dinner in the village?"

"I'm afraid that the SHO has already invited us," said Jim. About this time, a man in a powder blue *shalwar* chemise appeared to screw light bulbs into wall sockets near our camp area.

"I want to tell you my story. Please let me tour you in the village." I nodded and told him we would try, but as I spoke the man in the *shalwar* chemise suddenly turned around. The doctor gasped. It was the SHO.

"I propose that we take a tour of the town together," he said pleasantly. The doctor turned pale. "I do not know what stories my friend the doctor proposes to tell you, but I would certainly be honored to be present when they are told." He was smiling, looking deceptively placid in civilian clothes.

On the chaotic main street of the village, the SHO ordered us a round of sodas at a busy outdoor truck stop. An armed constable stood at attention just beyond the outer rim of tables. His head kept turning in slow sweeps across the crowded *shai* stand. The center of his sweep was the SHO.

We never did hear the doctor's story of corruption. After a quick soda, the doctor, now thoroughly agitated, excused himself and left. I wanted to follow him, but not while I was in the company of the SHO. When we had finished our sodas, Jim insisted that the SHO let us pay for the drinks. He started to pull out the group purse. "My friend, put away that money. You are my guests," he said cheerfully. Without paying anything, he stood up and walked away, back in the direction of the compound. I moved to pull a few rupees out of my money belt to pay the bill but lost my nerve under the cold stare of the constable. It was an embarrassing episode. The three of us felt like accessories to a crime as we sheepishly followed the SHO into the safety of the street and away from accusing eyes that we imagined were staring after us.

"Would you like some cigarettes?" asked the SHO on the way back to the compound. Without waiting for an answer, he casually picked up a pack of Red and Whites from the nearest stand. He did not pay or even speak to a wizened old man tending the stall. It was as if the man didn't exist. But I saw no anger in the man's face. Instead, I saw a sort of vacant expression that reminded me of certain bag ladies in New York City. It was a disturbing look to an American—a combination of defeat, poverty, and acquiescence. Jim and Don refused the cigarettes offered by the SHO. He already knew that I didn't smoke.

We didn't always stay in "cop shops." Almost every day we got invitations to spend the night from people on the road. As word was passed down the highway that three American bikers were on the way, the frequent villages often had someone on hand who spoke English to greet us. Typically, our greeting committee would offer us goat's-milk tea or a Coke, and invite us to spend the night.

One evening, in the city of Hyderabad, we stayed with a doctor's family as the guests of his two sons. Ali Fasiabad, the older brother, ran a small plastics factory. The younger brother, Achmed, was applying to attend Hyderabad University. They lived in a middle-class duplex built of concrete slabs and trimmed with blue tiles. The Fasiabad house had the feeling of an unfinished basement. The walls and floor were gray concrete. The furniture was the sort of worn, out-of-style stuff relegated to a downstairs rec room in a middle-class American home. In the living room was a black-and-white television, down the hall was a shower room, and next to the living room was a tiny kitchen containing a half-refrigerator and a bank of portable electric burners mounted on a concrete shelf.

After a supper of curried mutton and rice, Ali and Achmed took us on a tour of their neighborhood. On a wide, smoky street we drank *lassies*—curdled milk flavored with mangos. At a tailor's shop, Achmed had us measured for *shalwar* chemises. The man said they would be done in two hours. Next we visited the local hospital, bought some bandanas at a drug store, and went to see an Urdu-language movie. The Fasiabad brothers took great pride in the movie theater. We were taken upstairs to the viewing booth, where an immensely fat man ran an ancient projector. He delayed changing reels to serve us tea.

●●●

Another night we stayed with a college student in Khairpur who called himself Sexy Abdul. "Are you sexy?" he asked. "I am so sexy, the women cannot resist me." In his dorm room Abdul asked if we liked to fuck. "Please do not be shy," he said. "You can talk freely here about fucking. I love to fuck. Sex is my life. I love it. It is hard to find women who will fuck in Pakistan, but I know where to find them. Do you want a woman tonight? The best cost five hundred rupees (about forty-five dollars). If that is too much, I can get them cheaper. Some are just twenty rupees, but they smell."

Abdul was a small young man with a thin mustache and almond-shaped eyes that made him look slightly Chinese. He was the oldest son of an engineer who owned a fleet of Pakistan's kamikaze buses.

"My family is very, very rich," he told us. "We have a big house and a Betamax. I have one hundred recordings of American movies and American television. What is your favorite television program? I like 'Charlie's Angels,' because of the women."

After we had moved our gear into his room, Abdul slipped a tape into a cassette player. "I want you to listen to a new tape I received from Bangkok," he said. "I have a cousin in Bangkok. Ohhhhh, the women there! He tells me that they fuck Ping-Pong balls. If only I could go to Bangkok."

The tape started with a burst of hiss and then some dialogue between a man with a heavy Cockney accent and an Asian woman who could barely speak English. He was asking her if she wanted to make it with him, talking about his massive member and deft moves. The tape quickly dissipated into several minutes of grunts and squeals and moans, accompanied by a steady creaking noise that was supposed to sound like a bed. In the middle of a long squeal from the woman, Abdul abruptly pressed the stop button.

"Maybe you can help me," he said, looking very serious. "They are speaking so fast in English, I don't understand everything they are saying."

Jim and I looked at each other and started laughing.

After showers, Abdul proposed that we smoke some hashish. We declined, saying that we did not want to chance getting caught.

"Have you seen the movie *Midnight Express?*" I asked.

"Yes, of course," he lied. A few minutes later, he lit up the hash in a small hookha pipe.

"I would like to offer you some whiskey," Abdul said, "but with Zia, we can no longer drink in Pakistan. It is part of the new Islamic law. Do you know about the law?"

"Yes," we answered, hoping that we weren't going to hear another dissertation on Islamic law.

"I hate all of it—all of Islam," he said. "I only tell you because you are Americans. My father beats me because I don't believe in Islam. It is stupid and backward. They do not allow sex. Oh, I want to leave Pakistan." He rolled back his eyes and released a stream of blue smoke. "Someday I will go to America, where they have free sex." He leaned in close to us, like he had a great secret to tell. "Is it true that all virgins must have sex in America by age eighteen? I have heard that virgins will come to a man's door and demand to be fucked."

"Abdul, where the hell do you get your information?" asked Jim.

"I have a friend living in New York," Abdul said proudly. "He writes me about American women."

Another night in rural Pakistan we were invited by a boy in a black robe to sleep in a compound belonging to a poor farming family. The boy led us off the main highway on his heavy one-speed bike and down a dirt track in the direction of the Indus. With every step, we seemed to move further and further back in time. It was as if the highway was a thin outpost of modern civilization, with its pavement, its trucks, and its Coca-Cola. To turn off the highway was to leave anything resembling the modern world. Travel here was by foot or by donkey, and every task was done by hand or with the use of some beast. Work gangs carried man-sized sickles and burlap bags of produce, while women carried on top of their heads baskets of greens and dried dung for fires.

We turned off the dirt track onto a narrow path leading to the boy's adobe-walled compound. Like a primitive apartment building, the compound was split into six open-air sections, each belonging to a separate family. In our hosts' rectangular section were two buildings attached to the walls on either side of the rectangle. In the middle was a large space of hard-packed dirt. One wall was reserved for three large water buffalos, three goats, and several chickens. They had apparently been brought in for the night. Across from the gate was a large wheel with buckets to draw water out of a well.

These people were obviously poor, but not desperately poor.

Their buildings were constructed of bricks, and the well was equipped with a manual pump that lifted the water on a bucket wheel and poured it into a cement trough. Plastic was a way of life. The plethora of bright buckets, cups, plates, and scoopers was like a Tupperware party gone mad. The compound itself was scrupulously clean. A stooped woman spent most of her time sweeping the hard dirt floor with a hand broom. Every few minutes, she would scoop up any fresh dung produced by the animals and deposit it in a wooden box to dry, presumably for fuel.

Later in the evening, after another meal of curried mutton and rice, the boy in the black robe introduced us to his grandfather. The man was seriously ill with a number of maladies. His bare feet were swollen with elephantiasis to the size of small watermelons and his skin was pocked with open sores. He kept us up most of the night by wheezing and coughing.

As the days wore on, the hardships of biking through Pakistan began to wear us down. Almost from the start I was sick with dysentery. I had my first major attack just five days out of Karachi. We were relaxing after a lunch of gruel under a tree along the road. Don and Jim were napping, while a small crowd of Pakistanis simply watched. The attack came on abruptly in a spasm of pain. My sweat turned cold, and my head felt like hammers were slamming into each temple.

With my stomach feeling like glass, we biked to the next village, where we were lucky enough to find a doctor. Outside a small concrete clinic, ragged men and women stood in a long line. Inside, a fat doctor with a round face injected each person with a clear liquid. After each shot, he wiped the needle with a towel soaked in alcohol, refilled the syringe, and used it again.

"I can cure you in five minutes," he said, pulling out a syringe the size of a horse needle. The chamber was filled with a yellow liquid.

"What the hell is that?" I said, my eyes widening. "You're not using that on me!"

"This will cure you, my friend," said the doctor. I was suddenly feeling sick again.

"Don, tell him I'm not getting any fucking shot," I murmured, feeling hot, frustrated, and very ill.

"Perhaps you would instead like a pill?" said the doctor, giving up on the needle. "I have good medicine." He pulled out an unmarked bottle filled with red and white capsules. "I use these myself," he said. "Take one every two hours while you have dysentery, and two a day for three days after the dysentery goes away."

The pills did help. They froze my stomach muscles in suspended animation, although the dysentery would return again an hour or two after I had taken the pill. I never did find out what the pills were called.

Don and Jim both got sick soon after I did, although Don's illnesses were shorter and less frequent, and Jim got sick only a few times. At first we stopped biking to allow ourselves time to recover. In the city of Sukkur, we stopped for three days while each of us got sick one after another. But none of this helped. Gradually, dysentery became a way of life, as it was for most of the people we saw along the road. The longer we had the disease, the more manageable it became. Partly this is due to the remarkable facility of the human body to adapt itself to misery. We almost got used to the periodic explosions of pain every two or three hours, and the sapped, laconic feeling in between.

We weren't the only people sick in Pakistan. Millions around us were suffering from a lot more than just dysentery. The children who chased us through the villages sometimes had eyes crusted white with trachoma. Open sores bled and oozed as flies dug in by the dozens. Beggars missing limbs occasionally appeared on the edges of villages. Statistically, one out of ten babies in Pakistan fail to reach their fifth birthday. Most of them die of dysentery. Unlike the three white American bikers, they could not afford to buy medicine. As in Egypt, most of their mothers did not know that they should boil their drinking water or use iodine.

After eleven weeks in the Third World, the spectre of poverty and disease was assaulting us on a very basic level. I tried hard to maintain my perspective, reminding myself of what Gruffy Clough had said in Sudan, that I was here by choice. Yet more and more the adventure was being smothered in hardships. As the days rolled by, the situation approached the intolerable. Our anger had been growing steadily as we headed east. We loathed the hassles, the illnesses, and everything else. At the darkest moments, I found myself hating Pakistan—the land, the people, and the trip itself. I wondered why I had ever left home. Why was I torturing myself? Was it to help HOPE? I failed to see how my being miserable helped Project HOPE. Was it to prove something? Was it to learn? *Why had I come?*

For a long time, I tried to suppress these thoughts. They were ugly, pessimistic reactions completely out of character for an optimist like me. They violated everything I had been taught. Yet I found myself caring less and less about the unfortunates around me and more and more about myself. As we struggled to mitigate our misery, we adopted an attitude of us versus them. It became difficult for us to tolerate even minor irritations. We easily became infuriated at one another. If someone failed to call out a bump on the road, we screamed and cursed. If a stallkeeper tried to haggle with us and we weren't in the mood, we would curse him and throw a few rupees in his direction like some rich jerk in a movie.

Each of us became obsessed with specific annoyances. Flat tires irritated Jim. During our four weeks on the ragged roads in Pakistan, Jim personally scored twenty-eight flats out of our group total of fifty-three. Some days he had two or three flats in a row. It was like a nightmare for him to have to constantly break his cadence and hold us up in the heat to fix another flat. He got very good at it. Properly enraged, he could yank off his wheel, patch his tube, pump up his tire, and replace the wheel in about the time it took for us to refill our bike bottles at a filthy well.

Flies were what set me off. Descending from the sky in heavy clouds, they buzzed over us constantly, landing by the dozens to bite into our skin. I often put on quite a show for the locals as I grabbed my dust mask and spun around while shouting curses at the flies. I got to where I didn't want to stop for breaks because of the flies.

Don was incensed by the kids that forever gathered around us. One day, Don made himself a "kid mallet" out of a long stick. When we stopped, he would draw a circle around himself and wave the stick, daring kids to cross the line. One afternoon Don slipped and fell into a sewer when a kid accidentally tripped him. His scream pierced through the clamor of the village. Jim and I instantly dropped our bikes, thinking that someone had attacked my brother. When we found him, he was standing beside the sewer, his left side covered with a slick of sewage.

"Get it off me!" he screamed. I grabbed the first thing I could find, which happened to be Don's Budweiser towel. It was neatly folded on the back of his bike. He wiped desperately at the shit as Jim grabbed a water bag and started dousing him. Later Don got angry with me for ruining his Bud towel.

As the days stretched on, our daily kilometerage declined dramatically. During the first two or three days in Pakistan, we kept up a steady one hundred kilometers a day. By the time we reached our halfway point, our pace had dropped to only about fifty kilometers. We were hopelessly behind schedule. Leaving Karachi on April 9, we had planned to arrive in Lahore on April 23. But by April 23 we had only reached the border between the states of Sind and Punjab, about two-thirds of the distance.

Passing into the Punjab, we were sicker than ever. Feeling utterly exhausted, we began looking for a place to rest for a day or two. One afternoon, as we checked into a large cop shop in the town of Liaqatpur, we were offered a chance to stay on one of the large estates of southern Punjab. A "big man" named Munir Achmed Shah Khan happened to be visiting the police compound when we wearily pushed our bikes through the gate. He was a small, gentle man whose generosity would do much to revive us over the next couple of days.

"You look very tired," Munir said. "I think you can get much rest at my home. Please come and be my guests."

Leaving our bikes and most of our gear in a locked jail cell, we followed Munir toward his estate, which covered a stretch of land between the Indus and Liaqatpur. Walking through the main street of Liaqatpur, we passed a bank owned by Munir's uncle and a row of shops owned by his cousin. Turning off into a narrow, twisting side street, we emerged into the main courtyard of the Khan estate. It was an ancient courtyard with a dirt floor and old, crumbling walls and buildings. Water buffalo, cows, and chickens wandered at random in the yard. The only sign of wealth was the entrance to the main house. It was a Persian-style doorway covered with shiny blue tiles and flanked by potted *rabel* trees. Inside, we could see a tile floor and silk curtains. High above the house rose a television antenna.

"You will stay in our guest house," said Munir, pointing at one of the slowly decomposing buildings across from the main house. Within minutes several servants had laid out three *charpai* cots in front of the building, complete with fresh sheets and silk-covered comforters. "I know you are tired," our host said, "so I will give you a simple meal tonight and allow you to sleep. Tomorrow I will show you my estate. I think you will find it interesting."

In the morning Munir's servants brought us a breakfast of curried eggs and mangos. Then Munir performed an act of respect and admiration toward us. One by one, he lathered our faces, sharpened a straight razor, and shaved off our ragged beards (Jim, who still kept his beard, got a trim). After the shaves, Munir led us on a tour of his lands. Joining us was a small retinue of servants, family members, and a lawyer friend named Aurang visiting from Lahore. Our first stop was a field full of cut wheat gathered into man-sized stacks. We paused here so Don could take photographs of Munir standing in front of the wheat.

"This estate produces wheat, millet, and small crops of corn and peppers," Aurang told me during the photo session. "It is not a large estate, but it is also not small."

A half mile later we visited a peasant's compound on Munir's land. The scrupulously clean cluster of huts was the home of the estate's laborers and their families. Many peasant families have lived on these estates for generations, living, toiling, and dying like serfs in medieval Europe. The wall of the compound was constructed out of branches and grass. Inside were several individual homes, a community oven, and several chickens. The men and buffalos were out in the fields.

"My friends, will you come and help me make an old man happy?" asked Munir. He pointed to one of the homes. "The man who lives here, he is very ill with hepatitis."

A wrinkled woman in black answered Munir's soft knock. He spoke gently as she retreated into the shadows inside the sparsely furnished home (we saw very few women on the Khan estate). We waited, sitting on woven flax stools, while Munir spoke with the sick man in a back room.

"Please, my friends, I have told him that you traveled a great distance to wish him well," said Munir. "He is very honored that you have come."

We stepped inside a room reeking of sweat and sickness. Lying among heavy blankets was a man whose flesh barely wrapped his bones. But his eyes, despite their yellow pall, acknowledged us with a flicker of enthusiasm as he raised his skeleton fingers in a weak wave. Even in my hardened state of mind, I felt a rush of sympathy for this poor man.

"A *salame lakem*," we said, using the formal Pakistani greeting.

"*Lakem salame*," he whispered, twisting his mouth into a faint smile.

Our next stop was a quiet grove of eucalyptus trees on the bank of a wide irrigation canal. Small mounds of dirt, some of them with walls pressed flat, were laid out haphazardly under the trees. They were Muslim graves. Munir stopped to toss a *rabel* blossom onto one of the mounds. A boy in our party also stepped forward to throw a blossom. He then joined hands with Munir.

"It is the grave of Munir's brother," Aurang explained, "the boy's father."

As we walked on—the sun was getting hot now—Aurang told me that Munir's brother had been killed in the 1971 war with India. His two boys were being raised by Munir. "In Pakistan," he said, "the family is the most important part of our lives. The family helps us with every crisis. It is our strength."

"Is Islam as important as the family?" I asked.

"Of course. Islam and the family. These are the two foundations of our lives."

After about three miles, the sun was glaring directly overhead. The three of us were getting tired. Our feet were dragging and our muscles were starting to knot up. It had been weeks since we had walked so much. Our leg muscles were not used to exercise off the bikes. My stomach was also feeling a bit queasy.

Just as I was about to suggest a rest stop, we rounded a bend into another small grove of trees. Set up in the shade were five *charpai* cots outfitted with down-filled covers and pillows. Three servants stood nearby, holding tin tea pots, china cups and saucers, and biscuits.

"I noticed that you were tired," Munir explained, "so I sent a boy ahead to arrange tea. You may also want to sleep."

Munir supervised the tea and assigned cots to each of us—Aurang, Jim, Don, me, and then himself. While we were getting settled, he chatted in Urdu to the servants and to some field hands who had appeared to watch the show. After the tea was poured, Munir sat down on his cot, which was a signal for the servants and field hands to sit down on the ground.

That night, after a delicious dinner of roast chicken, we sipped goat's-milk tea and chatted with Munir and Aurang on cots in front of the Khan guest house. All day we had been discussing subjects ranging from American foreign policy in South Asia to the latest films in America. We enjoyed these discussions. It was refreshing to talk to people who had a broad knowledge of the world and who didn't hassle us about American visas, overpriced Cokes, or the details of our trip. In the evening, the conversation turned to the subject of Afghanistan. I told Aurang and Munir about VOA reports that the Russians were using mustard gas against the guerrillas.

"Of course the Russians are using gas," said Aurang.

"How do you know that for sure?" I asked.

"It is well known," he said. "But do not take my word. Why not talk to a freedom fighter yourself?"

"Talk to a freedom fighter myself?"

"Yes," said Aurang. "Our friend Munir is providing temporary homes for a small band of *mujahadeen* resting from the war. It will be a simple task to invite them here for tea."

A half hour later we were sitting in a circle near the guest house, surrounded by a dozen fierce-looking men in puggaree turbans and dark robes. "This man says that he killed three Russians last month," Aurang was translating the slow, deliberate Farsi of a young Afghani whose beard was barely a shadow on his face. Beards apparently count for a lot in Afghanistan. The young man's comrades, most of them in their twenties and thirties, had long, wild beards that wagged as they argued over answers to our questions.

"This is the story of how the Russians died," translated Aurang. The oldest member of the *mujahadeen*, a huge man in a wide, white turban, was now speaking. "This boy and five others planted mines in a road used by Russians. Russians are afraid in the hills; they only move in tanks. So the mines were very powerful to disable the tanks." The older guerrilla was waving his hands in the air as he told the story. "The mines exploded three tanks. The Russians inside escaped. That is when this boy started shooting. He killed three Russians personally. His group shot seven total. The other Russians ran away in their tanks."

"He is only seventeen?" I asked.

"Yes," said Munir solemnly. "Just a boy, by age, but a man by deeds." This evening would be full of such declarations— of what it meant to be courageous, to be a man, and to die for one's beliefs.

"I am prepared to die," Aurang translated for the boy. He had spoken these words with such conviction that his older compatriots had ceased their arguing for a moment to share tough looks of admiration with each other. The air was charged with a primitive, masculine energy. The boy, slightly nervous with all of this attention, absently fingered a silver good luck charm hanging around his neck. Inside the pendant was a passage from the Koran. "Some *mujahadeen* believe these charms protect them from Russian bullets," Aurang told me later.

"Why is he prepared to die?" I looked straight at the boy and spoke in a strong voice. The guerrillas seemed to respect this sort of toughness.

"The Russians are evil," Aurang was translating now. "They are against Islam . . ." The boy hesitated, trying to pick his words carefully. With a shout, the older man broke in, to the relief of the boy. He remained silent while the men began shouting out their opinions to Aurang, who continued to translate. "The Russians are godless. They spit at God and the prophet. They come into our villages and take boys for the Communist army in Kabul. They search all through our houses, even where the women live. We fight to keep the Russian away from our villages, and because the Russian has violated the honor of our women by invading our homes."

I asked what it was like to fight a war against such a powerful enemy.

"It is very difficult. The Russians send helicopter gunships. They are great trouble to us. When we get bombarded, we hide in those places that are rocky—in tunnels and caves. They sometimes drop bombs that look like rocks. These are mines. When lifted, they explode. So many men have lost arms and legs."

"Do they attack your villages?"

This question raised the level of the men's frenzy and the volume of their voices.

"No any building, no any place without burning. Every house they bombard. Our farms they burn. Our food they burn."

"How can you attack this enemy?"

"We hide to wait for Russians in tanks. When coming, we attack. We have rocket launchers to fight tanks, rifles, other small guns. These weapons we have got from Russians who have died."

I asked the guerrillas if they expected to win the war.

"Yes. We must win or die. It is holy war. *Jihad* is what we call it. The time will come when all Muslims will fight jihad beside us. The time has not come yet. Pakistanis will fight. Because if Afghanis all die, Pakistan has to fight. It is the jihad."

It took another five days to reach Lahore. Wrung out by heat and dysentery, we passed these days in a sort of lethargic haze. Each day we pedaled for most of the morning, stopped for lunch and long naps, and pedaled again until evening. Since the Punjab seemed safer than Sind, we spent the nights camping behind eucalyptus groves far off the highway. It was a relief to camp. We got little rest when we stayed with people, and exhaustion and short tempers were making it difficult for us to be polite or friendly. Even Munir, who was a superb host, wore us out with his tours and long talks.

We arrived at the slums encircling Lahore at dusk on May 3, twenty-five days after departing Karachi. Wearily we steered our bikes into town, through a traffic-choked maze of streets filled with tonga carts, scooters, donkeys, cars, and trucks. Long after dark, we reached our destination, a home belonging to a Pakistani family we had met in Karachi. The family gave us a wing of their large house, which included three beds, a bathroom, and a black-and-white television. For three days we slept in the soft beds. We woke up only for a couple of press interviews arranged by the U.S. consulate in Lahore, a few American-style meals at the Lahore Hilton, and a short tour of the Moghul mosques and palaces scattered around that ancient city.

On our fourth day in Lahore, we were still exhausted, but we had to get moving. In New Delhi, five hundred kilometers to the east, we were planning to spend several days recuperating in a three-star hotel.

On our way out of town, we stopped for one last meal at the Lahore Hilton. In the coffee shop we met a beautiful Pakistani woman in an Indian sari.

"You are the famous cyclists," she asked, "the ones that I read about in the paper?"

"I guess we are," I said, my mouth full of hamburger.

"I would like to offer you a deal," she said, introducing herself as the public relations manager for the hotel. "I would like to take your picture in front of our hotel, with your bikes. In exchange, I will offer you a free night here at the Hilton."

The three of us looked at each other and grinned.

"A free night at the Hilton!" said Don.

"You've got a deal!" said Jim.

The woman started by paying for our lunch. We then took the photos, straddling our bicycles in front of the gilded Lahore Hilton sign. Next we swam and had a glorious massage in the Hilton's Punjab Terrace Club. Later that night we had a dinner of steaks, baked potatoes, stewed carrots, and the first lettuce we had dared to eat since Israel. It was almost surreal to be enjoying such luxury. Just drinking ice water with no fear of contamination was hard to believe. It was like reliving memories that were familiar, yet slightly off. It took me a while to remember that the cloth napkin under my two forks was supposed to go on my lap and that the small knife was for butter. When our waiter asked if I would like the cork from our bottle of wine, I looked at him dumbly, having no idea what he was talking about.

After supper I took a bath in a clean, bright white tub under steaming hot water. The Hilton had issued us "non-Muslim drink permits" that allowed us each one bottle of wine and three bottles of beer. I was sipping my third beer in the tub, sloshing the foamy, bubbly, cold liquid over my tongue. My sunburned body was defracted into a red blob under the water as I ran my hands up and down my chest and stomach. It felt good to be naked in a tub. I hadn't really looked at my body for several weeks. It was skinny but still strong. I flexed my bicep and felt its hardness.

It was like a dream lying in that tub. For the first time in weeks, I felt that I was in a place resembling home. The only reminder of the road was a low, steady pain in my stomach, which I had learned to ignore. I closed my eyes and thought about Laura. What was she doing right now? Was she thinking about me? I tried to reach out to touch her mind far away, but I was too tired. Then, like a demon, a terrible thought flashed through my brain. "Eight months," said the demon, "you have eight months until you are home, until you can take a hot bath anytime you want to, until you can hold your Laura." I tried to flush the thought from my mind, but it wouldn't go away.

"Eight months! Eight months!" shouted the demon's voice. "And the worst is yet to come. Tomorrow is India!"

6. Indian Hell

After three months in the drab austerity of the Muslim world, we welcomed India—a twisting, vibrant mass of color, dust, and clamor. In the border city of Amritsar we saw Hindu temples alive with squirming, multiarmed gods and animals; we saw a couple of Buddhist priests in long gold togas carrying wooden bowls; and we saw the yellow-washed temples of the Sikhs, guarded by fierce-looking men wearing long knives, silver bangles, turbans, and wooden combs. We also saw women. They strolled the roads in saris blazing purple, crimson, and gold. Drops of gold and gems twinkled on nose rings, earrings, and bracelets. Red and green dots, signs of beauty and piety, were drawn in lipstick between sculptured eyebrows. Wide, beautiful eyes brushed with mascara studied us as we pedaled through the traffic. These women did not turn away like Muslim women when we looked at them. Nor were their rounded, full lips covered with veils. Their loosely wrapped saris revealed creamy brown stomachs and arms. It had been a long time since we had dared to even look at women.

New Delhi is 460 kilometers from Amritsar on the Grand Trunk road, an ancient highway cutting across northern India to Calcutta. Starting in Amritsar, the Grand Trunk runs through the Indian half of the Punjab, a wealthy agricultural state sometimes called the breadbasket of India. The Indian Punjab was a marked contrast to the areas of Pakistan where we had bicycled. Instead of camping or staying in cop shops, we slept in comfortable youth hostels and clean, inexpensive hotels in cities with names like Jullundur, Ludhiana, and Ambala. The food was also a relief. It was still spicy, but there was a tremendous variety of dishes for palates subjected to weeks of gruel and curried mutton.

We were desperate to get to New Delhi. Our tires were threadbare. By India we had already racked up a total of 334 flats in our group record book. Sixty-two of them had occurred in Pakistan. Our broken racks were held together with splints of wire and sticks. Sand and grit were slowly grinding down our cranks and cogs. Brake and gear cables were frazzled; I snapped my front brake cable one hundred kilometers before Lahore and had no replacement. In New Delhi a shipment of parts from HOPE was waiting for us at a shipping agent's office, or so we were told.

Physically and mentally, we were as worn out as our bicycles. The temperature was still rising every day, pushing up to 110 degrees in the daytime and 95 at night. The Indians call this time the *garmi marsam,* the Season of the Great Heat. Hundreds die from the heat in India during the month of May. We were also suffering from some of our worst bouts with dysentery. While waiting for our passports to be processed at the border, I had blood appear in my feces. But a couple of red and white capsules from Pakistan settled my stomach enough for me to keep going.

New Delhi is a grand, slightly dog-eared city built on a broad plain beside the ancient city everyone calls Old Delhi. Designed during the reign of King-Emperor George V in 1911, New Delhi's broad avenues, arches, marble colonnades, and massive palaces were intended as the ultimate expression of empire. The city is laid out on a majestic triangle. In the east is the India Gate, a triumphal arch commemorating Indians who died fighting for the British in World War I; in the west the buildings of Parliament and in the north Connaught Place, the commercial center of the city. But New Delhi was not completed until 1937, when Gandhi was demanding independence, Hitler and Tojo were massing their troops, and the idea of empire was in its death throes.

The Indian capital was another major stop for revamping the bikes, organizing visas and routes, meeting with the press, and relaxing. Near Connaught Place we checked into a three-star hotel called the Janpath. It offered room service, telephones, and Western-style bathrooms for eighteen dollars a night. It was expensive for our budget; in Pakistan we had averaged under eight dollars a day for all our expenses. But we desperately needed to rest and recover from our illnesses before tackling the rest of India. For several days we remained ensconced in the Janpath, sleeping, taking baths, and reading newspapers.

Every major news organization in the world has a bureau in New Delhi. Working with the press office at the U.S. embassy, we arranged interviews with everyone from the Associated Press to *People* magazine. During a press conference for Indian reporters, one man raised his hand and loudly asked if we were CIA spies.

"No, we aren't," answered Jim, "but I sure am happy to be back in a country where you can ask such a question."

In the course of our interviews, we got to know several reporters who introduced us into the active international community in New Delhi. The American segment of this community was a large, gregarious group composed of embassy personnel, journalists, business people, and a few influential Indians. One evening the NBC radio correspondent in New Delhi, Nick Hanks, invited us to have dinner at the American Club on the grounds of the U.S. embassy. In a miniature world of Americana, we consumed steaks and Budweisers, bowled on the club lanes, and learned about life in New Delhi.

"This is considered a hardship post," Nick told us, "but it's not that bad." He said that even on a reporter's salary he could afford a nice apartment and a chauffeured car.

"Hell, you can live like a king in this place," said a young UPI reporter at our table. "I'm having a guy make me an air hockey table. All I had to do was show him the table here at the club. Guess what it's costing me?"

"How much?"

"Six hundred rupees—seventy-five dollars. Can you believe it?"

The next night, Nick took us to a small party in an elegant neighborhood surrounded by fences and guarded by a private police force. Our hostess was a young Indian woman who bought Indian fashions for stores in New York City, London, and Paris. Her home reminded me of a large loft apartment in New York. Wide open spaces were ringed with balconies and a staircase of natural wood. Large ferns, natural fiber rugs, and framed posters from New York galleries reminded me of photographs in *Architectural Digest*. The house was also filled with gadgets that we had not yet seen back in the States. We saw cordless phones, a miniature stereo, and a clock radio that told us the time with a synthesized voice.

Cavorting in the privileged world of New Delhi was a refreshing change after the grueling weeks in Pakistan. We spent almost two weeks in the Indian capital, resting and waiting for our spare parts to clear customs. In the Janpath we stuffed our bikes and gear out of sight in closets and reveled in the comforts of an almost Western environment. We met several young Americans touring in New Delhi. Most of them hung out in a pizza place called Maxwell's in Connaught Place (it was across the street from the all-important American Express office). One day I shared a green pepper pizza with an American woman who had been living with a maharaja in the south. "He got into some kinky stuff, so I had to get out of there," she said. I also met an American professor studying Indian percussion rhythms and a man from Los Angeles who claimed to be a reincarnation of a sixteenth-century Indian guru.

For the first week in New Delhi I saw little of the city beyond the former imperial areas around the Janpath and the U.S. embassy. I knew that the wealth and privilege of the new city existed in tandem with the poverty of the old city, yet I wasn't anxious to see it with Pakistan so fresh in my mind. But after a while I grew curious about the Moghul temples and forts in the old city. One afternoon I took a bicycle rickshaw ride through old Delhi. Leaving the broad, quiet spaces of the former British capital, my rickshaw driver pumped hard as I sat on a seat mounted behind his bicycle. Gradually a spectacle of pandemonium and filth gathered around us as buses, scooters, tongas, bicycles, oxen, and myriads of people pressed and pushed and shoved in the narrow, filthy streets. I felt the sweat and smelled the odors. It brought back the long days on the bikes. But riding on that rickshaw was different. I was dressed in clean clothes and paying a boy to drive me around. I was living the privileged life of New Delhi, where people stayed in luxury hotels, played air hockey, and spoke on cordless phones.

It seemed grossly unfair. In the grand half of the city, an entire population lived in the palaces of their former masters as if they were on a vast island of privilege, even in the midst of intense poverty. Didn't they realize that they were surrounded? Had they seen the world that we had been biking through for the past several weeks? Were they doing something —anything—to close the gap?

Feeling overwhelmed, I closed my eyes for a moment, shutting out the frenzy around me. Then I realized why nothing was being done. It was for the same reason that Jim, Don, and I had become so nasty to people on the road. It was something called privilege. On the road, privilege had been critical to our survival. We had used our relative wealth and our white skin to get preferential treatment. This was excusable considering that we could do nothing about our skin color or background. But we had gone far beyond a passive acceptance of our position as Westerners. In Egypt and Pakistan we had begun to *expect* preferential treatment. Moreover we would expect it again once we were back on the road, especially in India.

After five months on the road, I still had a very basic question. Why should I be able to enjoy these privileges? Why were the people around me forced to live in poverty? I thought of Gruffy Clough in Sudan. She had told me that people had two choices when confronted with poverty. "You can freak out over the immensity of the problem," she had said, "or you can pick a little corner and try to help where you can." But Gruffy had left out a third choice, which is to ignore the problem, simply to forget that it exists.

I watched the bare brown back of my rickshaw driver glisten with sweat in the intense heat. About half my size, he worked painfully hard pedaling through the streets. Sitting in my privileged position on the back of his cart, I decided that I wasn't going to ignore this kid. I was going to help him. We had agreed on two rupees for the ride. Two rupees! It was only eighteen cents, and I had haggled with him as though it were eighteen dollars. I fumbled in my money belt and found two crumpled hundred-rupee bills. "I'll pay him a hundred times two rupees," I thought. It would be a gesture, an acknowledgment that I understood something about his life, that I had been traveling through his world myself for weeks.

We were nearing the Red Fort, my destination, so I signaled the boy to stop. Hopping off the rickshaw, I pressed the rupee bills into his hand. *"Namaste,"* I said, giving him the formal Indian acknowledgment. After assuring the delighted boy that I meant to give him the two hundred rupees, I watched him rush into the crowded streets of old Delhi and disappear. I felt good, but I also felt troubled. After all, I was a single white man standing on a frenzied corner of old Delhi among millions of people just like that rickshaw driver.

We left New Delhi during the hottest week of the year. At nine A.M. it was already over 100 degrees. Almost immediately our laundered riding clothes were saturated with the sweat and dust we had so despised in Pakistan. Not far from New Delhi we stopped to cut out the sleeves and bottoms of our T-shirts to help the wind flow over our bodies while we biked. It was the only way to keep remotely cool. Despite the chaotic traffic, we also took off our helmets as the prickly heat dug into our scalps like hundreds of sharp needles.

Swinging south and then east from New Delhi, we began a slow journey across the state of Uttar Pradesh, one of the most densely populated regions of the world. Over 3 percent of the world's population—110 million people, almost half the population of the States—live in an area the size of Nevada. The sacred river, the *Ganga,* the life-giver, rolls its slow, muddy waters through the center of the state, past the birthplaces of the Hindu hero gods Vishnu and Rama, and past Varanasi, the holy city where the Buddha delivered his first sermon. Monuments to a dozen great empires and religions line the highways. They are mostly in a state between disrepair and ruin, stripped of their marble and jewels, their original purposes forgotten. Hovels lean against brick walls that once housed kings. Flat stones that once felt the light footsteps of court dancers now prop up loads of wood or frame dung-patty fires. The architecture of Rome suffered a similar fate during the European Middle Ages.

For us, Uttar Pradesh was largely a continuation of Pakistan. We quickly returned to our daily routine. Waking at dawn, we pedaled until it became too hot and then stopped to take naps and eat gruel under shade trees beside the highway. In the afternoon we rode until dark when we found a cop shop or a guest house (the British built guest houses for their administrators all over India). As in Pakistan, thieves and bandit gangs made it unsafe to camp or sleep in most roadside hotels.

But everything that made Pakistan miserable seemed to double in intensity in Uttar Pradesh. The heat bore down as if focused by a magnifying glass on our flesh. Some days we couldn't even touch the metal on our handlebars without cycling gloves. Our already tan skin was baked a bright, painful red. The poverty and disease were worse than anything we had seen before. In several towns, whole families slept in clogged, filthy streets or on the tarmacs next to train depots and other public buildings. The food was bad, and water was still drawn from filthy, polluted wells or black canals. Outside of large towns, food consisted mostly of skimpy, withered vegetables. The fruit—mangos, oranges, and plantains—were left to spoil on unshaded carts along the road. Occasionally we paid a boy to pluck and cook a skinny chicken.

Day after day we pedaled past cities with names like Firozabad, Etawah, Bara Banki, and Faizabad. We passed Kanpur, an industrial city of sooty skylines and tangled slums, and Lucknow, where hundreds of British men and women died during the 1857 Indian Mutiny. The towns and bazaars in Uttar Pradesh were awash with the odors, dog yaps, shrieks, and clamor of a thousand towns we had biked through since leaving Israel. The same crowds of children in tattered tunics chased us around; the same wily vendors haggled with us over everything from mangos to pieces of cloth for dust masks; the same flies drove us crazy as they hovered in black swarms over everything.

We sometimes slept on the roofs of guest houses above the bazaars. These houses were often former British bungalows, once bastions of wealth now unrecognizable from decay and abuse. As we headed east and got farther off the tourist routes, these places got steadily worse. The rooms were filthy chambers completely bare except for old *charpais* and an occasional table. The toilet and water supply were often in the same place. To draw water from hand pumps, we had to reach over skids of black scum, feces, and vomit. In Pakistan we had doubled and tripled our quotients of iodine. In India we used so much iodine that it changed our water to the color of weak coffee. It

Expedition Photo Log

U.S. Capitol, Washington, D.C. Left to right: David Duncan, Donald Duncan, Jim Logan, Dave French. Send-off ceremony on a rainy December 1, 1981.

Photo: Patricia Duncan

Don in northern Indian village, surrounded by crowd.
Photo: David Duncan

Jim and Don, Sahara Desert near Kassala, Sudan. The bikes and gear weighed nearly 125 lbs. loaded with water on the desert. Temperature: 125 degrees.
Photo: David Duncan

At the Taj Mahal, Agra, India. Left to right: Don, David and Jim.
Photo: Donald Duncan

Don leading Jim in the Himalayan foothills near Pokhara, Nepal. We had 12 flats in 12 kilometers on this stretch of chewed-up road.
Photo: David Duncan

Crowd of Indians in Uttar Pradesh, India. This crowd gathered around us at the time of my "Day of Rage," page 145.
Photo: Donald Duncan

Khalil giving David his *kaffiyeh*, Occupied West Bank, Israel. See page 48.
Photo: Donald Duncan

Lalamba medical team, Abudah Refugee Camp, near Showak, Sudan. Hailing from my hometown of Kansas City, Lalamba operated a clinic for Ethiopian refugees. Left to right: village boy, Tweldeberhum Elazar, David, worker, Gruffy Clough, workers, Jim. Pages 101–104.
Photo: Donald Duncan

Afghan *mujahadeen* ("holy warrior") in Punjab, Pakistan. Only 17 years old, this man claimed to have killed three Russians. The necklace is a charm against bullets. See pages 132–134.
Photo: David Duncan

Ethiopian Orthodox
priest in front of refugee
church, Showak, Sudan.
Note Coptic cross on top
of hut, Jerusalem cross in
priest's left hand.
Photo: Donald Duncan

David repairing a broken rack in Pakistan.
Photo: Donald Duncan

David in Arab *kaffiyeh* in front of tent on the Sinai Desert. A scary night near a Bedouin enclave. Pages 59–60.
Photo: Donald Duncan

Postman lowering American flag in Old Glory, Texas, near where my grandmother was born in 1908.
Photo: David Duncan

Boy in military garb, Sukkur, Pakistan.
Photo: Donald Duncan

More than any other time on the trip, we were in a world completely alien to anything we had known in America. Looking back over the six months since leaving Washington, we saw that we had been gradually immersing ourselves deeper and deeper into the squalor and hardships of the Third World. From Spain to Egypt to Pakistan and now India, each step had taken us further from home. Our grand adventure had turned into a series of hardships that seemed to stretch on and on forever.

Just six months earlier, in a place halfway around the world, I had been a young college graduate from Kansas City dreaming about a bicycle trip around the world. I had talked about traveling to a place like India on a bicycle. I had wanted to smell it, to breathe it, to taste it, to understand it. Now my dream had come true. Against tremendous odds, I had managed to cross the stellar distance between Middle America and rural India. I *was* smelling, breathing, and tasting India, and I hated it. Slowly, gradually, it was driving me crazy.

My frustrations finally blew up on June 2, our tenth day out of New Delhi. In my journal I called this my Day of Rage. It began early in the morning when a crippled boy grabbed my ankle on a street in the city of Faizabad. We were loading the bikes at the doorway of a bungalow hotel. The kid had no legs and was covered with sores. His stumps were mounted on a greasy wooden skateboard, and he was whining for baksheesh. When he suddenly grabbed my ankle, I slapped hard at him, screaming obscenities.

All morning I lashed out at everything I could think of. I screamed at the sun, the ragged highway, and the water buffalo along the road. I screamed at the vultures overhead, my bike, and my sunglasses that kept getting smeared with dust. For a few hours I think I was close to insanity. Jim and Don were not far behind me. I heard them both yelling at the sun. "You fucking sun!" shouted Jim. "Go away! Get out of here!"

This was probably the lowest point of the trip, when the restraints of our upbringing had been thoroughly squeezed out by the hardships of the previous weeks. If it had been possible, we would have quit the trip that day. Fortunately, there was no easy way to do this. We were a long way from an airport, and the trains and buses were crowded, hot, and slow. Just after lunch, we took a break in a small village. While Jim and Don looked for a soda stand, I guarded the bikes. Slowly the usual crowd gathered, pressing in and grabbing at me and the bikes.

Suddenly a hand snatched a Buck knife off my bike. I leaped to my feet, but not fast enough. Soaked in sweat, I shrieked at the uncomprehending mob of Indian faces, each the color of a burnt sienna crayon. "Thief!" I screamed. "Can't you bastards understand the word *thief?*" I couldn't believe it. Someone had stolen my Buck knife! My father had given me that knife. I pushed my face, filthy and unshaven after days on the road, up against a random face in the mob like a drill sergeant about to roar at a recruit.

"Thief!" I screamed again, my voice shaking with rage. "Can you say it, old man?" The face was grizzled and wearing thick, frameless glasses, like Mahatma Gandhi's. He flinched at my loud voice and hot breath so close to his skin, but he stood his ground.

"Idiot!" I screamed, turning away from the old man. Sitting astride my bicycle, I grew more furious as the crowd swelled, shoving in on me. Two or three hundred turbans, some of them just piles of filthy rags, were bobbing up and down as their owners struggled to get a glimpse of the raving blond man on the battered red, white, and blue push-bike.

Overhead the burning sun of the *garmi marsam* fueled my anger and hatred—a hatred of this human mass; a hatred of the filth and the stench of open sewer troughs and festering cesspools; a hatred of children whose eyes were crusted white with trachoma and whose skin was pockmarked with sores; a hatred of the wretched food, the acorn-sized potatoes, the mangos, spoiled tomatoes, and searing hot peppers; a hatred of the flies, the dust, and the constant pain of chronic dysentery that slowly drained my energy and willpower. Most of all, the sun burned into me a hatred of my own impotence. I *still* couldn't believe it. Somebody had stolen my knife! In a rush of pent-up emotion, I made that old knife the symbol of my frustration and helplessness far from home in that miserable land.

Then the crowd opened up. A boy about sixteen years old called out to me, "You speak English?" He was wearing the black knit slacks, white shirt, and worked leather sandals of an educated man in rural India. "You have a problem, mister?" he asked. "Maybe I be able to help."

"I sure do have a problem," I answered, trying to control myself. "I've been robbed." He didn't seem to understand the word *robbed.* "Someone has stolen my knife," I said. "There's a thief here. I need to find a policeman."

"But mister, look here, so many peoples." He waved his hand at the crowd and shrugged. "Many thieves are living in India." He was smiling now. "It is impossible to find thief in crowd." He actually seemed amused at my anger. In the irrationality of my emotion, his smile seemed to be a sly, mocking grin. In an instant, this boy, who was only trying to be helpful, became the enemy. When he spoke rapidly in Hindi to the edge of the crowd, a low murmur passed the story back. Then they were all grinning and mocking me. "We have so many thieves in India," the boy repeated. "I am sorry."

I couldn't bear those mocking faces. My rage suddenly erupted. I grabbed the boy's clean white collar and shook him as hard as I could, screaming, "What is so goddamned funny?" I wanted to hit him, to feel the sensation of my fist smashing into his mocking face. He struggled, but I was much bigger and was holding on with the strength of a crocodile that has clamped its jaws around a victim. The crowd around me was quiet. I started raving. "I hate your fucking country," I screamed, almost hoarse now. "You're all bastards!"

I wanted to hit him. I wanted so bad to be free of my help-lessness that I wanted to kill that boy. My brain kept sending the command: Hit him! Hit him!

I didn't hit him. I'm not sure why. Maybe it was some last shred of decency that held back my arm. But it didn't really matter whether I hit him or not. The fact is that *I wanted to hit him.* I wanted blood. I wanted to kill. At that moment I became everything I had been taught to loathe. I became a fanatic, a bigot, and a murderer. For an instant I looked deeply into the dark side of my soul. I confronted the evil side of human nature that I had first observed in the shattered ruins of El Kantara on the Suez Canal. It was the evil that pits men against men, that justifies war and inequity. It was the evil that told me I was special, that I was white, educated, moneyed and, above all, American. *Goddammit, I'm an American! They can't treat me like this!*

Standing there in the hot, baking sun I continued to hold the boy as I wrestled with the turmoil inside of me. Suddenly a wave of nausea swelled in my stomach. My muscles weakened and my sweat turned cold. I could feel the explosion of dysen-tery forming inside me, draining my strength. My grip relaxed. I let go of the boy, who scrambled away into the crowd. Feeling faint, I bent over with my hands on my knees.

"Get out of my way!" I heard an American voice in the crowd. It was Jim. "Dave! Where are you?" he shouted.

"Over here," I answered weakly, just as my body started convulsing with the dry heaves. I felt the crowd step back. Jim was nearby. Now he was holding my shoulders. Gently he was leading me somewhere. I fell back onto a *charpai* cot. He helped me raise my legs onto the cot so I could roll into a ball, the least painful position during a dysentery attack. For a long time I held my eyes tightly shut as the pain tore through my stomach. I could feel Jim's hand on my shoulder. When the pain began to subside, I opened my eyes.

"Feeling better now?" he asked.

"Yeah," I said. I wanted to tell him about the knife but didn't have the strength. He was pulling something off his bike.

"I have a surprise for you," Jim said. I could see his red-bearded face smiling at me as he peered down. Then he handed me a Thumbs Up cola. I felt the intense cold register on my fingertips. I couldn't believe it was so cold.

When I recovered, I tried to find the boy among the dusty stalls. I was disgusted with myself. How could I have been such a jerk? I searched everywhere, desperate to find him, to tell him that I was sorry. I wanted to tell him that I had planned this whole trip to help people like him. "I'm working with Project HOPE," I wanted to say. "Don't you understand?" But even as I searched, I knew he wouldn't understand, nor would the people of his village understand. We were from two different planets. I was from a planet of privilege, and they were not. Maybe this was the answer to my question about fairness, about why I was lucky enough to be born an American. It was fate. It was the way of the world. It was dumb luck. Maybe a God somewhere had ordained it or maybe not. That didn't matter. What did matter was that the inequity was real. And it was not going away, because in the end, people like me were not going to give up our privileges.

This was not a particularly satisfying answer, but it seemed true. I had glimpsed evil in myself, and it had shocked and saddened me. Yet even at this low moment, I wondered if the world was really as horrible as I imagined it. I wondered what the future would bring. We still had half the world to cover, including the last leg of the trip across America. What would it be like to return home after my day of rage?

7. On Top of the World

We sighted the Himalayas on June 4, our twelfth day out of New Delhi. Through the heavy dust of the *garmi marsam*, the mountains appeared on the northern horizon as a low band of shadows that never moved.

"I see them! The Himalayas!" Don shouted, sounding more excited than any of us had for several days. We were hoping that the mountains would signal an end to our misery on the Ganges plains. To celebrate, we stopped under a shady eucalyptus tree to rest and drink gulps of lukewarm, iodine-dosed water. As we drank Jim sighted his first Nepalese bird, a bright green chestnut-bellied nuthatch.

We biked into Nepal a kilometer later, although we saw no customs house or sign or anything else indicating we had crossed an international border. Instead the border was marked by an abrupt change in the quality of the highway. The smooth paved road was replaced by a cratered, chewed-up, useless strip that even ox cart drivers avoided. Along with pedestrians and bicyclists, they steered their broad-backed beasts along a hard dirt path to the left of the road.

149

This road was supposed to be a shortcut into Nepal, through a town called Lumbini, where the Buddha was born twenty-five hundred years ago. About thirty kilometers to the east was the main highway running from New Delhi to the cities of Katmandu and Pokhara. A pharmacist in India had suggested this route. "The road is very good," he said.

Ten kilometers later, the pavement dissolved completely into a dirt path leading into Lumbini, a town filled with sloppy shacks built from coffee-colored wood. Tiny men and women with almond skin and round, Mongol-looking faces stopped to stare at the Americans on eighteen-speed bikes. They wore hats shaped like squashed Egyptian fezes colored with vertical stripes of red, black, yellow, and white. A flock of shy children followed us with awestruck looks.

As we stopped for Cokes and crackers, Lumbini appeared to be another dismal, poverty-ridden village. This was disappointing. We had heard wonderful tales about Nepal, about clear, snow-fed lakes, good food, and comfortable lodges. It was supposed to be a legendary haven of hippies and mystics, a mountain paradise where the Beatles and Buddhist monks had rubbed elbows in a magic kingdom. But Lumbini was no magic kingdom. Climbing wearily back onto the bikes, we pedaled toward the center of town, wondering if we'd ever escape the poverty of South Asia.

It only took another five hundred meters for Lumbini to become the Nepal we had expected. As if a light switch had been flipped, the town abruptly changed from a kingdom of squalor to a domain of magic. In a blaze of green grass and neatly tended flower bushes, we found ourselves in a park complete with benches and a steel pole flying the red, blue, and white flag of Nepal. A neatly printed sign announced that this was indeed Lumbini, the birthplace of the Buddha. According to the sign, the Nepalese Ministry of Tourism was responsible for this park. They were also responsible for a nearby complex of guest houses called the Lumbini Tourist Bungalow, which included a Western-style restaurant serving chow mein, water buffalo burgers, and Italian spaghetti. The beer was ice-cold, and the songs playing on a cassette recorder were from *Sgt. Pepper's Lonely Hearts Club Band*. It seemed extraordinary to find this tiny pocket of home after our disappointment with the southern end of Lumbini.

We found out later that the sudden intrusion of the Ministry of Tourism in Lumbini was part of a broad campaign in Nepal to transform the country from a medieval realm into a tourist mecca. Tourists were coming to Nepal in increasing numbers every year as word of the magic kingdom spread. Countries like America and Britain, eager to court a country poised between China and India, were building new roads, communications facilities, and hotels. India, anxious to develop Nepal's considerable hydropower resources (its steep river courses could power the entire subcontinent), was also pouring money into Nepal. We could feel the optimism for the future among the people of Lumbini, although it wasn't completely clear that they were benefiting from the trickle-down from tourist dollars. They were smiling and anxious to please us. Their exuberance and innocence was a stark contrast to the world-weariness of the Indians.

Peeking inside the restaurant at the Lumbini Tourist Bungalow, we smelled the greasy scent of burgers and saw a whole table of Caucasian faces. They were speaking English!

"Hey, where y'all from?" asked a young man in a straw hat, Levi's, and a checked flannel shirt. He looked like the farmers I used to see outside of Kansas City. What was he doing in Nepal?

"Name's Mike," he said. He was a Peace Corps volunteer from Texas. The others at the table were also American Peace Corps workers. Hearing them casually introduce themselves was an astonishingly normal event. I watched their facial expressions and listened to the inflections of their voices. Both were familiar and foreign—the casual smiles and the flat, twangy pronunciations. I suddenly felt happy and relieved to be in Nepal. It seemed like we were a little closer to home in the tourist bungalow eating spaghetti with American folks.

We continued to meet Americans as we pedaled toward the mountains. Outside of a restaurant-hotel called Siddhartha, we met two agriculturists from Cornell working on irrigation projects with the Nepali government. A couple of kilometers later we met two high school exchange students from California. As we talked to them, a jeepload of more Americans appeared beside them.

"Hey, you guys comin' to the swimmin' hole?" a woman asked the two students. She was in a tight T-shirt and had a deep tan. I ogled her—an American woman! "Who are these guys?" she asked, looking at us. I realized how filthy we looked in our ripped shirts and shorts.

"We're from the States," Jim said.

"We're biking around the world," I added.

"Hey, why don't you guys come on up to our swimmin' hole?" said a big guy about twenty years old. He had the ease of a high-school football player. "You can follow us up."

"I don't think we can, Dave," Jim said. "You know we don't have any Nepali cash, and we need to find a place to spend the night."

"Well, if y'all change your minds, just bike straight ahead for about four miles," said the football player. "The swimmin' hole is on your right. Look for a rocky creek under a bridge."

Nepal seemed to be overrun with volunteers from the States. As we looked for a hotel in Butwal, we were directed to an American-run guest house organized by the United Mission to Nepal, an umbrella group of U.S. churches sending aid to Nepal. This particular guest house was part of the Butwal Industrial Institute, a light-industry training center run by UMN missionaries and volunteers.

The supervisors of the institute's guest house welcomed us with the smiles and good humor of born-again Christians. The institute itself was a large tin building like a giant Quonset hut with a flat roof. Inside was a woodshop and a metal shop, looking a little like the shops in my high school in Kansas City. Lathes, jigsaws, table saws, die cast furnaces, and a host of light machinery filled the enormous room. College-age men were being trained by the missionary staff to use the tools and machinery, coordinate a production line, and market their wares. At the moment they were making folding chairs and tables to sell abroad. "We hope to break even in a year or two," said one of the smiling students in the woodshop.

The place felt like a Boy Scout camp. Everyone was smiling and clean-cut; everyone seemed to be accomplishing commendable tasks. Up a hill from the shops was a long building with small guest rooms, a meeting room, a library, and a casual, camplike dining room. We were given three of the small guest rooms for thirty rupees ($2.25) apiece.

While waiting for our dinner that night, I spent over an hour thumbing through books in the institute's library. The titles ranged from Christian books like *The Cross and the Switchblade* to a collection of Edgar Allan Poe short stories. It was wonderful to see so many English books all at once. I picked up a world almanac and looked up Nepal. I was surprised to see it was the poorest country that we had yet biked through. With fourteen million people, this country the size of North Carolina had an annual per capita income of $114. This figure compared with $150 in India and $280 in Pakistan. The Nepalese Gross Domestic Product for the last year was only $2 billion, a sum the U.S. generates every six hours. Two of the major industries were drugs—mostly opium and hashish—and tourism. Only nine thousand telephones were in use, the illiteracy rate was 81 percent, and the life expectancy was forty-two years. No one owned a television, because Nepal had no television stations.

After dinner, the institute's director, a Scotsman named John Finley, invited us over to his small home for a cup of real ground coffee and a chat about dung. "Dung is my specialty," John had told us earlier. His official designation was "bio-gas specialist."

"I'm working on a method for farmers to extract methane from cow and water buffalo dung," he said. John had a scraggly beard and a remarkably pale face for this climate. He spoke slowly and deliberately, yet I could sense his excitement. "I'm helping people help themselves," he said. It was refreshing to see his sincerity. I had almost forgotten people like him existed.

"If dung were utilized properly, South Asia would have no problem with fuel," he explained. "You see, it's quite simple. A farmer digs a circular hole about three feet deep and maybe six feet in diameter, depending on how much dung his animals create. Then a dome is built over the hole, preferably with concrete." He was waving his hands in the air to demonstrate. "You insert a small pipe with a seal that can be opened. Within a few weeks, the decaying dung will create methane gas, which can be captured in containers and used as cooking or heating fuel." He smiled. "We've already built twenty-two methane domes here in Nepal."

The Himalayas are the youngest major mountain range in the world. Twenty-seven million years ago, two immense plates of bedrock began to crash against each other, one pushing north from India and one pushing south from Tibet. Over the next two million years, the plate pushing toward India slowly overlapped the opposing plate to grow and buckle and ripple in waves of rock and soil. When the gradual violence of this geological warfare stabilized, a massive wall of rock 1,600 miles long and 150 miles wide had risen above the flat Ganges plain, very much as the Rockies rose above the Great Plains in America fifty million years earlier.

On the morning of June 5, Jim, Don, and I left the hot, dusty Ganges plains and began our journey into the Himalayas. Gray monsoon clouds hung low over the Gandak River valley, keeping the air cool but terribly humid. We were overwhelmed by the lush greenness of the mountains. *Green!* For months we had seen nothing but brown, in dusty skies, mucky roads, and dirty faces. Here we saw exotic, contorted trees rising straight up against the steep hills. Oriental-style houses were perched up and down the slopes on infrequent flat spots. Patchworks of rice paddy walls climbed up and down the slopes, while the gray, turbulent waters of the Gandak pounded and crashed far below our cliffside road.

We were climbing through the southernmost wrinkle in the Himalayan range, called the Siwalik. The Nepalese call these mountains hills because they are only four or five thousand feet tall. Rising in successively higher wrinkles are the Lesser Himalayas, which climb to peaks of thirteen and fourteen thousand feet, and then the Great Himalayas, culminating in Everest and Annapurna. These snowy, impossibly high peaks are two hundred kilometers to the north of the Siwalik. This was a surprise for me. From photographs in books and magazines, I had expected Nepal to be covered with snowy peaks. Jim had even worried about whether or not to bring thermal underwear. But most of Nepal is composed of dense, subtropical forestland that is nearly as scalding during the hot season as the Ganges plain.

A light drizzle fell over the Siwalik range as we pumped and grunted up the river valley toward the village of Tansing, fifty kilometers and four thousand feet upward from where the mountains begin. The tops of the mountains were obscured in swirling gray tufts of moisture. These monsoon clouds were also holding down a thick, humid mass of air that caused us to sweat as if someone were pouring water over our skin. Our faces turned bright red with exertion and, before long, our legs ached. It had been months since we had done any serious climbing. With few exceptions, from the Nile to the Sahara to the Indus to the Ganges the terrain had been flat as a table top.

We passed several small villages, groups of heavy wood

buildings lined up in narrow rows between the road and the lip of the cliff. Like the southern part of Lumbini, these villages were glimpses into the poverty of Nepal: the sewage, the animals and children playing in the garbage, and all the other familiar scenes. In between the towns were groups of Nepalese smoking cheroots—everyone was smoking, even the kids—as they toted heavy wood or canvas packs filled with dung chips, mangos, seed, and greens. These packs had no shoulder or waist straps. The loads were supported by strips of leather strapped across the forehead. Most of Nepal's commerce is transported in these cumbersome packs. With only twelve hundred kilometers of paved highway in the entire country, and most of that in the flat Terai region below the mountains, the only way to get around most of Nepal is over steep mountain paths. Distance here is not measured by kilometers, but by how many days it takes to walk from one village to another.

Our road out of Butwal was built in 1970, but the pavement already looked decades old. Heavy rains and a steady stream of trucks and buses had nearly chewed it to pieces. Sometimes the road settled into the drenched soil, creating a basin filled with muddy rainwater. Don was the first to discover one of these ponds when he went pedaling into what looked like a one- or two-inch-deep puddle. Before he could stop, his bike was half underwater.

The monsoon season, which had just begun, was the worst time of the year for roads in Nepal. Besides the rain, water also runs off from melting snow in the Great Himalayas. Avalanches routinely tear chunks out of the road or bury sections in tons of dirt and rock. In 1979 monsoons combined with a warm spring runoff to create a wall of water that burst down from the high range to kill several people and wreck Butwal.

It was slow going up the river valley. Kilometer signs, written in the elegant Nepali script, seemed incredibly far apart as we climbed up five kilometers, ten kilometers, and then fifteen kilometers. We stopped frequently to drink from streams of fresh, snow-cold water bursting out of cliffside rocks. A few of the streams had been caught in pipes that spilled out of beautiful brass spigots shaped like cow or bull heads. For the first time since Europe, we were using our special Avocet gearing. Dave French had been right about these ultralow gears. Without them it would have been next to impossible to pull our weight up the mountains.

At fifteen kilometers we reached the "swimmin' hole" that the Peace Corps volunteers had told us about. It was just in time. We were sweating and baking in the wet heat.

The water in the deep pool was an indigo blue. A thin, glittering rivulet of water fell from a stream about twenty feet above. Green ferns, hanging vines, and pink and violet blossoms grew over the edges. "It's a tropical paradise," I wrote in my journal. "Like Shangri-la." The icy water felt tingly to our naked skin.

As we lay on our backs in the water, I suddenly heard laughter. Standing above us, up where the water fell from the feeding stream, were three young women in light white dresses. Diamond pins twinkled in their noses. In Shangri-la, they looked like nymphs in loose muslin gowns. We stayed in the water to hide our nakedness while the girls dove into the pool beside us. Their thin gowns did little to cover their young, round bodies. While the girls shyly giggled and pointed at us, Don moved to the shore, picked up his towel, and covered himself as he grabbed his camera. He managed to capture those nymphs on film before they finished their swim and scurried away through the forest.

The final approach to Tansing was up a torturously steep series of switchbacks. My legs, pulling nearly a hundred pounds of gear, were aching and rubbery. Some kid ran next to me babbling in Nepali. I was breathing heavily and dripping sweat, but my escort was not even winded. When I got to a small snack stand about a kilometer below Tansing, I bought two cold Cokes and had the boy run back down the hill to give them to Jim and Don, who were a few hundred meters back.

Tansing, like San Francisco, was not embarrassed to have its streets rolling up and down at angles approaching ninety degrees. Its ancient, Tibetan-style houses and shops were perched nearly perpendicular to the hillsides. Only a smattering of the West had reached here. The sole hotel was a sloppy square structure with a curio shop selling hats, T-shirts, and pennants from the Moscow Olympics of 1980. These trinkets were an odd reflection of Nepalese politics. They probably came through India, which has close ties with Russia, although just up the hill from the curio stand was a bookstore selling books from Communist China. Nepal—a poor, landlocked nation sandwiched between neighbors the size of continents—had to try to please everyone.

In Tansing we stayed at another United Mission to Nepal project called Shining Hospital. Our hosts were a couple from Seattle, Neil and Clarissa Slovick. Neil was the pharmacist at Shining, and his wife was a nurse. Both were in their fifties and had lived and worked in Nepal for eight years.

The Slovicks were delighted to have us stay with them. "We have three sons of our own," said Clarissa, "but they're grown up now. With you boys here, it will be like having them home again!" We were hardly inside their house and cleaned up before she served us a meal of hamburgers and french fries with plastic dishes and tumblers with stars etched into the glass. It was like stepping into an American home.

"Clarissa, this is unbelievable," said Jim. We were trying to restrain ourselves from grabbing at the dripping, oozing meat while we waited for Neil so that we could say grace.

"I've got some ice-cold beer here," Neil announced, popping into the room. He put down a tray of Singa beers and sat down. "Now, let us pray," he said, bowing his head and grabbing the hands to his left and right. "Lord, thank You for this bounty and for delivering these boys safely into our hands. Watch over them, Lord, on their journey. In Your Son's name we pray, amen."

The Slovicks' house was a comfortable blend of American suburbia and Asian bungalow. Eight-by-ten glossies of the family covered one wall. Books covered most of the other walls. Several years of National Geographics filled one case. The Encyclopaedia Britannica and reference books ranging from an Oxford unabridged dictionary to a guide to English etymology filled another. On top of a large chest holding a few pieces of china was a toaster-sized shortwave receiver and transmitter powered by a large car battery. After supper Neil tuned in VOA. It only came in here for two hours each evening. Listening to these broadcasts was a regular event in the Slovick household.

Just before dark Neil took us on a tour of the hospital. "Shining is the only clinic in this area," he said, showing us the front room of the ramshackle complex. A dozen Nepalese, most of them women with children, waited with wide eyes on wooden benches around the room. Posters on the wall warned against walking in bare feet. Tapeworms Can Enter Through the Skin in Your Feet, said one poster, which had ample pictures to show the illiterate the danger of tapeworms. Other posters suggested the ingredients for a proper diet, the reasons for boiling water, and a daily regimen for keeping clean.

In the main hospital, roller beds and wheelchairs lined the corridors. On one roller a wrinkled man moaned what sounded like incantations. The smell of ether was strong in the air. A young doctor in green surgical apparel stood over the patient.

"That man's had a leg removed," whispered Neil. "It's from smoking."

"Smoking?" I said.

"You must have noticed those wretched cheroots everyone smokes around here. Even tiny kids smoke them. You wouldn't believe how many cases we get where some poor fellow's arteries have clogged up with nicotine and cut off the blood to an arm or a leg. By the time they make it here from their village, the leg or whatever has turned black. All we can do is chop it off."

We stayed with the Slovicks for most of two days, eating Clarissa's home cooking, drinking beer, and reading books out of their extensive library. I read every *National Geographic* article I could find on Nepal. The earliest one was about the 1951 climb up Mount Everest, an event that introduced Nepal to the world. I also skimmed through several volumes of the *Encyclopaedia Britannica*. I had a plethora of unanswered questions from as far back in the trip as Egypt. They were random questions: When was Napoleon in Egypt? What was the Meroe civilization in Sudan? What was the history of Sind in Pakistan? It had been frustrating trying to write about these places when I had no way to answer these questions. As a rainstorm rattled steadily against the roof, we lost ourselves in the splendor of words from the Slovicks' shelves.

That first night, after a dinner of pork chops and mashed potatoes, we accompanied Neil and Clarissa to the weekly Bible study at Shining, held in a one-room school building near the hospital. It reminded me of Campus Crusade for Christ meetings in high school. We sang pop-sounding songs about sunshine and Jesus and love. Several times we joined hands for long, personal, rambling prayers delivered by whomever the spirit moved. Several prayers asked God to protect the three bikers staying with the Slovicks.

I noticed during the meeting that no Nepalese were attending. After it was over, I asked Neil why. "It's very frustrating," he said. "In Nepal every citizen is required by law to be Hindu. It's against the law to convert to another religion. Each of us working for the United Mission to Nepal has to sign a document swearing not to proselytize here."

"Do you know Nepalese who are Christians?"

"Sure, but we have to be really careful. They don't come to our meetings, because it could land them in jail."

"It sounds like it's tough to be a Christian out here."

"Sure it is," he said, "but it's always tough to fight for what you believe in. We believe it does a whole lot of good just being here to help spread God's goodness to these wonderful people. That's our purpose—to live the life God has planned for us."

From Tansing the ragged highway became a series of steep up-and-down switchbacks. Neil had told us a tragic story about a French cyclist who had been killed on this road by a bus. "He was zipping down a hill and smacked into the bus, right between his eyes." Thinking about the Frenchman, we biked slowly down the hills. Despite the terrible humidity, we wore our helmets. Every break, I changed a sweat-soaked bandana, attaching the wet one to a rear bungee so it would dry in the wind as I pedaled.

The roads were disastrous for the bikes. Every three or four kilometers someone had a flat. We set a group record of eighteen flats in one day. In one stretch of road Jim had eight flats in eight kilometers. In two days Jim broke six spokes, Don broke three, and I broke two. Jim's rear wheel was so out of true that he had to loosen his rear brake housing to allow the wheel to spin freely.

But biking through the Himalayas was not all bad. After weeks of heat and illness, we were gradually shaking off our lethargy. The mountain air cleared our heads, and good food strengthened our bodies. In a burst of energy, I began scrawling in my journal during free moments. Don spent hours cleaning the Ganges plains dust out of his cameras with fine tissue paper and a small aircan. He took thirteen rolls of slides in three days. Jim sighted at least a dozen birds between Butwal and Pokhara. One afternoon a lammergeyer—a huge, hawklike bird with an eight-foot wingspan—soared just a few feet above us as it sought out a rodent in the valley below.

"Did you see that!" shouted Jim. "God, it was only six feet away!"

It took two days to cycle to Pokhara, where we were planning to take a couple of days off. The first night out from Tansing we camped on a ledge overlooking a steep ravine. The second night we stayed in a Thalaki lodge in the village of Waling (the

Thalakis are the traditional tribe of innkeepers in Nepal). The lodge reminded me of what a medieval European inn must have looked like. Inside was a low-ceilinged tavern room with a fireplace on one side and two long tables with benches. Two boys served unmarked bottles of beer and food in wooden dishes to three truck drivers whose Bedford rigs were parked outside. Climbing a ladder into a sort of attic area, one of the boys showed us a tiny room with ankle-high cots and pitchers of water. The latrine was a ditch out back. It was all scrupulously clean and neat and cost only two Nepalese rupees—about fifteen cents. For another two rupees we got a traditional Nepalese dinner of *dhal, bhat,* and *takari*—lentils, rice, and lightly curried vegetables.

Warm beer and exhaustion put us to sleep by eight o'clock, despite the oppressive humidity and the mosquitoes in our rooms. But at nine that night I was suddenly awakened by several radios blasting at once in the tiny village. A cacophony of twangy Indian tunes blew into the night. Laughter and loud talking erupted from the tavern room below. Through the floorboards I could see the bright lights of several gleaming lanterns. A few minutes later all of the roosters and dogs in town started crowing and yapping in response to the music. It was like the *paseo* in Spain or the *promenade* in France—the time in the evening when the people of Waling pulled up a beer and relaxed with their friends.

I lay in bed for a few minutes feeling utterly weary. I wished that the music, the yapping, the mosquitoes, and the humidity would disappear. I noticed that Jim, on the next cot, was adding his snores to the melee. How could he be sleeping through all this noise? Not wanting to suffer alone, I shook him and told him to stop snoring.

"Huh?" he grunted.

"You're snoring!" I shouted over the other noise.

"Sorry," he muttered, turning over and going back to sleep.

A day later we reached a high pass overlooking the Pokhara valley, an intricate bowl of latticelike paddies filled with new shoots of rice. The fresh, dark greenness of the valley was sharp against deep gray clouds still churning a few meters above us. To the north, where the sky was clearer, we could barely make out the dark shadows of the Annapurna range, one of the snowy, outrageously high ridges in the Great Himalayan range. With a cheer we climbed onto our bikes and raced down the steep road into the valley. Many of the tales about the magic kingdom of Nepal centered on Pokhara. This was one of the prime spots for the hippies who invaded Nepal in the early seventies. They had come here by the thousands, disenchanted with life at home and searching for love and freedom and hashish in these exotic, Edenic hills. Pokhara was famous for good food, comfortable mountain lodges, bookstores, and lots of Western women.

In the valley we turned toward a suburb of Pokhara called the Lake Phewa district. Phewa is the resort area of Pokhara, where most of the Westerners stay. The turn to Phewa was at the Pokhara Airport, which had a grass runway, a small terminal, and an orange bag-flag to indicate the direction of the wind. Tall, faded billboards with cartoon characters advertised flights to Europe and the USA via Katmandu and New Delhi.

Near Phewa we stopped at the Baba restaurant, which looked like a bar in Hawaii or the Caribbean with a large, thatched roof and no walls. Under the roof we ordered Star beers and perused a menu that included Mexican, Italian, and Continental dishes. I ordered a bean burrito, french fries, and French onion soup. While we ate, two Western hippies sat down nearby. One was bald with a long goatee and about twelve tiny earrings in each ear. He looked like some of the hippies we had seen in Egypt and Sudan, wearing a caftan, *baruka* pants, and sandals. His friend was also bald except for a small blond tail of hair at the crown of his head. He was swathed in a gold robe. They were absorbed in conversation.

"Hey, who did you say your teacher was?" I overheard the robed man say.

"Oh, he's Guru Mahosi Harnalasi."

"Oh, hey, isn't he into the purity of virtue in all things, and not just the random happenings of truth?"

"Yeah, you should come to one of our meetings."

"What is his opinion on the guilt of nirvana?"

"Man, come to the meeting!"

Just beyond the Baba, more men in gold robes and tails of hair chanted, tapped drums, and tinkled finger cymbals behind a gate at a Hari Krishna colony. Then came the main cluster of hotels, stalls, and coffee shops at Phewa. Pasty, anemic-looking hippies mixed with clean-cut tourists at outside tables in cafés with names like The Hungry Eye and The Cuckoo. Hotels charging three dollars a night had names like Annapurna and Snowland and featured "solar-heated showers." The place was an odd blend of Berkeley in the sixties, summer camp, and Appalachia. The Rolling Stones, Deep Purple, and the Grateful Dead blew out of tinny speakers and dusty cassette players mounted in every hotel and coffee shop. Wooden stalls topped in corrugated tin sold everything from hash pipes and rice paper stationery to used books and yak-wool trekking packs. Nepalese in jeans and T-shirts were hawking hashish and LSD, saying "hey, man" after every other word. One hippie in a jeans vest and muslin skirt strolled blithely around the cluster, quietly inquiring if anyone wanted to have his ears pierced. "It's clean and safe," he said. He also did tattoos of Krishna or a Tibetan dragon, if you'd go with him to his cabin down the road.

Lake Phewa is sacred to Nepalese and Tibetan Buddhists. On a small island just off the shore of the lake is a tiny temple with two bronze monsters and a bronze bell standing among a grove of low trees. Young boys rented heavy canoes to tourists so they could paddle out to the island or other parts of the lake. Like the swimmin' hole near Butwal, the snow-fed lake was freezing and tingly in the heat and humidity of the Nepalese summer. After checking into the Snowland, we grabbed our towels and took a dip. Then we returned to the hotel to take solar-heated showers. But the water was freezing.

"Hey man, I am sorry about the shower," said a Nepalese boy behind the Snowland's front desk. He was listening to Iron Butterfly's "In-A-Gadda-Da-Vida." "The sun is behind monsoon clouds for many days," he said. "Without sun, we get no solar-heated shower."

We rested in Pokhara for two days. Jim insisted on it. He was complaining loudly about needing time alone. Personal conflicts that had been building for several weeks were beginning to erupt now that we were free of India's miseries. Jim was making annoying lists of everything again, I was getting compulsive about wanting to bike fast, and Don was becoming stubborn about taking photos. "I need to spend at least forty-eight hours without looking at you guys," said Jim. "I don't even want to hear your voices. For the next two days, I'm on vacation."

The next morning, Jim left to take an overnight trek into the hills around Pokhara. Don sneaked around Phewa trying to snap shots of hippies and mystics. I scrawled notes in my journal and reflected on life. Soon after Jim left, I hired a dugout from a kid named Thalaki. I wanted to go out to the middle of the lake to think. I took with me two bottles of Star beer, a towel, my journal, and a book of short stories by Graham Greene.

Out on the lake, the water was a floor of green, reflecting the jungle in patches of color like a painting by Monet. From the shore flew great white egrets. High overhead a crested serpent eagle was circling, looking for water snakes swimming close to Phewa's surface. It was sunny directly above the lake, but the Annapurna range was still blocked by clouds. In the peace of the morning, all I could hear was the splash of my paddle and my steady breathing.

In the middle of the lake the boat began to drift as I lay in the sun and felt a cool breeze blowing off the mountains. It was a perfect setting for thinking. Now that the miseries of Pakistan and India seemed to be behind me, I wanted to try to sort out what had happened over the past few weeks. I had left India feeling angry and disturbed. My day of rage had had a profound effect on me. It seemed to reveal a basic ugliness inside of me, an intolerance that I found revolting. I stared at the calm water. What did it all mean? What had motivated me to attack that boy in India? Did this indicate that I was a bad person? Was I evil? This was a frightening possibility. Maybe I wasn't the good, kindhearted person I had always believed myself to be. Maybe I was no better than people like Louisiana Bill with his whip and the SHO in Pakistan. I hoped this wasn't true. After all, I had not been casually cruel. It had taken an extreme situation to make me lash out against an innocent boy. I had had to sink very low before I could allow myself to be overtly cruel. Perhaps there was a lesson in this. On my day of rage, I exposed a part of myself that every person should see just once in their lives. I understood that evil is real. It exists within us, and it must be faced.

This may seem like an obvious conclusion, but it had never been particularly obvious to me growing up in the States. At home I had never taken evil seriously. To a kid who watched television and read comics, evil was Darth Vader or Emperor Ming breathing heavily and threatening to blow up planets just for fun. Good was Luke Skywalker and Flash Gordon. Beyond these fantasy depictions, I had never absorbed a clear idea of good and evil. I could read about evil, about madmen like Hitler or ruthless dictators like Stalin. I could go to church and hear sermons about the evils of Satan. But none of this was real in the world of Middle America, a world that has managed to insulate itself from many of the more blatant evils in the larger world. Growing up, I had never had a Hitler or a Stalin ruining my life; nor did I have to face the evils of tyranny or war or poverty or disease.

Yet I had to stop concentrating on evil. For several weeks, since the shock of seeing El Kantara, I had been thinking mostly about the ugly side of human nature. I had felt cynical and pessimistic about the plight of the world. But now I was pulling out of this phase. Nepal seemed to offer a fresher view of the world. Here was an intensely poor country filled with people like John Finley and the Slovicks. Like Gruffy in Sudan, these people were here to help. They offered a concrete example of goodness, even if their type of goodness was rare and always threatened by the darker forces at work in the world.

In the midst of my musing I noticed that my boat had drifted far away from the sacred island and the Phewa enclave. I grabbed my paddle and started scooping the water. I paddled hard, taking in deep breaths of mountain air. I felt exhilarated and free as the dugout cut through the water. As I worked, the monsoon clouds obscuring the high Himalayan ridge suddenly blew away. I stopped paddling to stare at the snowy peaks hovering above the valley. They looked almost translucent against the blue sky. They were a magic ridge, a far pavilion of heaven. But they only appeared for an instant. When the clouds had rolled back over the peaks, I stood up in the boat, stretched, and dove into the tingling waters of the sacred lake.

Leaving Pokhara on June 11, we took two and a half days of hard, up-and-down riding to make Katmandu. The first night out we stayed in another Thalaki lodge. On the second night we camped near a river as a heavy monsoon beat down on the tents and soaked everything. At about ten A.M. on the third day we reached the approach to Katmandu Pass. Before attempting the pass, the three of us stopped to eat a lunch of steaming *dhal, baht,* and *takari* at a cliffside lodge. Monsoon rains rattled against the tin awning. Water poured off the roof in thin sheets against the red earth. A squat stone marker outside the lodge pointed toward Katmandu to the east, Pokhara to the west, and Mount Everest to the northeast.

"We're only about twenty-five kilometers from Katmandu," I said, studying our map.

"I'm guessing it'll only take us a couple of hours to get there," said Jim. "This pass doesn't look too bad."

Four hours later, we had pedaled only twelve kilometers. The road had turned upward just a few meters east of the lodge. The grade was 14 percent in some spots, and the pavement was a ragged strip of craters and ground-up asphalt. The ceiling of fog had risen a few meters, but the rain was falling in heavy, swift drops. A mass of swirling gray clouds still obscured the top of the steep pass, so we had no idea how far up we had to pedal. At one point, we struggled past a road crew of villagers repairing a caved-in section of road. It looked like a giant creature had taken a bite out of the highway.

"Dave, hold up!" Jim suddenly shouted from behind me. I was pumping hard, trying to make my legs take me a few more meters before I had to stop and rest. "Dave," Jim shouted again, "stop!" I put out a leg quickly to stop myself against the steep hill. Just then, another piece of road cracked, crumbled, and caved in a few meters ahead. I looked back at Jim and realized that he had probably just saved my life.

After topping the Katmandu Pass—we pedaled three thousand feet up in about nine miles—we sped down into the broad Katmandu Valley. Soaked by monsoon rains, the dark green plains were pocked here and there with villages leading to a gray mass of smog and airborne muck marking the city of Katmandu. As we got closer to the city, splashes of the twentieth century appeared among the ramshackle villages. We saw a line of microwave dishes, then a row of modernistic shopping stalls, and then a lot full of new Toyotas and Datsuns apparently waiting for someone to buy them.

Katmandu itself was a mix of ancient streets, hundreds of shrines and pagodas, and pockets of modern hotels and shops. Narrow streets were lined with coffee-colored lodges and filled with statues of Hindu gods, their stone foreheads smeared with red ghee and their shoulders covered with mountain blossoms. The Nepalese in the streets wore mostly Western clothes, while the Westerners wore mostly Nepalese and Indian clothes. In the central Durbar Square, a forest of small temples housed doll gods draped in silk robes. Rising above the square were the Oriental tiers of the Basantpur tower, part of the royal palace complex built in the seventeenth century. Hawkers stood under the the palace walls selling everything from curved Gurkha knives to recently published "underground" guides to Nepal.

Just off Durbar Square was a cramped alleyway the Nepalese had nicknamed Freak Street. It was the major hippie colony in Nepal during the golden age of hippiedom. In the mid-seventies thousands of hippies had lived in cheap bunk houses while frequenting restaurants and shabby cafés with names like Peace, Delight, and Eden. It was a place of utter abandon, a place where no government or parents told anybody what to do. It was Berkeley and Haight-Ashbury multiplied a thousand-fold, a place where everyone could worship exotic gods, legally smoke the excellent hashish, and live like a king for a few dollars a week.

We pushed our bikes through the crowds on Freak Street to see if anything of the hippie legend remained. Cafés like the Happy and the Paradise still served vegetarian food and played sixties music. The street was still lined with shabby stalls where Nepalese merchants sold caftans and saris, Tibetan calendars, and ragged copies of everything from *Little Dorrit* to the *Bhagavad Gita*. The crowd was mostly composed of young tourists and long-haired Nepalese trying to sell them hashish. (Since 1975, hash has been illegal in Nepal, but this hasn't stopped the thriving business.) "Hash here, hash here," they whispered. Few bona fide hippies walked the streets. I think that most of them had retreated to Pokhara or had vanished into the past.

After a beer at the Paradise Café, we left Freak Street and headed uptown to an area called Thaimel. Our Nepalese guidebook advised us not to stay on Freak Street, unless we enjoyed "filthy, lice-ridden bunks." Thaimel had replaced Freak Street as the "place to be," according to the guide. We biked down a confusing array of streets until we emerged at a small street with newsstands selling *Time* magazine, the *International Herald Tribune* and the Asian edition of the *Wall Street Journal*. Up ahead was the Katmandu Guest House, "the finest in clean, modest housing," according to our guide. At the desk, a clean-cut Nepalese man checked us into three separate rooms opening onto a grassy area in back. We immediately fell asleep, setting our watch alarms so we wouldn't miss dinner.

Jim, Don, and I explored the city over the next six days, peeking into temples and shops and eating every sort of food—from vegetarian enchiladas to water buffalo burgers—in the earthy restaurants. One night we attended a spaghetti dinner at the U.S. embassy. Another night we gambled at the Katmandu Casino, where I won four hundred Indian rupees (about forty-five dollars) on the roulette wheel and then promptly lost it playing blackjack. I spent most of my mornings at the American library, where the U.S. press officer gave me a typewriter and a small office to work in. I spent several hours in the library's reading room, researching Pakistan and India for possible articles or just reading random magazines and books.

Katmandu was one of those charming cities, like Jerusalem and Aswan, where we could have stayed forever. But we had to move on. Since leaving Karachi seventy days earlier, we had not thought much about the overall schedule for the World Bike for HOPE. We were now almost six weeks behind my original itinerary. With HOPE and our sponsors getting more and more interested in publicity and fund-raising events, it was becoming imperative that we devise a realistic schedule and stick to it. It was time to get to work on the business of running the World Bike for HOPE.

We had hoped to bicycle into China, from Katmandu to Beijing. But like Saudi Arabia, China had consistently turned us down. We had worked for several months in Washington trying to get permission. We had negotiated with the Chinese ambassador in Washington, written letters to officials in Beijing, and used all of the influence HOPE could muster. Laura and HOPE had continued to try for a meaningful route in China, but it was apparently not going to happen. We were asking to bike through parts of Tibet and central China that no Westerners had visited since the 1949 revolution. "It is impossible for you to bicycle from Katmandu to Beijing at this time," the First Secretary of the embassy in New Delhi had told us. When we asked why, he told us that tourist facilities were not available.

"But we don't need tourist facilities," I said.

"I'm sorry," said the First Secretary. "Perhaps in a few years."

Excluding China from our route posed a serious problem. How would we get across East Asia? South of China the route to the Pacific ran through eastern India, Bangladesh, Burma, Thailand, Cambodia, and Vietnam. It was obviously impossible to travel in Cambodia and Vietnam. With the monsoons coming in July, it would also be close to impossible to travel in eastern India or Bangladesh. So we decided to bypass eastern India and fly to Burma, where we would head south into Thailand and Malaysia. On June 20 we biked to the Katmandu airport and boarded an Air Burma flight to Rangoon.

EAST ASIA

Donald Duncan and Jim
Logan on Himalayan
mountain road, Nepal.

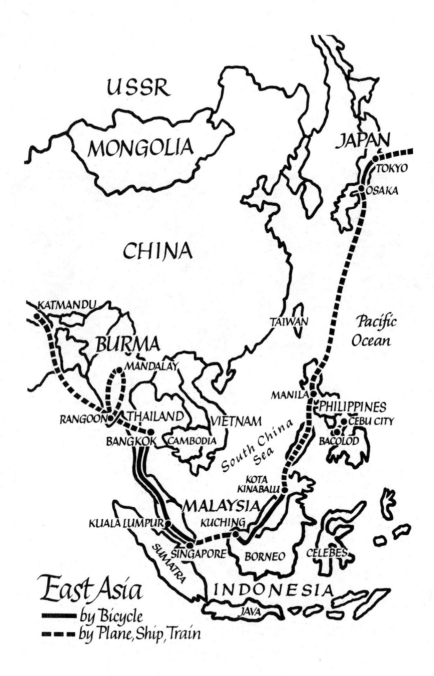

USSR

MONGOLIA

JAPAN
TOKYO
OSAKA

CHINA

KATMANDU

Pacific
Ocean

BURMA

TAIWAN

MANDALAY

MANILA
PHILIPPINES

RANGOON
THAILAND
VIETNAM
CEBU CITY

BANGKOK
CAMBODIA
BACOLOD

South China
Sea

KOTA
KINABALU

MALAYSIA

KUALA LUMPUR
KUCHING

SINGAPORE
BORNEO
CELEBES

SUMATRA

East Asia
— by Bicycle
- - - by Plane, Ship, Train

INDONESIA

JAVA

8. Land of the Monsoons

In the Rangoon airport, tiny men with skin the color of polished walnut pushed our bikes through a baggage doorway. Thanking them, we inspected our machines for damage. When flying, we never disassembled the bikes. Instead we left all the panniers in place to use as padding.

"You, what are those bicycles?" said an impatient Burmese officer in an olive green customs uniform. He stood over us as we worked on the bikes.

"What? These are our bicycles," I said, not quite understanding the question.

"Bicycles are forbidden in Burma!" barked the man. He spoke sharply in Burmese to two soldiers standing nearby. One was tiny enough to be a toddler playing soldier. Looking tough, this midget grabbed my handlebars like they were water buffalo horns. Another midget soldier, playing Laurel to the other soldier's Hardy, tugged on my rear load. Jerking hard, he suddenly fell backward when a bag snapped loose from its bungee.

"Hey! What are you doing?" I shouted. My voice filled the small terminal, turning every head in our direction.

"What is the trouble over there?" asked an officer with three tin stars on his shoulders. He stood behind a worn customs counter in the middle of the dingy room.

"These guys are trying to do something to our bikes!" I shouted back. The impatient man added something in Burmese.

"Please come over here," said the officer. While he perused our passports and scanned our latest newspaper clippings, we mentioned our plan to bicycle from Rangoon to Bangkok.

"I am so sorry, but that is completely impossible. Completely."

Jim told him that Air Burma in Katmandu had assured us that we could bike from here into Thailand. The officer's laugh sounded like an engine rattling. "My friends, no road has existed to Thailand since the war."

"But our map . . ."

"Your map is wrong."

"Can we bicycle north to Mandalay?"

"No, no. It is illegal for foreigners to travel by road. You must take a train or airplane. You leave bicycles here. We have a vault. Everything is very safe."

I wondered if this man could be bribed. Burma was notorious for its underground economy of bribes and black market deals. A young German on our flight had just bribed a customs guard after being caught with a pouch full of illegal gems. All over the airport, black marketeers were haggling with foreigners for everything from liquor to blue jeans. Other black marketeers were trying to sell Burmese kyats for half the official rate. This was all happening *inside* the airport.

"Sir, can I offer you a present?" I tried not to look like a novice briber. "What kind of present would you like to allow us to take the bicycles?"

"I tell you, it is impossible." The man gave me a deep, worldly look. "I want to help you. But you must leave your bikes here if you stay in Burma."

Frustrated, we pushed our bikes away from the counter so we could talk. Eventually we decided to lock the bikes in the airport vault and take four days off to see Burma by train. But the Burmese refusal to let us bike was disappointing. First Saudi Arabia, then China, and now Burma. The list didn't even include the countries we had simply skipped because of wars, politics, or turmoil—countries like Syria, Lebanon, Iran, and

Afghanistan. Back home in Washington, a U.S. State Department officer had warned us that the world was becoming more and more chaotic, and travel options more and more restricted. In my optimism I had not believed him, because I had thought that anything was possible. But now we were facing the reality that large portions of the world were closed off to three Americans biking for charity.

Flying to Bangkok a few days later, we suddenly found ourselves in a new and unexpected part of the world. Hoping to bike through China, we had never seriously considered Southeast Asia as an alternate route. Consequently we knew little about Bangkok, Thailand, or Southeast Asia. How were the roads? What was the weather like? How much money would we need?

From Thailand we decided to pedal south toward Malaysia and Singapore, because that was the only route open to us in a country bordered by Burma on the west, Laos on the north, and Cambodia on the east. From Singapore we again had only one choice if we wanted to continue in an easterly direction—the string of Pacific islands that roughly follow the coast of Asia. From Singapore these islands are Borneo, the Philippines, Taiwan, and Japan. With the exception of Taiwan, we planned to pedal around Asia on these islands, hopping by boat or airplane over the waters dividing them. We hoped this route would compensate for the disappointment of missing China and would roughly equal the kilometerage we had planned for East Asia.

In downtown Bangkok we checked into a comfortable, high-rise hotel called the New Amirin. Exhausted by the long weeks in South Asia, we wanted to rest and rid our bodies of the stubborn parasites still making us ill. Pushing our bikes into the stylish lobby we were suddenly confronted by an unexpected display of modern prosperity. Having just arrived from the Third World, we were astounded by the fantasyland of plush carpeting, ferns, mirrors, and high-tech trim. It would not have been a dramatically ostentatious lobby to anyone coming straight from the States, but to us it was a dazzling display of the comforts and privileges in a world that we had not seen for months. Television monitors with news and travel information hung from the walls. Computer display terminals peeked over the top of the registration desk. Muzak filled the air, which was cooled by air conditioning. A mix of Oriental and Western businessmen and tourists strolled through the lobby, looking remarkably normal in their suits, knit shirts, and blue jeans. In the far corner of the lobby was a coffee shop, where waitresses in neat uniforms served hamburgers and tall ice-cream sundaes topped by red cherries.

"I'm going to eat ten cheeseburgers," said Don.

"I'm going eat ten banana splits," I said.

"I'm going to sleep for ten days," said Jim, "after eating ten cheeseburgers *and* ten banana splits."

That night, after several hamburgers, banana splits, and beers, Don and I both woke up in the middle of the night with intense stabs of nausea. It was hard to tell if these attacks were from overeating or from tenacious South Asian dysentery. We spent the rest of the night trading off on the toilet. But at least we had a toilet to sit on, our first "American" toilet since New Delhi.

When we began moving about in Bangkok, I was impressed by the level of development in the city. "We are not part of the Third World," a Thai businessman told me in the New Amirin coffee shop. "We are in the Two-and-a-Half World." Telephones, running water and electricity all worked twenty-four hours a day. The smooth performance of these basic infrastructures was a given for most of Bangkok's population. Banks, hotels, and the plethora of travel agencies were computerized and decorated in the flashy, high-tech style popular in the States. Stores and shopping centers were stocked with everything available in America and Japan, from Cuisinarts to Levi's jeans, although many of these items were half-price bootleg copies made in Taiwan, Hong Kong, or South Korea. Hawkers on the streets sold even cheaper, homemade versions of items like polo shirts and cassette tapes. Each of us bought several bootleg Izods for two dollars apiece. They were perfect copies, right down to the color of the threading in the alligator.

In this modern setting, Jim and I quickly recovered from our illnesses by taking medicine dispensed at a U.S. embassy clinic. We also restricted our diet to the clean food and water at the New Amirin. But as Jim and I improved, Don got worse. He was still functioning, but the pains in his stomach were intensifying. "It must be something I'm eating," he said. "I'll try eating real bland stuff, and maybe the pain will go away."

•••

After a couple of days of eating, resting, and walking around the streets near the New Amirin, we began taking care of business. I spent almost an hour on the phone with the director of publicity for Project HOPE, a man named Scott Patton. He had been in charge of our trip for several months. Discussing future publicity and fund-raising plans for the World Bike for HOPE, he told me that it was time to shift the focus of the trip. For the past seven months, our energies had been devoted to bicycling. In the context of the project, this time had been necessary to establish our credibility as world bikers. Scott now considered the "credibility phase" of the trip finished. "It's time to capitalize on your accomplishments," he said, telling me that he was putting together press materials on our Southeast Asian leg to coincide with interviews being arranged by the U.S. embassy in Bangkok. This effort would be a build-up for major publicity campaigns in Japan and San Francisco, where we planned to arrive in late September.

When I hung up the telephone, I felt excited over the success of the trip. From a publicity point of view, everything was happening perfectly on schedule. Yet it felt strange to be suddenly thinking about our journey again in terms of publicity and credibility. Somehow it reduced the significance of the last few weeks. It reminded me of my life in Washington before the trip, when matters like press attention were critical issues for the expedition. Now the business side of the trip seemed less important than other priorities. For one thing, I was spending most of my time trying to write about South Asia, pondering the lessons of Pakistan and India, trying to figure out what had happened, although the experiences were still too close to make much sense on paper.

Two weeks earlier I had been scrounging to find decent food and water. I had been ill and close to quitting the trip. Now, whisked into this land of comparative plenty, everything seemed all right. Like magic, I was sitting in a nice room with clean clothes and chatting about business on the phone. It was like flipping on a light switch in a darkened room. Yet it was hard for my emotions to keep pace.

On one level, I loved it. Like a prisoner released from hard labor, I was suddenly free. I could eat hamburgers and pizza all day. I could drink cold, uniodined water with ice. I could call Laura on a direct-dial phone and talk about New York, ice cream and movies. But on another level, I felt traces of anger at myself. I didn't want to lose what I had learned in India. I knew I would eventually return to my former life of comfort and privilege in America. I knew I would have to confront the inequities and naiveté of my homeland with regard to the rest of the world. Worst of all, I would have to face who I was before the trip. I would have to look at that twenty-three-year-old kid who had dreamed of romance and adventure and charity. I would have to reconcile the wants and desires of this kid with what I had learned over here. It was not a task I looked forward to.

Bangkok is famous for two things, its temples and its red light district. The many Buddhist shrines are decorated with curving, gilded roofs, tall statues, and walls of glittering, colored glass. Yellow-robed monks drive in and out of the temple compounds in Toyotas and switch on bright spotlights at night to illuminate their complexes. The main red-light district, known as Patpong, is equally glittery and prosperous, at least at night. Originally established for U.S. soldiers on R & R from Vietnam, Patpong is now a major draw for the million or so tourists who visit Bangkok each year. "If you are so inclined, visit a massage parlor while in Bangkok," one of our guidebooks suggested. "They are clean and orderly in a country that encourages certain Oriental pleasures."

On our third night in Bangkok, Jim, Don and I took a taxi to Patpong. Don almost didn't come, because of his stomach. But we told him not to let a little sickness get to him. "I've been sick for most of five months, and *I'm* still alive," I said.

At the New Amirin entrance, a doorman in a maroon uniform hailed us a taxi, telling the driver that we were going to Patpong.

"You want fuck?" asked the cabby as soon as we pulled out into traffic. "You want sex show? Live show? I get you anything you want, Joe." As we weaved through traffic, the cabby launched into a well-rehearsed harangue in pidgin English describing women screwing Ping-Pong balls, bowling pins, and guitars. We could have ten women at once. Men too. Any age, any size, any color.

Arriving at Patpong, we entered a swirling mass of tourists and Thai women in glittering G strings and microscopic tops swaying to flashing pink and red neon. Policemen in trim, American-style uniforms stood every few feet, watching the crowd with serious faces.

"Come on in, Joe, you want good time?" the women asked, trying to lure us into disco bars with names like Crystal Palace A Go Go, Bangkok's Soul Bar, Bottoms Up, Pit Stop, and Safari Disco-Bar. The thumpa-thumpa of sophisticated sound systems blasted from doors covered in pink velvet and silver sequins. Aging women carried tall boards covered with cigarettes and cigars, while pimps roamed the sidewalks muttering replays of our cabby's performance. Everyone called us Joe, because of the U.S. soldiers that used to come to Patpong during the war.

As the guidebook said, Patpong was surprisingly clean and new-looking. The paint was fresh and expertly applied to signs, and the sidewalks were swept and mopped. The women standing beside the bars were young and attractive. The clientele ranged from youthful preppie tourists from the States to sleazier men with greasy hair and dirty clothes who hungrily eyed the women as they prowled the streets.

We strutted up the short street, peeking into each open doorway, feeling like kids who had just discovered a *Playboy* in their father's desk. It was an intoxicating place for three men who had just arrived from South Asia. We attacked it as we had the hamburgers at the New Amirin. Even Don felt better—at least for the moment. Like most of the men on the street, we were grinning like little boys. Buying cigars, we started telling locker-room jokes and laughing as loud as we could.

Jim finally decided on a bar called Mississippi Queen, because it was playing "Satisfaction," which he considered appropriate for the occasion. Before we were even in the door, six women in almost nothing gently slid their arms under ours. "Hello, you are so good-looking," they said, leading us to bar stools under floating platforms where women swayed to the pulsating music. It was a tiny, alley-sized bar that splintered into a confusion of mirrors and flashing disco lights. Every man had at least one woman on his lap. They were jiggling their breasts and seductively licking their lips. A few were toying with their G strings and caressing their customer's thighs. But the customers did not touch the women. Giant thugs, most of them Caucasian, lurked around the edges of the Mississippi Queen.

"You take me home tonight?" said one of the women on my arm. She called herself Dee. She ran thin fingers along my thigh, very close to my crotch. "You stay in big hotel?"

I must have looked like an idiot. All I could do was grin and shake my head while trying to puff on my cigar without choking on the smoke. I looked over at Jim and Don to see what they were doing and noticed that Don was gone.

"Jim, where's my brother?" I shouted over the music. I was worried that he was getting sick again.

"I don't know," said Jim. "Maybe he's in the john."

Later that night, back at the New Amirin, Don was lying in his bed, holding his stomach and moaning. His face was twisted in pain. "Something's really wrong with me," he kept saying. "This is not like dysentery. The pain just keeps getting worse." About midnight we called the hotel doctor, who advised us to take Don to a British-run clinic in downtown Bangkok. At the clinic Jim and I drank coffee in an empty waiting room. In the silence of the heavy tropical night, we were both thinking the same thing. Ever since the trip was conceived long ago in Washington, one of our greatest fears was that one of us would get hurt or seriously ill far away from home. After almost eight months of minor injuries and illnesses, I think we had begun to believe that nothing serious was ever going to happen. We had developed a false sense of invincibility that was now crashing down around us.

"I'm afraid your friend is very ill," the doctor told us after finishing his examination. "We believe he has appendicitis, and may have some other problems as well."

"Appendicitis?" we gasped. "What does that mean?" I blurted out, knowing damn well what it meant. It meant that Don was very sick and that the trip was over for him, at least for several weeks.

"You see, his appendix is quite swollen," said the doctor. "Now, an appendectomy is a fairly routine operation, but we suspect that there may be complications. We'll have to run more tests. But I should warn you. If these complications do develop, and it comes down to surgery, I would recommend sending him to Tokyo, or even better, back Stateside if he can handle the trip."

That night the doctor called my parents. When my mom answered, the doctor told her that Don might have to come home. "He's very sick," the doctor said, "although we are unclear right now about how sick." After the doctor finished, I got on the phone and talked to my mom. She was thunderstruck by the news.

"My God, Dave," she said, "I'm practically in shock. You

have no idea how afraid I've been that this would happen to one of you boys. For God knows how many months your father and I have been so worried." She paused, and I could hear her take a deep breath. "Listen, I can't talk now," she said with a choked voice. "I need to call your father. *Please* call us back in a half hour and talk to us again."

Don remained in the hospital for the next several days, but his condition stayed about the same. On July 11 the doctors at the British hospital decided he should go home. "He seems to have appendicitis, but something is not right," they said. So we booked my brother on a flight to Kansas City, via Manila and Los Angeles.

That night we took Don and his bike to the Bangkok airport. He was pale and slightly doped up, and he said little as we processed him through the airport and took him to his gate. Before leaving Don gave me his two Nikons and his equipment. "Take some good shots," he said. While a flight attendant stood by to help him get on the plane, I gave him a tender hug.

"Take it easy," I said, holding him close to me. He looked so pale it scared me. "Are you okay to take this flight?" I asked him. Jim was also looking very worried.

"I can make it," Don said, smiling weakly. "But I'm worried about you guys. Are you going to be okay?"

"Sure, as long as Dave behaves," Jim said, smiling.

"I'll be back soon enough," Don said. "As soon as I'm well, I'll be back."

"I'm sorry," interrupted the flight attendant, "but the plane is leaving. I must get this man on the airplane."

"Take care," I said as the attendant helped him out of the gate and onto the runway. A moment later Don was gone.

At noon the day after Don flew home, Jim and I packed up our battered bicycles and pedaled out of Bangkok. It was a relief to be riding again, to feel the physical sensation of steering my heavy bike and pumping my legs. We had been off the bikes for more than three weeks since arriving in Katmandu. The faster I pedaled, the better I felt, as though the frustrations and setbacks of the last few weeks could be dissipated by just a little physical exertion. Shifting into our highest gears, we sped along as the concrete architecture of Bangkok gave way to patches of jungle, fields of bright green rice paddies, and an occasional small, modern town. This highway was taking us to the Gulf of Thailand, where we would jog west and then south to follow the Malay Peninsula all the way to Singapore, nineteen hundred kilometers away.

Jim and I made a decision in Bangkok to concentrate on one thing during this leg of the trip—speed. We had several reasons for wanting to pedal fast. First was our obligation to Project HOPE. Under the new publicity schedule we had worked out with Scott Patton, Jim and I had to be in the States by September 26, which was only eleven weeks away. Arriving late would throw off the U.S. publicity schedule and cost HOPE and our sponsors a lot of money.

But pleasing HOPE was not the only reason we were speeding south. Jim and I were also smelling home. After all the months on the road, home suddenly seemed within reach. On that first day, we covered the thirty-six kilometers to the sea in only ninety minutes. Using our Casio timers, we figured that our speed had averaged close to twenty-five kilometers an hour, a World Bike for HOPE record. This was the first of many speed records made and broken between Bangkok and Singapore. Taking minimal breaks and lunch stops, we were shooting for a daily average of one hundred kilometers. At that speed we would make Singapore in only twenty-five days, including breaks. Jim called this fast-paced style the "macho school of biking," a line he had picked up from Dave French.

Thailand's wealth confronted us everywhere on the road. Japanese cars and motorcycles had completely replaced the oxen and donkeys of South Asia. Public buses were air-conditioned. Many of the stores were fronted in glass and abundantly stocked with everything from color televisions to Wrigley's chewing gum. In most of the larger towns all of the basic Western infrastructures were in place. This was a surprise. In other Third World countries these basics seldom appear outside of major cities. Electricity was dependable, sewers were covered, sidewalks were in good repair, and services like telephones and post offices were at least as efficient as in Spain and Greece. We did see substantial pockets of poverty in enclaves of straw-topped huts, but to eyes accustomed to the Third World of South Asia, this country seemed like a bastion of extraordinary wealth.

The prosperity of the Thai countryside became the fuel for our sudden burst of speed. Prosperity meant good food, comfortable beds, and smooth roads. It also meant that we had more time to concentrate on biking. Since Israel our days had been dominated by hustling for food in dusty markets and searching for safe places to sleep at night. Ragged roads had popped our tires and almost wrecked our bikes. Disease had stolen our energy and drive. In India our riding time had dropped to only four or five hours a day. In Thailand our time in the saddle almost doubled.

With the appetites of gluttons, we amazed waiters up and down the Malay peninsula with the amount of food we consumed. Typically we ate three full dinners a night; the courses were fried rice, eggs, chicken, pork, and strips of beef, all soaked in sauces that blended the curries of India and the sweeter flavors of China. We spent all but two nights in cheap hotels. It was common for them to have air conditioning, plastic shower stalls, and a TV in a main lounge.

Our first night out from Bangkok, we slept in a small town called Samut Songkhram, a typical town with a central shopping area, a movie theater, and an air-conditioned hotel charging only one hundred baht (about five dollars) a night. Checking in, I offhandedly asked the tiny manager if I could make a call to the States.

"Of course, mister," he said. This seemed too good to be true after countries where we couldn't even place calls in major cities. I immediately called Kansas City and asked my mom if Don was all right. Jim was leaning over my shoulder.

"Don is still on the plane," my mom said, "but we had a real scare in Manila. He almost had to have his appendix out right there, it was hurting so much. How did he look when he left you all?"

"Not good," I said.

"You and Jim be careful," she said. "If anything happens to you, it will devastate us."

"Mom, we'll be all right," I said. "We've made it this far."

The next morning, Jim and I woke up to a monsoon rain rattling against the roof of the hotel. It was monsoon season in Thailand, an awful time to be bicycling. On a typical day, the clouds would start thickening in the morning as the air become more and more moist. By mid-afternoon, the sky would be almost black, and the air would be thick with humidity as the rains suddenly fell in great sheets of water.

Southeast Asia's monsoons form over the Indian Ocean toward the end of April, when the tilt of the earth shifts the summer season from the southern to the northern hemisphere. As the sun's most powerful rays pass north of the equator, the winds over the Indian Ocean abruptly change direction from a calm northeasterly to a violent southwesterly. A low pressure system over the ocean slams into a high pressure system over India. By May a hot, damp, tropical wind is blowing hard into Asia, swirling in a backward C shape from Southeast Asia and Southern India north into Burma and Central India. Thailand and Malaysia, being near the start of the C, tend to have the longest monsoon season, stretching from the end of May to the end of July. As we pedaled south from Bangkok, almost one hundred inches of water had already fallen on Southeast Asia. The land we cycled past was often flooded with gray-brown stretches of water. Houses in these places were usually on high bamboo stilts. People got around in rowboats or in long, narrow boats powered by engines that shot out water like jet streams.

The macho school of biking largely ignores minor inconveniences like monsoons, although the rains did keep most of our things perpetually soaked. The water also damaged some of our equipment. As the days progressed, all of the places on our bikes where the paint had been scratched off began to turn the red-brown color of rust. After a week of dampness, a cloud of moisture appeared inside my watch. Clothes started to smell of mildew. We had each bought two boxes of Ziploc bags in Bangkok, but they didn't help much.

Occasionally the rains fell hard enough to hurt. When this happened, Jim and I stopped in an open-front coffee shop to sip cold sodas with the local men idled by the floods. They seldom spoke English, but we had a good time speaking to them in sign language about the bike trip, the rain, women, and American movies. Thai men loved American war movies. "Green Beret?" they would say.

"John Wayne," we would answer. Then one of them would point his finger like a gun and start shooting.

The days passed quickly as we dashed south through towns with names like Phet Buri, Hua Hin, Bang Saphan, Ranong, and Trang. We passed a plethora of tall Buddhist temples roofed in plastic blue tiles, watched several Chinese martial arts movies, and continued to sample a rich variety of food and drink. The land remained flat along the gulf until our road crossed the low, green mountains of the Bilauk Taung Range about 450 kilometers south of Bangkok. The mountains run down the middle of the peninsula, like the ridged back of a giant reptile's tail. We stayed nearly every night in a cheap hotel, trying to maximize our time on the road while avoiding camping out during the drenching evening monsoons.

The further south we got, the more the jungle thickened. Vines and moss hung from tall trees with tan bark, while locusts cackled, frogs bellowed, and macaws screeched. Far in the distance, an occasional jaguar would scream like a house cat with a five-hundred-watt amplifier. The gulf areas smelled like dead fish, while the jungle interior smelled musty and, occasionally, like rotting flesh.

Jim and I were good buddies during most of the Thai portion of the trip. Free at last from the miseries and hassles of South Asia and from the disappointments of missing China and losing Don, we relished a chance to enjoy each other's company. As in the first days of the trip, we revived our practice of having long discussions about random topics. But even as we enjoyed ourselves speeding south, the seeds of discontent were forming. The problems were not new. They involved old arguments about a restrictive schedule, the budget, and petty items like where to take a break and how far we could go on a given day. But the context for these arguments was different now. Without Don, Jim and I had no buffer between us when one of us was in a bad mood. Even two people that like each other are bound to start feeling friction when thrown together for long periods of time. Another new feature of the trip was the inflexibility of our schedule and the intensity of our pace. At first it gave us a sort of high to be able to bike so fast and so hard, but after a while our compulsions about pace and schedule began to wear us down. Neither of us had much free time. I had purchased an eight-pound portable typewriter in Bangkok to carry on my bike, but I was finding little time to write. Jim had little time to study his birds or to read his small library of books. It was as if we had been awarded our freedom only to have it taken away.

Our journey through Thailand ended in the town of Hat Yai, a district capital tucked into the corner of a jungle valley near the Malaysian border. This is a wild, unsettled corner of Thailand. Our guidebook called it a "Thai version of the wild west." For years bandits have robbed trains on lonely stretches in the jungle. Like Butch Cassidy and the Sundance Kid, they fell trees across the tracks, force the passengers outside when the train has stopped, and then rob them of their money and jewels. The jungles also hide bands of revolutionaries, most notably the Communist People's Army of Malaysia (the CPM), who were fielding as many as seven thousand troops armed by the Chinese.

When we arrived in Hat Yai the Thai army was engaged in an offensive to oust the Communists. Thai troops in full battle dress were rushing around the city and into the countryside. The day before, the army had fought a major skirmish with the Communists. According to the *Bangkok Post*, a Thai sergeant had been killed and a captain and a private wounded. "An undetermined number of CPM insurgents were killed and wounded," reported the *Post*. Weeks had passed since we had seen a city so tense. The serene and confident faces in Bangkok were absent here. As in Karachi and Israel, we saw that look of routine apprehension, of always having to look over your shoulder.

"It okay you ride to Malaysia," said a police captain at the Hat Yai station. "Only ride in daytime. No night. Stay on road, and you be safe." He assured us that the skirmish was over, and that the countryside was safe. He worried more about thieves than battles. "No stop between Hat Yai and Alor Setar, in Malaysia. Only eighty-five kilometers. Many thieves. Very dangerous."

We were on the road just after dawn the next morning, watching for signs of thieves, Communists, or soldiers. The road was almost empty, an ominous sign. Then Jim bounced over a ragged pothole and snapped two spokes. His rear wheel butterflied. Without a word we began replacing the spokes as the sun peeked out from behind the clouds. With the sun beating down on our heads, we moved under the shade of giant fern blades hanging like dark green knives over the road. Weird whines and bird calls emanated from the jungle. They sounded spooky, like a sound effects record of jungle noises. Then, suddenly, a high shriek pierced the air just behind us. We jumped up and looked at each other.

"What the hell was that?" I asked.

"It sure as hell wasn't a Booby-chested nuthatch," Jim said.

At noon, our run of bad luck continued when my derailleur snapped. "If that spring in your derailleur is busted, we are up shit's creek," Jim said. We had no spare derailleurs. In Bangkok, Thai customs had refused to release our drop box without the payment of a ridiculously high duty. Fortunately the spring inside the derailleur was not broken. It had merely lost its tension and needed to be reattached and wound up, a task that would take at least an hour because we had to take the whole derailleur apart.

As we worked the jungle filled suddenly with the sounds of a machine—a low, fluttering noise that stirred a tree full of macaws into fits of screaming and chattering. We froze to listen.

"Helicopter," said Jim.

A moment later, as the fluttering noise got louder, a large helicopter gunship slowly dipped out of the clouds a quarter of a mile away. Its wide bay doors were open. We could see soldiers inside peeking out as wisps of smoke burst out around the belly of the craft, closely followed by sharp snaps like firecrackers. Jim and I dropped to our knees behind the bikes as the echoes of automatic weapons ricocheted across the valley. It seemed like several minutes before the shots stopped and, like an apparition, the floating gunship disappeared into the clouds.

We didn't reach the Malaysian border until five o'clock, closing time for customs. On either side of the road, stretching off into the jungle, were cleared paths filled with mines. The skull and crossbones sign we had seen long ago on the Sinai was mounted on high, barbed-wire fences on both sides of the path. It was a frightening place, especially after the helicopter attack.

We had to use a threat to convince the customs guard to stay open long enough to process our passports. "We are going to Alor Setar tonight," I said. "You will have to arrest us to stop us. We have no place else to go, and we will not stay here."

I suppose he believed us, and wanting to avoid trouble, he became very friendly. He offered cigarettes, which we refused. "You boys are very brave to bicycle here," he said. "Communists are in this jungle. But you are only thirty minutes from Alor Setar." We told him that thirty minutes by car was two or three hours by bike.

"You boys are so very brave," he said again, stamping our passports. We hadn't heard anyone say that since Sudan.

In Southeast Asia, dusk never lingers. Like an electric light being switched off, the sun suddenly blinks out. Deep, moving clouds of gray, steamy mist settled over the dark jungle as we sped south, pushing hard toward Alor Setar. We only paused to mount flashlights wrapped in clear plastic bags between our handlebars. We passed a couple of small enclaves raised up on stilts as in northern Thailand. Outside electric lights shot beams into the mist, creating ghostly visions that moved and twisted in eerie panorama. We sped on, ignoring these refuges for our goal, Alor Setar. I don't know why we didn't stop in one of these villages. It was as if these mist-spirits had possessed us and were pulling us into their nighttime dance, propelling us through the haunted, drenching night.

We didn't slow down until we reached Alor Setar. Approaching downtown, we found ourselves in a dusty colonial city filled with British-style colonnades and open-front restaurants. That night we stayed with a middle-aged Chinese woman named Doris Wong and her fourteen-year-old son, named Richard Nixon Wong. "He was born the day Richard Nixon was elected president in America," said Doris, who had a habit of giggling like a young girl. We followed her home to a neat, middle-class house with a carport and manicured lawn. Exhausted, we ate a delicious meal of Chinese noodles and fell asleep on Richard Nixon's bunk beds.

Waking up in Alor Setar the next morning, we found ourselves in another prosperous, partially Westernized country. But it was different from Thailand, where most things appear to have been built in the last fifteen years. Malaysia's prosperity was older and more casual. The architecture seemed to have sprung out of a Somerset Maugham novel. We passed airy, sprawling bungalows, arched shopping arcades, and banks and train stations covered with Victorian gingerbread. I could easily imagine sahibs strolling the streets of Alor Setar in white linens, waving straw fans and jovially discussing the fine points of cricket.

The only departure from British influence was the frequency of signs and placards covered with Chinese characters. We soon discovered that the Chinese are a dominant force in Malaysia. Running a close second in poplulation to the native Malays, they tend to dominate the nation's economy. The Malay people, a Polynesian race who embraced Islam in the fifteenth century, dominate the political arena. The other major population group, the Indians, run Malaysia's railroads and other transportation systems. This division of responsibilities was established by the British and, despite serious racial strains that appear every few years, the system remains intact.

At night in Malaysia we slept in Chinese-run hotels with names like Four Lions, China Inn, and Loo Wong's Little Paris Hotel. These hotels charged two dollars a night. They were usually large, warehouse-sized rooms split into partitioned areas like rows of oversized toilet stalls. Ceiling fans whirred overhead, keeping away mosquitoes and pushing the hot, tropical air out the large windows and open doors. At night men of all races argued, swore, and spit in their stalls. Occasionally we heard the muffled sounds of a woman.

Every religion on earth seemed to be represented in Malaysia. Mosques predominated, followed closely by an assortment of bright red and blue Chinese temples, where the Chinese practiced a confusing blend of Taoism, Confucianism, and Buddhism. Dozens of Christian churches, many of them left by the British, had full congregations. One night I stood in the back of a Baptist church and listened to the congregation of Chinese in starched white shirts and black pants sing something that sounded like "Onward, Christian Soldiers." A tiny Chinese preacher, also in white shirt and black pants, delivered a quiet sermon in Mandarin. In Kuala Lumpur, Malaysia's capital, we would see the carved gateways of Hindu temples and the yellow, open-walled temples of the Tamils.

As we pedaled south toward the equator, the temperature dropped into the mid-eighties and the monsoons softened from heavy squalls to cloudbursts that splashed cool water over our hot skin. Our highway took us past the rolling hills of Malaysia's plantation region, where mangos and plantains scented the air, date palms spread green leaves like fountain sprays on top of husky trunks, and neat rows of rubber trees stretched from the edge of the road for miles in all directions. Men in loincloths and straw hats worked the trees, tapping them with hollow tubes that carried the white, gooey sap into plastic buckets. Rubber is a primary source of Malaysia's wealth, along with tin and oil. As if to reinforce the importance of rubber to Malaysia, thuggish guards armed with shotguns and pistols patrolled the road. They glared at us as we sped by, daring us to camp or even set a foot in the domain of the rubber barons.

Malaysia's prosperity nearly killed us. Only fifteen minutes out of Alor Setar we had our first "dive" alert in Southeast Asia when a white Toyota and a Mercedes came racing side by side, topping out at somewhere close to ninety miles per hour. Traffic signs were everywhere, but were seldom observed. Malaysia's fast, sleek cars and giant trucks careened unimpeded along the excellent roads. In ten days we saw four crashes. One afternoon a Nissan came roaring past as we slowly rounded a long curve in the highway. A split second later I heard a screech of tires. Looking up, I saw the Nissan fishtail toward a gasoline truck straddling the road. As if in slow motion, the Nissan slid sideways, crashing into a heap of splintering metal and glass. I slowly braked, sickened by the loud, echoing *Crash!* A moment later we pulled up to the car. Several policemen were already on the scene. Luckily their office was just a few meters from the accident. The truck driver and the police were trying to force open a bashed door on the Nissan. The driver lay slumped and unconscious inside. I saw no blood, but the man must have been seriously injured. The car was mangled all around him. When police cars began arriving, we left the crash site.

Jim and I pedaled into Malaysia's capital city of Kuala Lumpur on July 31, after biking fifteen hundred kilometers in just nineteen days. As in Pokhara, we were planning to check into separate rooms, because our close proximity was driving both of us crazy. Passing from the plantation country into the neat suburbs of Kuala Lumpur, we steered our heavy cycles along the edge of the crowded streets, looking for a cheap hotel suggested by *Southeast Asia on a Shoestring.* Turning a corner in the frenetic traffic, we spotted a large yellow sign that we had been secretly craving for months to see—McDonald's: Over 45 Billion Served.

Forgetting our fatigue, Jim and I shot across an anarchic intersection and walked into a plastic world filled with smiling Malaysians sitting in red chairs. We spent two hours eating Big Macs, twig-thin fries, and aerated thick shakes. We rubbed the nose of a plastic Ronald McDonald for good luck. Everything was there. The menu was lit up over the stainless steel counter, the french fry machine beeped politely when the fries were done, and the teenaged employees wore baseball-style caps and polyester uniforms. Slick Grand Opening posters told us that this restaurant was the first McDonald's in Malaysia. To celebrate, McDonald's had shipped in a gang of American "celebrities" to play a "celebrity tennis match" against Malaysian tennis stars. On our placemats were several familiar faces framed in stars—Jonathan Winters, Peter Graves, Richard Roundtree, Trini Lopez and the reigning *Penthouse* Pet. As we ate, a few of the teenagers behind the counter moved onto the floor to hang up McDonald's bunting and welcome posters. "The movie stars are to be here soon," one of them told me as we left the restaurant to find a hotel. "Is it not exciting?"

The next night, we met the "celebrities" at a party given in their honor by the U.S. ambassador to Malaysia. We arrived at his sprawling bungalow just in time to hear Trini Lopez sing "Georgia on My Mind." Jonathan Winters was out on the patio telling dirty jokes about some Marines in World War II, and Richard Roundtree was looking Hollywood bored at a table out back. A servant in a white jacket handed us gin and tonics with tinkling ice cubes as the ambassador came to greet us and offer congratulations on our "incredible effort." He was a big man wearing a Hawaiian shirt and white pants. This attire and his booming good nature made him seem more like a bar owner in Florida than an ambassador.

"Hey, you boys want to meet a real princess?" The ambassador winked and led us through a crowd of overdressed Malaysians and underdressed Americans. He was about to introduce us to three striking Malaysian women when he was called away by another guest.

"And who are you?" said the woman in the middle. She stared for a moment at our frazzled clothing and then seemed to lose interest. Like her friends, she was dressed in expensive clothes and draped with a great deal of jewelry.

I explained who we were and then asked them who *they* were. "The ambassador said that one of you was a 'real princess,' " I said laughing. When the women looked mildly surprised at this pronouncement, I explained that *princess* is a derogatory term for women in America like *cupcake* or *dish*. The women's mildly surprised looks shifted almost imperceptibly to expressions of pity.

"Do you know who this is?" asked the woman to my left, referring to her friend in the middle. "This is Her Royal Highness, the daughter of the reigning sultan of Malaysia. She *is* a real princess."

Feeling like social slugs, Jim and I quickly escaped from Her Royal Highness to gorge ourselves at a long table heaped with American-style barbecue, cole slaw, and potato chips. After eating our fill, we were moving toward the door when I met a woman who introduced herself simply as Amanda. She asked me to dance.

"I haven't danced in months," I said.

"That's okay," said Amanda. "I haven't either."

Amanda was the daughter of the embassy's political officer and a junior at Columbia University. "I'm here visiting Dad for the summer," she said. As we jitterbugged and discoed, Amanda and I discussed politics, theater, and F. Scott Fitzgerald—that is, when our faces came together long enough between twirls and loops to speak sentences. I was surprised that I remembered how to dance.

During a Rolling Stones medley, Amanda told me that she was working for the summer as a volunteer English instructor in a Vietnamese refugee camp—a "boat people" camp—outside Kuala Lumpur. I told her that I was interested in writing an article on refugees and would love to visit the camp.

"Are you a journalist?" she asked.

"Sort of," I said.

"It's hard," she gasped as I twirled her around. "They don't like foreigners around, especially reporters." I swung her into a "pretzel," which winded both of us. Taking a deep breath, she said, "But I think I can sneak you in."

The next morning Amanda took me to the Sungei Besi Refugee Camp on the edge of Kuala Lumpur. "My friend is interested in seeing the camp," Amanda told a Malaysian captain at the camp's gate. "He might want to volunteer. May I show him around?" The captain eyed me suspiciously, asked for my camera and passport, and warned us to stay away from the dorms. "Do not talk to any people," he said firmly, "or you will be removed from the camp."

Sungei Besi was a "transit camp," which means that the five thousand refugees living there had been moved from larger camps after being tentatively accepted for emigration by a host country. The camp was split into rows of barrackslike dorms named Australia, France, Canada, and America, depending on where the refugees were going or hoped to go. The United Nations, Red Crescent (the Muslim Red Cross), and other relief groups had provided the buildings, bunks, blankets, food, clothes, and the school where Amanda was teaching. They had also provided a basketball court, soccer goals, and toys for the hundreds of orphaned kids. Several local businesses had donated supplies. Children were running around in A & W Root Beer and Esso T-shirts. The Malaysian government's contribution was less altruistic. They provided the high walls, barbed wire, and armed guards who kept the refugees from leaving

Sungei Besi. After two years and over a million refugees, the government wanted no more boat people.

The camp reminded me some of Abudah in Sudan, although conditions here were considerably better. The similarities between Abudah and Sungei Besi could best be seen in the faces of the refugees. Like those of Gideon in Gedaref and of Tweldeberhum in Abudah, the eyes of the boat people were tired and dull, with the same frustration hidden under masks of calm. I asked one of Amanda's refugee friends if the people in Sungei Besi were happy about finding new homes.

"They are happy, of course," said Mr. Phoc, a thin young man whose father had been a high-ranking officer in the South Vietnamese army, "but they are only happy on the surface. It is a tragedy, what my people have endured. We can never go home, never see our families. This is sad." I remembered that Tweldeberhum Elazar had said the same thing in Sudan.

Like many of the refugees, Mr. Phoc and his family were persecuted in Saigon because of their connections to the South Vietnamese regime. After the South surrendered in 1975, the Communists sent Mr. Phoc's father to a reeducation camp in North Vietnam. They took the family's car and money, leaving only their house and a few bits of furniture. "They did not let me get job," said Mr. Phoc. "I am trained in two years of engineering school. They would not let me continue school. I had no future in Vietnam, so I leave." He was twice put into jail trying to escape. "I did not pay big enough bribe to the soldiers," he said.

I asked him how he could talk about all this so casually.

"I am numb," he said, shrugging.

As we talked to Mr. Phoc, a tiny woman about thirty years old jogged over to us from the other end of "America." She was shouting for Amanda. "Amanda, I have such good news." She paused, overwhelmed by her emotions. Amanda took her hand.

"What is it, Huin?" she said softly.

Tears were coming down Huin's delicate cheeks. "I am going to a new home. I am going to Australia," she said. "I have just been given the news!" Amanda hugged her for a long time. As my eyes misted over with emotion I snuck a glance at Mr. Phoc, but he just stood there, looking numb.

In Kuala Lumpur we finally got word about Don. The news was surprising.

"He didn't have appendicitis at all," said my mother. "He

had a rare strain of salmonella—food poisoning. The symptoms are almost identical to appendicitis."

"Is he all right?"

"Sort of," said my mom.

"What does that mean?" I asked. "Is he still in the hospital?"

"No. It's embarrassing," she said, "but Don had an accident. We checked him out of the hospital last week, and he went swimming with some friends. They were diving, and well, Don landed wrong. He broke his shoulder."

"Broke his shoulder? You're kidding."

"I'm afraid not. He won't be able to bike until you guys get back to California."

"Where is Don now?" I asked.

"He's on his way to Washington, to see Scott Patton at HOPE and *National Geographic*. He's going to help Scott with PR for your trip."

In other calls, Laura told me she was arranging a few days alone for us in San Francisco when I arrived in September, and I learned that HOPE was about to fire its public relations firm for being ineffective. We also received a special delivery telegram from Scott Patton announcing that *People* had published our article. Eight million people were reading about the World Bike for HOPE. *Eight million people!* I could hardly believe it.

Pedaling the four hundred kilometers to Singapore was a repeat of previous days on the Malaysian road, except that Jim and I were more edgy than ever. The major source of frustration was the traffic. Cars and trucks sped by in continuous lines that created powerful drafts. Columns of cars coming from the opposite direction created headwinds that cut down our speed by almost 25 percent. Then, just as we got frustrated, a line of cars coming our way would suddenly cut off the headwind and blow us forward on a tailwind. We felt like Ping-Pong balls.

On August 7, twenty-six days after leaving Bangkok, we crossed a wide causeway over the Singapore Straits and entered a huge enclosure dripping with dozens of lion-crested Singapore flags. Two officers pulled us over from a row of customs booths lined up like a platoon of twenty-four-hour photo stands.

"You are dirty," said one of the officers in a uniform with creases as sharp as knives.

"You have very long hair," said the other man, who scrutinized our passports. Singapore customs are legendary for turning away foreigners who did not conform to their strict code of hair length, cleanliness, and attire. Handing the man our Chinese-language articles from Kualu Lumpur we promised to take a bath as soon as possible.

"Please take a bath very soon," said one of the men. He stamped our passports and waved us through.

Singapore is like an architect's scale model of a sterile, futuristic community where every tree is evenly spaced and nothing is older than brand-new. The buildings rise like file cabinets and butcher blocks between manicured grassy stretches and concrete parks. Large fines are levied for dropping a toothpick or a chewed piece of gum in the street. Tossing a cigarette butt can cost as much as five hundred dollars in fines. Police participating in the government's latest "courtesy campaign" are directed to be friendly when giving tickets for littering. But if the offender isn't polite in return, there are also fines for being discourteous.

Singapore was a great disappointment. Before World War II it had a reputation as one of Britain's most pleasant colonial cities. Imperialists in white pith hats had once strolled through streets lined with bungalows, ornate hotels, and whitewashed shops. Near the docks had been a huge, twisting Chinatown that rivaled parts of prewar Shanghai for intrigue, mystery, poverty, and commerce. But almost none of this romance remains today. In the zeal to purify this little island, Singapore's history has been literally paved over. The result is a cold, sterile city, a distortion of the West that made us very uncomfortable.

Pedaling through the faceless canyons of steel and glass, we found, appropriately enough, another McDonald's. But the crowd in the restaurant seemed oddly subdued. Someone behind the counter told us that everyone was waiting for the American celebrities to arrive, the same group we had met in Kuala Lumpur. "They are an hour late," said an elderly Chinese man sipping on a shake. "It is very rude. We do not like rude people in Singapore."

After hamburgers at McDonald's, Jim and I rode to the American Express office to get our mail and to check on airline reservations to Borneo. The American Express office is in the center of Singapore's shopping district, a place overflowing with tourists on shopping sprees. Every year hundreds of thousands of tourists crowd street after sterile street in search of bargains on just about everything made in Japan—cameras, calculators, stereos, watches, and video machines. In the free port of Singapore, merchants can sell these things for as little as half their usual price.

At the American Express office we were pleased to discover that at least one element of colonial Singapore still existed. In a rack of brochures was a pamphlet on the famous Raffles Hotel, where Kipling and Maugham both stayed and where the Singapore sling was invented around the turn of the century.

"We've got to stay there," said Jim, adding that he was sick of the cheap, spare Chinese hotels that we had been staying in for most of the last twenty-six days.

"Jim, it's got to be way over our budget," I said.

"I don't care," he said. "I'll pay for it with my own money. I mean, this is the *Raffles!*"

Staying at the Raffles fulfilled our fantasies of a tropical paradise, even if it was slightly run-down. All of our frustrations and petty arguments were forgotten there. On a veranda overlooking lazy palms and banana trees, with wooden-bladed ceiling fans whirring, we ate roast duck and drank beer as the steady fugues of Bach filtered through the warmish night. A Chinese in tails and spats played a polished Steinway grand piano. After supper we retired to the billiards room for a brandy and bought thick cigars to have a smoke at the Long Bar, birthplace of the Singapore sling. It was a glorious evening of romance and fantasy that reminded me of the early days of the trip, when everything had seemed like a wonderful adventure.

Jim and I stayed in Singapore for two days, enjoying the colonial fantasy world and getting a good rest. We only strayed twice from the Raffles, once to meet with the press at the U.S. embassy, and once to go shopping. I bought a Casio calculator watch with three alarms and a game for nineteen dollars. Jim grumbled about having to leave the Raffles and bought nothing.

9. Pacific Doldrums

After a quick nighttime flight from Singapore, Jim and I arrived at the Kuching airport, a dumpy, one-room terminal surrounded by the thick jungle of northeastern Borneo. We knew almost nothing about Kuching, or about Borneo. Like Thailand and Malaysia, Borneo was never seriously researched in Washington as a place to bike. We weren't even sure if good roads existed. On a map the huge island (Borneo is the second largest island in the world after Greenland) is shaped like the profile of a trimmed turkey, with Kuching in its rear. Jim and I planned to bicycle across the back and up the neck of the island, along its northern coast to a city called Kota Kinabalu. It was a twelve-hundred-kilometer route through dense, virginal rain forest broken occasionally by jungle towns with names like Simang-gang, Sibu, and Miri. These rain forests were the homes of the Dayak and Iban tribes, who lived in villages of longhouses and, until recently, chopped off the heads of people they didn't like. Tourist brochures told of headhunter longhouses that still had the dried skulls of tribal enemies rattling in the rafters.

On our first morning in Kuching, we woke up to a river city of fading colonial colonnades and sprawling bungalows stained by decades of jungle sweat. It reminded me of descriptions in Conrad novels of lazy, humid, isolated towns where white settlers in sweat-drenched safari suits drank bad whiskey, cussed at natives, and gathered raw materials for far away companies in the West. But this older Kuching existed in the shadows of a newer Kuching, a Kuching built on the wealth of North Borneo's oil boom. It is filled with contemporary mosques, shopping arcades, air-conditioned hotels and offices, and modern dock facilities. Boxy sedans, cassette players, and televisions poured in from Japan, and plastic toys and Western-style clothing poured in from Taiwan and South Korea. Like the Malaysian mainland, north Borneo was impressively modern, an area firmly in the ranks of the developing world.

Modern Kuching was founded in 1839 during the heady days of colonialism, when a man could leave England as a petty wage earner and wind up being a king. In Kuching's case, the petty wage earner was an agent of the East India Company named James Brookes. When Brookes helped the Sultan of Borneo put down a revolt in Sarawak, the Englishman was awarded suzerainty over the formerly rebellious state. Brookes set himself up as the White Rajah in Kuching and began a jungle dynasty that ruled the country for over one hundred years, until the Japanese invaded in 1942.

We stayed in Kuching three days, resting and trying to figure out the feasibility of biking across Borneo. The initial information was discouraging. Maps at the Sarawak Lands and Surveys office showed a nice road colored red stretching almost the entire route between Kuching and Kota Kinabalu, but local Kuchingians told us that the maps were wrong. In several places, they said, the road was next to nonexistent, although they disagreed as to exactly where those places were. Apparently, North Borneo had never felt a strong need for roads, because the intricate system of rivers on the island worked much better as a transportation system. "On Borneo, rivers are our highways," said the Chinese manager of our hotel. "The jungle is too thick to make good roads."

"Will we be able to bike across Borneo?" we asked.

The manager shrugged. "I do not know," he said. "But you may try, if you wish."

On our last night in Kuching, Jim and I had dinner in a fast-food place called American Fried Chicken. A sophisticated replica of an American franchise, it had logos, a secret recipe for the chicken, and a jingle printed on everything. Just as Mc-Donald's says, "You deserve a break today," or Kentucky Fried Chicken claims, "It's finger-lickin' good," American Fried Chicken boasted, "It's makes your lip watering."

"It's sure does makes *my* lip watering," said Jim as he bit into a drumstick.

Later that night, after a couple of beers at a Chinese bar, I took a walk through the deserted, foggy, Conradian streets of old Kuching. It was a spooky place, a great set for a thriller starring William Powell or Humphrey Bogart. I could almost imagine Bogey in a trenchcoat leaning up against one of the thick plaster columns, blowing out a cloud of cigarette smoke. Thinking about thrillers, I suddenly realized that someone was following me in the empty streets. Turning quickly, I saw the lithe figure of a Dayak woman in a thin dress and blouse. "Good evening," she said. "Are you American or British?"

"American," I said, thinking this woman was far too beautiful for a whore. She asked me what I was doing in Kuching when I suddenly recoiled. *This was not a woman.* The Dayak realized that I had seen his trick, but he smiled anyway. "Do you do things with boys like me?" he asked seductively. I fought an impulse to flee. Instead I shook my head and walked slowly away, slipping through the damp, sweating streets of Kuching toward the safety of our hotel.

Jim and I left Kuching with a sense of frustration mingled with deep weariness. It seemed likely, from the information we had gathered, that our route was unbikable. This news was just one more item in the long series of logistical hassles. As we pedaled past a neighborhood of bungalows, the rain forest quickly closed in an unbroken chain of razor-edged ferns, shrubs, and overhanging moss. Again we were bombarded by the catcalls and screeches we had heard in Thailand and Malaysia. Here and there, green hills and ridges of limestone poked through the canopy of treetops. When the oceans covered much of Borneo ten thousand years ago, these were coral reefs. The pavement often took us straight up these hills with no switchbacks. A few of the grades were ridiculous. In the sweltering heat, we began to lose our tempers as our skin became caked in sweat and dust. Prickly heat burst in pinpricks on our scalps and flies attacked us by the dozens.

Few houses or people appeared on the road, and very few

cars or trucks. The buildings we did see were dark, wooden houses stuffed with racks of Coca-Cola and outland gear. Close to lunchtime, Jim hit a pothole and snapped three spokes just a few meters from one of these outback shops. We bought sodas, doused our sweaty heads under cups of cold well water, and pulled out our tape players. Jim had bought a tape player in Bangkok, and I still had my Aiwa from Washington. We had been listening to these machines frequently since coming to Malaysia, slipping on the headphones at every opportunity.

The rest of that day and the next were repeats of our earlier Malaysian routine. We biked hard through the hot jungles, slept at night in Chinese hotels, and continued to amaze waiters at restaurants with our appetites. Then, on our third day, the pavement suddenly ended ten kilometers beyond the city of Simanggang. Large, crushed rocks and hard-packed earth replaced the asphalt. We thought about turning back but decided to go on, hoping the road would improve. But we were not optimistic. The rocky road slowed us down to about three-quarters our usual speed and the rocks gouged our deteriorating tires. That night, feeling tired and angry, we set up a sloppy camp beside the road. It seemed unfair that the road had forced us to camp when we could have been in a hotel sipping beers and eating lots of food.

The next day, the road deteriorated even further. The hard earth softened, and the gravel mixed with swampy mud. It was clear that this road was unbikable. "It is foolish for you to bicycle from this place," an old Dayak told us in the next big town, called Sarikei. He suggested that we travel by riverboat. "The rivers are our highways," he said with a grin. I think he was amused at two Americans trying to bike across Borneo.

"Do the roads ever get better?" Jim asked.

"I do not know," said the Dayak, a tiny, Polynesian-looking man with wrinkled skin. "Why not you take boat to Sibu and try biking from there?" Looking at our maps, we saw that Sibu was the next major city to the east. A river called Batang Rajang connected Sarikei with Sibu.

The "express boat" to Sibu was a long, sleek vessel shaped like a cigar cut in half down the middle and bolted to a barge. The cabin was air-conditioned, but we established ourselves on the roof where our bikes were lashed down along with several crates and bundles. For three hours we swerved around curves of overhanging jungle, disturbing huge egrets and raising screeches from the foliage. The boat cut a white, flaring wake through the muddy, khaki-colored water. Occasionally we passed villages of shabby huts raised on stilts. Women in ragged sarongs washed tin pans and clothing in the filthy river. Naked children splashed and played in the water. Strings of native longboats with old Johnson outboards rocked and bobbed as our wake swelled against the village docks. A few of the huts had "garages" for their boats. They were roofed platforms on stilts with gangplanks lowered into the river. At one point we passed massive islands of floating logs being dragged by tugs.

Sibu, like Kuching, was a mix of an old colonial jungle town and a bustling, oil-rich pocket of modern buildings, Japanese sedans, and Western-style clothing. But unlike Kuching, Sibu had no real roads leading out of the city. The commerce of the city was completely dependent on the river and on air transport. Deciding that our effort to bike on Borneo was growing futile, we decided to try one more spot to the east before giving up and heading on to the Philippines. Riding out to the small airport at Sibu, we took a Fokker prop plane to Miri, the next big city to the east.

In Miri, the roads were as bad as in Sibu. We probably could have tried to slog it out on the wretched jungle roads, but it seemed pointless. But we did have four more days left on the big island, according to our schedule with HOPE. Since neither of us felt like rushing to the Philippines to bike again, we decided to use our four days to take a vacation.

"I'd like to get out and see what the rain forest is like," said Jim. "We've been biking through these forests since Bangkok and have never really taken the time to look at them."

"What did you have in mind?" I asked. He pulled out a brochure on a place called the Niah National Park. According to the brochure, Niah was a large rain forest preserve. It was also the site of a major archeological dig, where the remains of men living here forty thousand years ago were discovered in a huge complex of caves.

"This place is only a few kilometers south of here," said Jim, "and they have a hostel we can stay in."

Leaving our bikes in a hotel, Jim and I left for Niah that afternoon. For supplies, we took a tub of American Fried Chicken, a case of Carlsberg beer, a deck of cards, and several paperbacks. Our prime goal at Niah was to relax and try to forget about schedules, bad roads, and biking.

A bus took us south about ten kilometers to the town of Batu

Niah, where a longboat with a Johnson outboard motor ran us down a rust-colored river to a dock below a neat bungalow with a sign out front: Niah National Park Visitors Hostel. A yellow dog ran down and licked our ankles. A large hornbill with a yellow throat was strutting proudly on the veranda of the hostel, looking like the Froot Loops bird with a tan beak. It was a comfortable spot with all the attributes of a tropical paradise.

We paid a native housekeeper two Malaysian dollars a night per person for three nights and were provided bunks in a small dorm room. In the hostel was a large kitchen and a sitting room filled with posters identifying butterfly species, trees, reptiles, and birds. Once we were settled in, Jim stopped to compare the bird charts with his *Birds of Borneo.* I sat in a deep wicker chair on the veranda and watched the sun set in a blaze of pinkish hues over the jungle. This was primeval rain forest, a dark, canopied, misty jungle full of large lizards, buzzing insects, phosphorescent butterflies, oozing mud, and birds of stunning colors. Absorbed in the beauty of the sunset over the trees, I felt an immense sense of calm settle over me. I stood up and left the veranda to take a slow walk through the jungle. Following a park path marked in blue, I felt the warm, dark mists engulf me. With the darkening sky filling with cackles and screeches, I breathed in a strong odor of decay. Walking faster, I felt the savage power of the forest. Like the deserts of Africa, this was a place untouched by human hands, an ancient, wild, invigorating place where survival was at a fundamental level of life and death. Slipping against the moist path, I walked even faster until I broke into a run. In the dusky forest, trees and outcrops of rock passed in phantom shadows, but I kept running, reveling in the primitive vitality of the jungle. It was a glorious, fantastic feeling to feel my heart pounding, my lungs working hard, and my sweaty, dirty legs tearing along the trail.

Finally, when the woods were almost dark, I fell exhausted on a fallen log. I wondered how far I had run but decided that I didn't care. I felt close to the untamed pulse of this place and almost hoped I was lost so I would never have to leave. I could stay here and never have to face going home. In some ways I dreaded going home almost as much as I yearned for it. I dreaded facing my friends, parents, and even Laura, because I wasn't sure if they would be the same people I had known before. I felt caught between two worlds—the world of America, of my past, and some other world that was not yet clearly defined. It was a world where innocence is unacceptable, a place of extreme contrasts, of rich and poor, of privilege and oppression, of good and evil. It was a world that confused me, because I wasn't sure where I fit in.

Five days after arriving at Niah, Jim and I touched down in Manila. Neither of us was anxious to face another country. In the early days, beginning a new journey had been an exciting moment. Now we dreaded having to acclimate ourselves once again to a new culture. We had already biked close to 15,000 kilometers (9,000 miles) in fifteen countries. In 305 days, we had biked on four continents, across three deserts, and over four mountain ranges. We had fixed 389 flat tires and had set up and taken down the tents over two hundred times.

Landing in Manila, we feared that the possibilities for bicycling might be as limited as they were on Borneo. As a nation of islands, the Philippines was not a likely spot to find a continuous, satisfying route. But, as always, we would try.

With a typhoon churning in the South China Sea, Manila was drenched in ash-gray rains. A jeepney taxi drove us and our battered bikes downtown from the Manila International Airport. (Just before leaving Borneo, I had shattered my derailleur, so we were unable to bike into town.) Like trucks in Pakistan, the vehicle was painted in elaborate, colorful designs and trimmed with glittering plastic strips and decals. Six chrome horses were attached to its hood. Our driver, his teeth clenched on a cheroot, started punching a switchboard of different horn squawks and squeals as we turned into the snarled traffic leading into Manila. His noise joined in a fray of colorful jeepneys, some of them with eight or ten chrome horses on their hoods.

Following Manila Bay, we drove along Dewey Boulevard, named after the American admiral who destroyed the Spanish fleet defending Manila in 1898. On the right side of the road, across from the bay, was a neighborhood that reminded me of poor areas in Southern California. Rows of dilapidated, neo-Spanish houses lined streets filled with palm trees and concrete row shops of bars and discount stores. Everyone wore American T-shirts—Property of the L.A. Rams, Close-Up Toothpaste, and "Gee, Your Hair Smells Terrific!"

On the left side of Dewey, our driver pointed out a large, modernistic auditorium. "Imelda did that," he said.

"Imelda?" I said. "Who is Imelda?"

"The wife of Marcos," he said with a sneer. "She build the Philippine Arts Center. It cost sixty million dollars. Can you believe it?" The driver blew out a choking cloud of cheroot smoke. "Imelda is ruining the Philippines."

Imelda Marcos was the Philippines' Minister of Redevelopment and the wife of President Ferdinand Marcos. In the short time we were in Manila, we heard her name mentioned everywhere. People talked about the billion-dollar monorail system under construction. "*That* was Imelda," they said. They talked about the bulldozers that came one day to move an entire slum so that a park could be built with lawns and flowers. "*That* was Imelda," said the people. One man in the YMCA where we stayed compared Imelda to the sister-in-law of South Vietnam's former Premier Ngo Dinh Diem, a woman notorious in Southeast Asian history for her insensitivity and lavish tastes.

Manila was a city on the edge of discontent. We could feel the energy building in the way people talked. Marcos had been in power for sixteen years, presiding over the gradual demise of democracy in the Philippines. After being a dictator for a decade and doing little to mitigate the poverty and high unemployment in the islands, he and his wife were unpopular with just about everyone we met—waiters at restaurants, taxi drivers, students, and even Philippine staffers at the U.S. embassy. But this unpopularity had not yet ballooned into any sort of active opposition in the city, partly because Marcos was adept at squashing overt opposition, and partly because the people were not yet upset enough to turn to violence. "We want Marcos to give up peacefully," a jeepney driver told me.

Earlier in the trip, this talk would have stirred my journalistic impulses. I would have actively sought out this story of discontent, taping interviews on my microcassette recorder and chasing down facts at the American library in Manila. I would have written a "Letter from Manila" for the *Kansas City Star*. But I was too exhausted. I had reached a saturation point on this journey and just couldn't take anymore. Besides, we had another job to get done. Somehow, Jim and I had to muster the energy to bicycle in the Philippines.

That first night in the city, we ate dinner at a Shakey's pizza parlor. Both of us were quiet and pensive as we munched on a large deluxe pizza. Pushed to one side of the table was our map of the Philippines, a map we were reluctant even to look at.

On the way home that night, the trip nearly ended for me.

After pizza, Jim and I slowly strolled through the damp, hot streets of Manila, traveling through an elegant hotel district filled with men and women in evening wear. We passed a large Catholic cathedral and then several ponderous federal buildings constructed during the Roosevelt administration in the 1930s, when the Philippines was an American colony. Just a few meters from the YMCA, a belt of rain suddenly crashed down from the sky, pouring water over the streets. We ducked low to run for the Y building. Suddenly my legs slipped out from under me on the oily wet pavement. I went down hard on the asphalt, landing on my hand. A bolt of pain shot up my arm. Standing up, I was sure that I had broken it.

"Shit," said Jim. "That's all we need."

The next morning an X ray at the Makati Medical Center in Manila told me that I had a hairline fracture in the heel of my hand. A young doctor named Antonio Riviera told me I would have to wear a cast for a couple of weeks. I groaned and asked him about bicycling.

"You want to bicycle?" he asked.

"I suppose I do," I answered.

"Then hold out your hand. The broken one."

He asked me to show him how I grasped my handlebars, and told me that he could construct a fiberglass cast that would fit onto my bars. But he warned me to be careful. "You have only a hairline fracture," he said, "but you could hurt it much worse if you are not cautious."

Again we had logistical difficulties with organizing a decent route. Just as we were trying to deal with the difficulties of island hopping, the typhoon blowing in from the South China Sea began intensifying over the northern half of the country. Towns north of Manila were warned on the radio and in the newspapers to haul their boats onto shore and to prepare for a serious storm. The typhoon effectively eliminated the main island of Luzon from our consideration. Mindanao, the large island near Borneo in the southern Philippines, was also ruled out by the U.S. embassy. They had issued a travel warning to American citizens because of agitation by Communist guerrillas based there. With all of these problems, Jim and I ended up choosing a route based on the schedule of ferry ships traveling to the central islands. We were told that the next ship out was to the island of Negros, about six hundred kilometers to the south of Manila Bay. From Negros we would again check shipping schedules and take ferries to other islands in the area.

On August 26, Jim and I bought two second-class berths on the *Santa María*, a large steamer with two open decks of canvas bunks divided into sections for men, women, and families. We locked our bikes and gear against two bunks in the rear of the upper floor, next to a speaker playing American Top 40 songs from seven A.M. to ten P.M. It was a hot, steamy ride with babies crying, Barry Manilow blasting, and soggy food in a small dining room. Rain fell for most of the trip, but it didn't cool the heavy air on the sleeping decks. I made an effort to write by setting up my typewriter on my bunk, but it was too hot. I eventually discovered a crew's dining room where the ship's officers let me work. But the work was uninspired. When the crew turned on a videocassette of *Patton*, I gave up on writing to watch George C. Scott rant and rave in the helmet and jodhpurs of General Patton. I smiled, remembering the SHO in Pakistan. He must have seen this movie, because he had had the swagger down just right.

For four days we biked on Negros, almost circling the peanut-shaped island from Bacolod City to San Carlos. The time went by quickly in a progression of soda breaks, nights in bungalow hotels, and boredom. Despite Dr. Riviera's skill, it was difficult biking with a cast on my hand. I could rest the cast on the top bars, but could not really use the hand to steer or operate the brakes. Any major bumps or gyrations felt like somebody was squeezing my hand with pliers. The cast itself was also frustrating. I couldn't write longhand, because the fiberglass had been set wide for biking. Even worse, the humid, steamy climate in the Philippines caused my arm to sweat inside the cast. Little droplets trickled and itched under the hard surface. I couldn't wait to get the cast off back in Manila.

One diversion on Negros was the scenery. Beautiful vistas of sugarcane fields stretched inland, punctuated by small hills rising like bumps in the distance. Every few kilometers the fields were interrupted by small, neat villages and roadside bungalows. The people here were generally poor, but not nearly as poor as people we had seen in South Asia. They seemed well fed and clothed, although some strong strains of the Third World existed in pockets here and there. Occasionally, piles of garbage attracted huge swarms of flies, and many of the shacks had no electricity or ready sources of water. But the people were friendly. Many of them made an effort to chat with us in surprisingly good English. As in Manila, they mostly talked about politics and their dislike of Marcos, although the atmosphere was much calmer than in the capital city. Feeling generally apathetic, we were polite but didn't say much.

After circling most of Negros, we arranged to take a ferry to the nearby island of Cebu. On our last night on Negros Jim and I met three fifteen-year-old school girls in the town of San Carlos. They wanted to be our pen pals. The girls found us sipping San Miguel beers on the porch of a small boarding house and began asking questions about California. They asked about the beaches, about Hollywood, and about rock stars like Tom Petty and Michael Jackson.

"You are asking so many questions!" Jim finally said. The girls giggled and told us that they never met Americans before. "We have only seen Americans on TV," they said. Then one of them showed us a creased photo of a small Philippine woman standing next to a large blond man in a Lazy Boy–style chair. "This is Esmelda," said one of the girls. "She is my cousin living in Los Angeles."

"We all want to marry Americans," said Esmelda's cousin, "and live in California." The girls were blushing now. "You can be our pen pals," said one of them, "and later you can pick one of us you like, and maybe we could get married." She whispered the last words as the girls giggled.

The next morning, as we biked toward the ferry dock in San Carlos, Jim and I were surprised to find a huge metal globe placed like a statue in the city square. Painted blue and green, it was about the height of a person sitting on someone else's shoulders. Climbing off my bike, I stood back to stare at the world. Had we really traveled most of the way around it? Stepping forward, I put a finger on the cold metal at Washington, D.C. Tracing an invisible line with my finger, I walked in a circle, passing through Europe, the Middle East, South Asia, Southeast Asia, Borneo and the Philippines. Then I traced a line from the Philippines along the globe to Japan. I was anxious to get to Japan, because my parents and Don were planning to fly over to greet us in Osaka. We were also planning a large-scale press blitz for HOPE in anticipation of the U.S. publicity effort. This would be the beginning of our big campaign, the one we had been planning for months. From Japan I traced a line across the wide Pacific to San Francisco, where we would land in just twenty-three days. That seemed impossible. Only twenty-three days? From San Francisco I traced my finger across the States to New York City, where Laura was just about to get home from work.

It took an hour for our ferry to chug across the Tanon Strait between Negros and Cebu. Pulling into the city of Toledo, we stopped for omelets in a greasy diner called Dave and Eve's Luncheonette. The last thing we felt like doing was bicycling. Pulling out our maps, we decided to take a shortcut. Instead of biking all the way around the island, which is shaped like a long finger, we decided to cut straight across from Toledo to Cebu City, the Philippines' second largest city. From Cebu City we would take a boat back to Manila.

Leaving Toledo, we climbed a series of abrupt hills and entered another steamy tropical forest. Neat grass huts with woven straw walls and thatched roofs appeared on shelves cut into the hills. Now and then we passed a cluster of huts selling sodas and snacks. At one store a boy was playing basketball against a bamboo backboard. He got Jim to play him one on one and soundly beat him in five straight points.

About noon, when it was clear that we would make Cebu City by the end of the day, we realized that this was our last day biking in the Third World. The sudden realization made us both slow down and take a last look at the huts, the jungle, and the occasional water buffalo as we pedaled up and down the jungle hills. I looked at the flat, dark faces of the people and at the makeshift churches and colorful trucks roaring by. I felt the calm serenity of this backwoods pocket of the Third World. As in the forest at Niah, I had the sense that we were far away from the rest of the world. In a strange way, I felt almost comfortable here.

I looked down at my bike. After ten months on the road, the blue paint that had been so shiny and new in Washington was scratched and battered. The handlebar tape was worn to tatters. The teeth on my cogs were worn down. My panniers were faded to a pinkish red, and the racks were broken and splinted at every joint. The equipment secured to my racks was worn and bleached by the sun. The tent and sleeping bag were covered with patches, my clothes were threadbare, my cameras and tape player were clogged with dust, and my helmet was battered and permanently dirty. My bike bottles were still wrapped in dirty denim from Sudan, the bandanas I bought in

India were ripped and filthy, and my Nepalese flip-flops, tucked under a frazzled bungee, were almost worn through with walking.

Next I looked at myself. Like my gear, I was a bit battered. Besides a broken hand, I had brown skin covered with tiny scratches and splotches of dirt. My shorts and shoes were bleached and torn. My stomach was very flat on the outside and still irregular on the inside. But my body was stronger than it had ever been in my whole life. This made me feel good.

Pedaling closer and closer to Cebu City, I realized that a chapter of the trip—and a chapter of my life—was closing. Very soon I would be seeing firsthand the shining city on the hill called America. Since Nepal we had gradually been making this journey back to the West. Step by step we had come from the intense poverty of India. Thailand and Malaysia had been steps up in terms of prosperity and expectations. In a couple of days, Japan would continue this progression as a prelude to America. In a few days, I would be going home.

I wondered what I would find.

10. Nippon

The international arrivals section in Osaka International Airport was separated from the visitors' waiting area by two long rooms and two doorways guarded by policemen in white gloves and spats. But none of this stopped my mother from forcing her way in to meet her son. A small phalanx of flustered Japanese guards raced after her, trying in their polite way to say she was in a restricted area. "David!" she screamed, turning several heads in the busy customs room. "Is it really you?" She ran to me, grabbed me, and burst out crying. "I'm sorry about the crying," she said, "but it's been so long." The Japanese, who have a deep regard for the love between a mother and son, stood back respectfully as I patted my mom lightly on the back and told her that it was true. Her boy was here, and he was all right.

Once through customs, we were intercepted again, this time by Japanese reporters. As we wheeled our bikes out into the visitors' area, a half-dozen photographers punched whirring motor drives and flashed strobes in our faces. Reporters asked questions about our journey. Hovering in the background was Don, with a sling for his broken shoulder. "How yah doin', bro?" I asked, glad to see him. He looked healthy despite the arm, and had put some weight on his thin frame. In a turtleneck, cords, and round, wire-rim glasses, he looked like the young photographer from Maine who had come down to Washington, D.C., ten months earlier to join the trip. I wondered if I would look that normal after a few weeks back in the States.

It is an old truism about the Japanese that when they want to do something, they do it with all their heart and soul. The Japanese are also said to be absolutely loyal to their friends. In our case these two maxims coalesced in the person of a Japanese woman named Atsuko Ise Sugahara. She had arranged for the reporters to meet us at the airport, which was the first step in her plan to boost us and Project HOPE in Japan.

Atsuko had befriended my parents when my father was a U.S. naval officer stationed in Sasebo during the mid-fifties. While my father was out to sea, Atsuko and my mother had traveled all over Japan. At that time she was a young woman living between two worlds. Before and during the war, she had been the daughter of an admiral in the Imperial Japanese Navy. Atsuko's great-uncle was Count Heihachiro Togo, the admiral who defeated the Russians in the Russo-Japanese War of 1904–5. She traced her family back twelve centuries to an ancestor who founded the Ise Shrine, one of the holiest places in the Shinto religion. As a teenager she had watched her home and neighborhood firebombed by American B-52s. After the war, with her family's fortunes ebbing, Atsuko married and became a piano instructor for the children of American officers in Sasebo. But she still retained her family name and her energy, which, as we would see, combined to form a one-woman public relations firm that mobilized what seemed to be the entire public apparatus of Nippon.

Jim and I met Atsuko in the five-star Royal Hotel in downtown Osaka. We were dirty and smelly after our ride to the Manila airport and two hours on the airplane, but Atsuko hugged us anyway. She was a short woman with delicate, beautiful features. It was hard to believe that she was almost fifty years old. "Welcome to Japan!" she repeated several times as we checked in. Because Atsuko was our guide, an immaculately dressed desk clerk, bell captain, and bellboy never questioned what two filthy, long-haired kids were doing in their expensive hotel. They didn't even protest when we wheeled our dirty bikes across the elegant lobby toward the elevators.

In my room a complimentary *Yukata* robe was folded neatly with bath salts on top of a deep Japanese bath. Near the door was a panel of controls—a timer to regulate a heating lamp in the ceiling, a digital dial to tune in Japanese radio stations, and a buzzer to summon the maid in charge of our floor. The room had a silent air conditioner, a color TV, and three telephones. One of them was in the bathroom. English-language magazines, travel guides, and newspapers were stacked on a table by the sliding glass door that led off to a small balcony. This was an intensely civilized room that made even the New Amirin in Bangkok look almost primitive. I felt like a mountain man returning to civilization after years of living in the dirt and squalor of the wilderness.

Over the next five days, Atsuko told us, we would be interviewed by every paper, radio station, and TV station in Osaka. We would receive a VIP tour of the main SunTour plant (SunTour was the company that manufactured our derailleurs, brakes, and gearing). We would also have an audience with the mayor of Osaka, see the Osaka castle, visit the old capital city of Kyoto via the bullet train, and receive an honorary membership in the Japanese Adventure Cycling Club.

About one A.M. that night, my father arrived from America. He looked older than I remembered him. At fifty-two, his face was tired and his hair was grayer. His plain brown architect's suit was rumpled after the long flight. In his hand was a small, worn briefcase with HED stamped in the corner. I felt awkward about how to greet my dad, because I owed him so much. Without him the trip would not have been possible. Several times he had wired me money when I got low on dollars. He had also encouraged me to keep going during the planning stages in Washington, when it seemed as though the trip would never get off the ground. I reached out my hand to shake his, but he took it and pulled me into a hug.

Late that night I called Laura on my bathroom phone as I soaked in the hot water of the tub. We talked about Japan, a weekend she had spent on the Jersey shore, and my arrival in San Francisco. We were planning to spend a couple of days alone in a cabin outside of the city before announcing our "official" arrival in the States.

The next morning, we began a whirlwind public relations tour through Osaka. Unfortunately, we spent so much time in taxis and in front of microphones that we hardly got a chance to see the city. But we still saw enough to be overwhelmed by Japan and the Japanese. After nine months in the Third World, the streets of Osaka were refreshingly familiar. Everyone wore Western clothes, drove cars, used sit-down toilets, liked hamburgers, and owned televisions. We could place phone calls to just about anywhere in the world from a phone booth on the street. Everything seemed absurdly easy. Elevators whisked us up tall buildings and vending machines produced Cokes and snacks for just a few hundred yen. Machines were available to shine shoes, direct traffic, tell fortunes, and instantly cook any sort of food. It was a society designed for maximum convenience and efficiency.

But in Japan these familiar surroundings seemed slightly distorted. First of all, everything in Osaka was too small. The people themselves were tiny. Men came up to my neck, and women to my chest. Cameras were tiny, stereos were tiny, roads were alleys, and shops were closets. Osaka was also too clean, especially after the shabby, dirty villages and cities of the Third World. Cab drivers wore clean white gloves, every sign was freshly painted, cars were undented and scrubbed clean, and hardly a cigarette butt scarred the spotless roads and sidewalks. No sidewalk vendors hawked vegetables or live chickens or tin pots from push stalls, and no cyclists on clunky one-speeds clogged the streets.

But Osaka had avoided the sterility of a city like Singapore, a city that had taken the Western penchant for organization and cleanliness and extended it to an obsessive extreme. In Osaka the glass and steel of the modern towers were tempered by shoji rice-paper screens in shop windows, paper lanterns and streamers, and origami figures decorating doorways and streets. The hard lines of concrete were trimmed with the gentle, up-turned edges of traditional Japanese architecture. Trees and bushes in parks were shaped like the mountains and hills we saw in Japanese prints. We also saw gardens everywhere. Our hotel had a small garden enclosed behind a high wall in back. The carefully constructed greens and browns, the small stream, the bonsai trees, and the small, stone lantern suggested a miniature mountain valley planted in the middle of the city.

When we pedaled out of Osaka, the mayor and his entire staff assembled on the steps of city hall to see us off. This was our last Osaka publicity event. They waved as Jim and I pedaled back and forth along the street for the cameras. Don stood with the mayor, waving. His shoulder would not be well enough for biking until we reached the States. He was going to join my mom and dad on a train trip around Japan.

Pulling out of the crowded suburbs of Osaka, we climbed a steep hill and suddenly biked into old Japan. Traditional wooden houses with shoji doorways and ribbed, ceramic-tiled roofs were perched here and there on steep, pine-covered ridges. This was a peaceful view, with quiet homes and gardens arranged like a scene in a woodblock print.

It was a hot, sweaty climb up the hill. Compact trucks and cars passed us, blowing an invisible cloud of effluents over the road. Part way up, it started to rain. We didn't know it at the time, but this was the beginning of another typhoon.

That night we slept in a youth hostel near the city of Nara, Japan's capital in the sixth, seventh, and eighth centuries A.D. After a simple dinner of fish and rice, we watched ourselves on the hostel's television leaving the mayor's office in Osaka. Fortunately, no one recognized us, and we didn't tell anyone who we were. We were tired of answering the same questions over and over again. "We're just biking around in Japan," was our line between Osaka and Tokyo.

Leaving Nara, we embarked on an eight-day, eight-hundred-kilometer ride along the Pacific underbelly of Honshu, Japan's main island. Tucked between a series of steep ridges and the pounding waves of the open sea, we followed Japan's National Highway One. It was by far the worst road we could have picked for cycling in Japan. Cutting through the industrial heartland of the nation, the route followed gigantic factory complexes in an almost continuous line from Osaka to Tokyo. The region produces everything from Yamaha pianos to Mitsubishi supertankers. Twenty-five million people live along this highway in one of the most densely populated areas in the world. Despite its left-side traffic, it reminded me of another Highway One, which runs up the Atlantic Coast in the States through industrial cities like Baltimore, Philadelphia, Newark, and New York City.

We picked up Highway One on our second day out of Osaka. Turning off a minor road, we found ourselves on a crowded, multilane stretch of asphalt that slowly rose on a causeway over the city of Nagoya, the home of Toyota. A murky gray drizzle and a steady wind washed over the road as the heavy traffic kicked up sprays of water and gritty dirt. Gradually the highway shoulder shrank to a space two feet wide between a concrete sidewall and the wall of traffic. It was a deadly place to be biking. With Jim in the lead, we bent low over our handlebars and pedaled hard, trying to keep our bikes from being sucked under semis or from crashing into the retaining wall. We pedaled and pedaled as water gradually soaked through our rain gear. Then, up ahead, we saw an exit ramp. Jim signaled to turn, but as I lifted my head to look at him my front wheel hit an inch-high steel reflector and, suddenly, I pitched right toward the traffic. Jerking left, I almost smashed into the concrete wall. But somehow I managed to hold on and steer a straight line between the wall and the traffic. Shaken, I followed Jim down the ramp and onto a road that followed Highway One under the causeway.

After Nagoya, the superhighway melded into the Tomei Expressway, and Highway One broke off to become a continuous strip of junk food joints, car dealers, newsstands, gas stations, and cheap clothing stores. Thousands of roadside vending machines sold everything from chicken rice soup to hard-core pornography. It was an intensely gray corridor of steel, neon, oil, and glass. Gray permeated everything—the road, the buildings, the people, and the sky. I started thinking about all the highway strips we had pedaled past around the world, and realized that a major difference among them was color. In the Third World, highway strips are dusty and brown. In the industrialized world, they are oily and gray.

One problem that we hadn't anticipated in Japan was the almost complete absence of English. It was the first country we had encountered since leaving Europe where English was not at least a second language. The Highway One strip was a jumble of Japanese characters—slashes and crosses and tic-tac-toe boards. Fortunately, Japan did use standard Arabic numerals, or we would have been completely lost. As it was, we had to memorize the Japanese characters for cities we were pedaling toward. Nagoya had three characters. One of them was a box with a cross on top. Nara had a cross with a skirt. Tokyo, appropriately, had two television screens on stands under roofs.

Jim and I rode like maniacs to get to Tokyo. Because of the publicity plans, we had only eight days to bike eight hundred kilometers. We pedaled at least one hundred kilometers a day. The only thing slowing us down were the frequent stoplights along the highway. Nothing destroys a biker's cadence more than frequent stoplights. Every ninety minutes, we stopped for a cup of coffee or a Coke, often in a vending machine rest stop. For lunch we ate everything from hamburgers to noodle soup, depending on what sort of fast-food we were in the mood for. About five, as the sun fell over the green mountains to the west, we would start asking people to point us to the nearest *ryokan* inn. *Ryokans* are usually family-run, offering small, traditional rooms walled in by sliding shoji doors. The floor is covered by woven tatami mats. A low Japanese table sits on the floor, along with a television and a traditional ikebana flower arrangement.

Immediately upon arriving at a *ryokan*, we would strip off our sweaty clothes and climb into the communal bath. These baths kept Jim and me sane through the morass of Highway One. The public tubs had scalding, scented water soothing to exhausted muscles. At first I always took a book with me to read while bathing, but a Japanese man bathing with us one night told me, "No book in bath! You relax here, clear mind, be at peace."

One evening, we turned off the road to try a country *ryokan* in the mountains. After a steep climb through a misty forest, we arrived at a large inn on top of a high knoll. Vast green forests stretched in all directions, a total contrast to Highway One. The large community bath had corner walls made of glass facing the forest. As the sun fell, we soaked in the bath and watched the fading twilight fall over the trees. Far away, the silvery light glimmered off Ise Bay, named for Atsuko's ancestor. After our baths, we heard a party going on at the end of the hall. Peeking into a small banquet room, we found two dozen Japanese men and women in their twenties and thirties dancing to American songs and drinking Asahi beer. "Come, join us," said an attractive woman with a long green dress. A skinny man with a broad smile handed us beers.

For two hours we danced and drank with the Japanese, taking turns singing American songs over a small PA system. The songs were from a kit that included the music of well-known songs without vocals. As the music to Beatles songs, Barry Manilow, and Rod Stewart played, we sang the words from lyrics included in the kit. Few of the revelers spoke English, but they could all sing the English lyrics. As everyone got drunk, some of the older women started trying to lift our kimonos. Having just come out of the bath house, we had nothing on underneath. "Sleep with you tonight?" asked one of the women, pointing at herself and four other women. We demurred, saying that we were too tired.

On the fourth day out of Osaka, the wind and rain of the gathering typhoon began to bend trees and crash the Pacific surf against the shore of southern Honshu. As we approached the city of Hamamatsu, almost halfway between Osaka and Tokyo, a gust of wind suddenly knocked us both into the slimy ditch along the road. Covered with muck sticking to our skin and clothes, we climbed back onto the bikes and struggled against a crosswind reminiscent of the winds in northern Spain. Finally we reached a large building on the edge of Hamamatsu. Rushing inside, we found ourselves in a place the size of a bowling alley. It was a *pachinko* hall. *Pachinko* is a sort of vertical pinball game played fanatically by the Japanese. Players near the front door stared for a moment at two mud-soaked men in helmets, phosphorescent vests, and riding tights. Then they returned to their games. No one bothered us as we relaxed and drank coffee from a vending machine. When we felt rested, we returned to the gale outside and managed to bike into the center of Hamamatsu, where we checked into a hotel, had a bath, and ate Big Macs for dinner.

The next morning we suited up to leave Hamamatsu but decided that the wind was too strong. We were told that the typhoon was now directly over southern Honshu. Just after breakfast, the electricity flickered and went out in the hotel. A few emergency lights went on, but it was very dark inside. Moving over by the door, we watched the rain splatter against the glass doors as it blew in great sheets across the city square outside. Through the rain and the gray, we could see pandemonium reigning outside. Civil defense police in white helmets were running about, heaving sandbags over the entrances to doors and trying to direct traffic and people dashing from building to building. Twirling red lights on emergency vehicles blinked in the darkness, and sirens wailed against the roaring wind.

For over twelve hours, the storm completely shut down the southern shore of Japan. No trains ran. Every computer was shut down. Phone lines were dead and electricity was out. The huge complex of modern technology that powered this area was a useless mass of components. It was remarkable how fragile this system was in the face of nature. For a brief time Hamamatsu was on a par with the little towns we had passed through in countries like Pakistan and Sudan. When I mentioned this to Jim, he disagreed. "I'd rather be in Pakistan," he said, "because Pakistan can function with or without electricity." He pointed at an electric vending machine shut down by the storm. "I can't even get a Coke in this place."

We woke up the next morning to the blue skies and fresh, clean atmosphere that always follow a typhoon. But as we pedaled out of Hamamatsu, the impact of the typhoon was all around us. Trees had crashed into houses and power lines. Cars had flipped into ditches. Road signs were bent and folded like omelets. At one point, Highway One was blocked by a twenty-foot avalanche of mud and tangled trees. On the Tenryu River floodplain, about ten kilometers east of Hamamatsu, civil defense crews were trying to clean up a carnage of smashed houses, cars, and garbage that had been deposited by the flooding river along its banks. Later in the day we read that twenty-three people had died in the typhoon and dozens more had been injured.

It took another four days to reach Tokyo. Each day we got more frustrated over the never-ending gray and the heavy traffic. This was the perfect impetus for Jim and me to escalate our petty fighting and arguments about schedules and pacing. One morning Jim got so angry over the schedule that he threatened to split off and head for the mountains. "Why am I doing this?" he kept asking. "We're bicycling through this industrial waste-land so we can get to a bunch of publicity bullshit on time. I came along on this trip to see *birds* and *trees*, not exhaust pipes and vending machines."

The last day into Tokyo was the worst of all. It began in Fuji City, one hundred miles southwest of the capital city. Normally we would have taken two days to pedal a hundred miles, but our public relations blitz was scheduled to begin the next day. Atsuko had arranged everything. At dawn we began riding through a progression of cities that suddenly ended when we began a steep climb up a series of switchbacks. It was a frustrating uphill, one of the worst of the trip. Jim compared it to the climbs into Jerusalem and up the Katmandu Pass in Nepal. Up and up we went as the industrial valley below spread out under a gray haze. Sweaty and irritated, we stopped at a scenic overlook and bought Cokes. A Japanese motorcyclist told us that the top was just a few meters away. He was wrong. We kept climbing and climbing. Then, finally, we came to an enclave of souvenir stands that marked the crest of Hakone Pass. In eight kilometers we had climbed twenty-five hundred feet.

Heading downhill, we raced around wooded switchbacks in Hakone National Park. At one point we saw Mount Fuji, pointing toward the sky in a perfect cone. At the bottom of the hill we stopped at a deep blue lake called Ashino Ko, where we found *another* steep uphill. Swearing loudly, we shifted down again into our smallest chainrings and went up and up to the top. When we stopped for a Coke, two Japanese men on bicycles approached us.

"Hello, you must be David and Jim," said the older of the two men. "We have come to escort you into Tokyo."

"What?" we said. "Who are you?"

"We are from the Japanese Adventure Cycling Club," explained the man, who introduced himself as Masao. The other man was Aki.

"How did you know we were here?" I asked.

"Atsuko Sugahara tell us your route," said Masao.

We still had ninety kilometers between us and Tokyo, so we started off immediately down another steep, winding hill. Masao and Aki, who had no equipment on their bikes, moved much faster than we did. I explained to them that we could not keep up their speed.

"I understand," said Masao. "Please forgive. I, too, bicycle with heavy equipment. Next year, I plan bicycling trip around world."

"Around the whole world?" I asked.

"Yes, I take five years, go sixty thousand miles."

"That's incredible," I said.

"How can we talk you out of it?" said Jim.

We shot down the far side of the Hakone Mountains and biked into the densest highway strip yet. Our guides continued to pedal much faster than our usual pace. But Jim and I, not wanting to appear less than heroes to these guys, fought to keep up. Traffic was heavy but steady. At twilight we stopped to don reflector vests and to bungee flashlights onto our rear loads. Calling my mother and Atsuko in their downtown hotel, I told them we would arrive about ten o'clock. Well after dark, the four of us finally pedaled into downtown Tokyo. Following our friends, who were steering us through a labyrinth of streets and highways, we passed under the brilliant, colorful neon lights that decorate the capital of Nippon. Pink, orange, green, yellow, and blue lights twinkled on the damp streets.

Finally, after one hundred miles and fifteen hours of biking, we pulled into the driveway of the Okura Hotel in central Tokyo. Atsuko, my mom and dad, and my brother ran outside to greet us, followed by three or four reporters and a couple of photographers. "Welcome to Tokyo," said Atsuko. Stepping off my bike, I could hardly stand, my legs ached so much. I turned wearily to face the press. It was then that I suddenly realized we were finished with the overseas portion of our journey. For months, I had been dreaming of this day. Like magic, my legs grew lighter and a broad grin appeared on my face. Could it be possible we were done? Had we really biked ten thousand miles? Were we really going home?

RETURN WEST

*State Highway 62 near
Twentynine Palms,
California.*

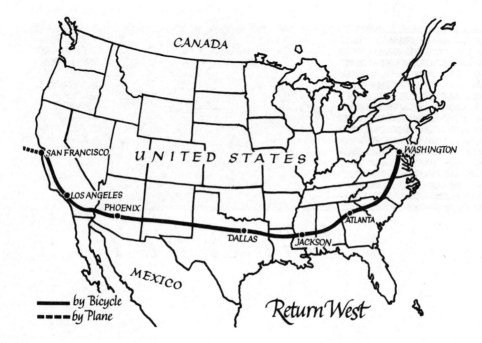

11. Across America: Stranger

My first glimpse of home in 296 days came as our Japan Air 747 arced downward in the sky over California's Napa Valley toward San Francisco Bay. Pressing my face against the airplane's tiny plastic window, I felt my eyes mist up. "There it is! America! Home!" I wrote quickly into my journal. "It's rainy and gray. The surf is breaking on the beach. I can see buildings, and cars, and highways flashing like gray ribbons. It's all still there!"

As I watched the earth slowly rise up to my window, thoughts raced through my head. I felt a mixture of fear and happiness. What did everything look like? What had changed? What was I going to eat first? I was also thinking about Laura, who had flown in from New York to meet me here.

Outside the airport terminal, Laura was waiting in a Mercury Marquis, a station wagon the size of a house. The car belonged to her mother, who lives just south of San Francisco. She jumped out of the car to hug me. Tears fell, and everything seemed all right, at least for the moment. "I've got something for you," she said, pulling a single yellow rose out of the car. This was my usual gift for her in Washington.

As we steered onto the Bayside Freeway, America rushed at us from all directions. To my left, rows of tidy houses reached up into the hills. On my right were factory complexes stretching to the blue waters of the bay. Huge cars zoomed past, filled with children in baseball caps and T-shirts. Billboards were everywhere, flashing a carnival of familiar images: a San Francisco Giant was slugging a ball, smiling teenagers were having a great time drinking Coke, and a nice-looking grandmother was reaching out to touch her little grandson (Call New York City for $2.43!). Then we turned around a broad curve and saw the gleaming white buildings of San Francisco and the tops of the Golden Gate bridge. Jim and I grinned, feeling over-whelmed to be home, to be back in America.

Downtown I marveled at the clean streets, the cable cars, and the white faces. Unlike Japan, America was sized to suit us; cars were big, people were big, and stores were big. We were taking Jim to a friend's house so that Laura and I could spend the next couple of days alone.

I realized that Jim and I were going to be separated after ten months together. It was an odd sensation. I was tired of being around him, but I knew I would miss him. As my cell mate over the last few months, he was the only one who could really understand what it meant to be home.

I spent the next two days with Laura in a small cabin at her mother's country club about forty-five minutes south of San Francisco. Most of the time was spent trying to sort out what had happened over the last year. Gradually we became com-fortable with each other. She told me about being lonely for months after I left. "I was in love with you," she said, "and then you left me. I could rationalize that you had to take this trip, but it didn't help. I compensated by working harder. I established a routine of working until eight or nine at night, then going home and reading or listening to music. I did this almost every day. I have learned to enjoy being by myself in my little apartment in New York. I can take a long bath, or read a magazine, or sleep, and no one is there to bother me."

"So what does that mean?" I asked.

"I don't know," she said. "I guess it means I'm feeling inde-pendent, but at the same time I want to get to know you again. I'll be honest. I dated other guys while you were gone, but none of them was like you."

"Is that good or bad?" I smiled. We were lying next to each other on a small bed in the cabin.

"It's good, you idiot," she said.

Laura and I resolved very little about our future plans together. That would come later. But we did get to see each other, to touch and sense each other, to hear each other breathe and sigh, to feel each other's skin and hair. After communicating through the tenuous means of international telephone lines or month-old letters, we spent most of our brief time together just holding each other. Our plans for the future would be decided over the next three months when we could talk for hours on the phone as I biked east.

During the two days I spent with Laura, as we tried to figure out our relationship, America continued to rush at me. In some ways I felt like Oliver Twist suddenly whisked into the glittering, polished world of Mr. Brownlow. I couldn't stop grinning as I rediscovered wonders like homogenized milk and FM radio. I had to make decisions like which television channel I would watch or whether I wanted to wash my clothes in a warm wash/cold rinse or a hot wash/warm rinse. I sipped good California wine and was sure that the taste was more intense than I remembered. I ate linguine, steak, hamburgers, shrimp scampi, and gooey cheese omelets. In fact, I ate everything I could get my hands on. I also rediscovered hair care products. On our first morning in the Menlo Park cabin, I found three plastic bottles in the shower—shampoo, creme rinse, and moisturizing conditioner. Then I heard Laura's blow drier snap on. After ten months of minimal bathing, I had completely forgotten about creme rinse and blow driers. Before the trip, I had sometimes spent fifteen or twenty minutes on my hair. On the trip, I washed it with bar soap, combed it, and didn't think about it again.

My weekend with Laura ended on Sunday night, September 26, when Laura caught the all-night "red-eye" flight back to New York and I moved into a hotel in downtown San Francisco. Scott Patton from HOPE met me in the lobby. He was a handsome man with a mustache and a playful smile. Jim and Don (just in from Tokyo) had already checked in. The next morning we began gearing up for the San Francisco PR campaign. One of our sponsors, Eddie Bauer, was providing a public relations man from a local firm to help coordinate everything. Jim dubbed him Smilin' Jack, because he never stopped smiling.

Smilin' Jack had put together a slick folder full of World Bike for HOPE information, including a new WBH brochure and two-by-three-inch cloth patches with our World Bike logo. It had press releases, clippings, HOPE pamphlets, and "fact-sheets" listing our total mileage, route, number of flats, injuries, occupations, and marital status. Don also had put together a slideshow of the first half of the trip, using his best slides from *National Geographic.**

It was strange to see these materials about the trip, to see our exploits recorded on neat sheets of paper and in still images. One photograph caught an instant of misery in Pakistan: I'm sitting in the midst of my dissembled bike in the hot sun, looking as if I'm about to throw up. The day came back vividly in my mind. Other shots depicted the ragged crowds of India and a spectacular Egyptian sunset. We also saw friends like Khalil in Palestine and Munir in Pakistan. It was exciting to see these photos and to read the impressive record of our journey, but it was also strange to find our active, dynamic trip transformed into a set of memories frozen in time.

Our media blitz began at three A.M. on September 29 when a stretch limousine drove the three of us to the KABC-TV studios for an appearance on "Good Morning, America." For the next five days, the interviews never stopped as Smilin' Jack dragged us across the bay to Oakland, up to Marin County, and ninety miles south of Frisco to a "very important radio interview." We gave seminars on biking at each of the Eddie Bauer stores in the metropolitan area and held a fund-raising banquet organized by Laura's mother at the Menlo Park Country Club. Kids asked for our autographs and asked us how they could plan their own trips around the world. Local TV stations filmed us packing our bikes and riding through the streets.

I enjoyed all this activity, although our efforts to publicize the journey still seemed to trivialize our experiences. Reporters asked mostly obvious or sensational questions like "Would you ever do it again?" or "Did you ever feel like your life was in imminent danger?" No one really asked how we felt or what we had learned. A few times I suspected we were merely fulfilling a newspaper's or a television station's quota for adventure stories. Yet there was a positive side to the publicity. For the first time, we seemed to be getting the message across about

---

* *National Geographic* donated film and cameras to the expedition.

HOPE. For most of the trip, the effort for HOPE had seemed distant; it was hard to tell, when biking in the middle of Sudan, how effective we were. But now we could call a press conference, talk about HOPE, and see the results the next day in the newspapers.

Several newspapers and a TV station saw us off from downtown San Francisco on October 5. Pedaling away from an Eddie Bauer store near our hotel, we rode through the skyscraper canyons of the center city, past the stately Victorian townhouses in Pacific Heights, by a battered corner of Haight-Ashbury, and down a long side of the Golden Gate Park. A light, cool wind blew off the sea as we left the suburbs and pedaled along high, grassy cliffs.

I began pedaling hard that afternoon, sailing over the rolling hills, leaving Jim and Don far behind. With the wind in my hair, and my muscles pumping smoothly, I felt free, as if I had been suddenly released after months of hard labor. I felt renewed. For the first time in weeks, I started singing as I had done in the first weeks of the trip.

Free. Freedom. Freedom! Biking down the California coast, we embraced America. We were suddenly free to bike at any speed without worrying about staying together. We were free to camp in dozens of campgrounds along the coast with no fear of thieves or kids harassing us. These campgrounds mostly had running water, flush toilets, and showers. We were free to eat anything, to listen to the music we wanted to, to talk to anyone, and to buy whatever we wanted. It all seemed so absurdly easy. At roadside stands and on junk food strips we acted like gluttons, buying M & M's, Fritos, sodas, and hot dogs. It took only fifteen minutes to buy groceries in supermarkets, compared to an hour or two in a Third World market. With a Bell Telephone credit card, I made two hundred dollars' worth of long-distance calls to my friends in four days on the road. Any time we burst a tube or broke a cable, a bike store with replacements was within a few miles. In a frenzy of appreciation for the bounty of America, we bought everything in sight.

It took ten leisurely days to bike the 430 miles from San Francisco to Los Angeles. We treated the journey as a well-deserved vacation and as a chance for Don to get back in shape. Each morning we woke up early in our campsite and got most of the biking over with before lunch. Jim and I continued to ride at our fast, Southeast Asia pace. At prearranged spots we waited for Don. For lunch we carefully chose fast-food spots, usually looking for a Mexican place, since we had been craving tacos and enchiladas for so long.

At lunch and on breaks, each of us worked on projects. Jim still had his birds, and Don was snapping three or four rolls of film a day. I scratched notes in my journal, worked on HOPE business, and read every newspaper I could find. As we biked down California, the papers were filled with two very American events—the 1982 elections and the American League play-offs between the Milwaukee Brewers and the California Angels. Californians were passionate about both. In the race for the U.S. Senate, Governor Jerry Brown was accusing his opponent, Mayor Pete Wilson of San Diego, of supporting nuclear war. Wilson was calling Brown a flake who dated rock stars. Californians were also voting on two emotional propositions. One would severely restrict handguns; the other was the nuclear freeze referendum. Bumper stickers saying Yes and No were stuck on every other car along the highway. In the play-offs, California was supposed to win, but the Brewers were putting up a good fight. I bought a Vote Yes on the Nuclear Freeze button and pinned it to my handlebar bag. Despite my loyalty to the Kansas City Royals, I bought an Angels pennant and planted it in my rear load.

Under the California sunshine, Jim and I forgot most of the arguments and fights that had been building up in East Asia. Having Don back as part of the team also helped mitigate problems. Jim and I still argued about everything we could think of, but the tone was far less caustic than in Japan. Don was amused by our arguments. "I can't believe the stupid things you guys fight about," he would say. "Who gives a shit how many HOPE pamphlets each of us is carrying? Who cares if we spend five extra minutes for breakfast?" This was a strange reversal of roles for Jim and Don. In Europe Jim had been the mediator for the group.

We were astonished by our reception along Highway One. Many of the people we met had seen us in the news. Restaurant managers donated meals, bicycle shops donated spare parts, and snack shops gave us free Mountain Dews (our current favorite). We sold almost three hundred World Bike for HOPE patches and gave away hundreds of HOPE pamphlets and contribution cards. We also answered people's questions, even if they were asking the same questions that had been asked over and over again since at least Cairo. It was nice just to be able to talk to people, after all the months of sign language and broken English.

We met an astonishing array of people along the road. On our first night, in a youth hostel at Half Moon Bay, we met George, an aerodynamic engineer from L.A. who said he was earning "close to six figures." His sunglasses were Vuarnets, his pink shirt Ralph Lauren, his turquoise pants Merona, and his bike a silver Trek worth about fifteen hundred dollars. George told us that he was bicycling one hundred miles a day to get home as quickly as possible, because he had run out of cocaine. The next morning we biked with George and an aging hippie named Lou. Lou looked like Neil Young in about 1973, with a leather vest, waist-length hair, and beads.

A couple of days later, near Monterey, we met a beautiful, blond senior from UCLA who told us that she loved to butcher geese and other fowl. In Carmel we met a deeply tanned, fortyish woman who had seen us on television and invited us to a hot tub party at her beach house. Near Pigeon Point we stopped by the Gazos Creek Beach House, a shabby bar that looked like it had been transported from somewhere in central Kansas. Burly farmers in flannel shirts and straight-legged denims wore straw cowboy hats with the front brims crinkled into sharp hooks. Others wore baseball caps with wide bills that said everything from International Harvester to I'm a Moonshine Mama. The jukebox had songs like "Elvira" by the Oak Ridge Boys, "The Devil Came to Georgia," by Charlie Daniels, and "A Good Love Died Tonight," by Conway Twitty. All of the pickup trucks in the lot outside had stickers reading Vote No on Proposition 15, the anti-handgun referendum.

"So you boys went all the way around the goddamned world," said a guy sitting on one of the vinyl-topped stools at the bar. "Hell, that's no big deal. We go round the world here every fuckin' Friday night if we get enough whiskey." He introduced himself as Jack, a "hick farmer."

"What do you grow?" I asked.

"I grow a little corn and a lot of hooch," he said.

"You grow hooch?"

"Sure. We plant it between rows of other crops, like corn." He paused to take a long drink of beer. "But don't y'all go looking for any hooch in any cornfields," he said to me. "Farmers'll shoot yah for trespassing. They do it all the time to the hippies who drive up and down the highway here."

Near Morro Bay we met Pappy, a sixty-four-year-old hobo who had been riding back and forth between Florida and California on a Western Auto bicycle for seventeen years. His bike was loaded with ancient leather bike packs covered with buttons saying things like "Who says you can't have everything! I'm here!" and "Dirty old men need just as much sex as dirty young men." A duck carved out of pine was mounted between his handlebars.

"This is Fred," he said, introducing his duck. "He keeps me company when I'm on my bike."

While we cooked a Kraft macaroni and cheese dinner on our stove, Pappy cooked a TV Dinner in a stone barbecuer.

"I was born in 1918," he said, "and became a hobo when I was fifteen years of age. That was durin' the Depression."

"What exactly *is* a hobo?" I asked him.

"Back then, it was all the folks out of work and wanderin' around lookin' for work. You jumped the trains, ridin' 'em 'cause there weren't no other way to get from town to town. But that was long ago. Now I'm seein' the country by bike, 'cause it's the best way to travel if yah got the bug, and I got the bug. But my gosh, you boys done more than I've done. I guess I oughta get your autograph."

"Pappy," we said, "we oughta get yours."

Almost everyone we met on Highway One had some sort of cause they wanted to talk about. With little prompting, we heard long, passionate dissertations on handguns, nuclear war, EST, vegetarianism, the American flag, cars, Ronald Reagan, and God. A thirty-five-year-old photographer I met near Monterey was convinced that if the whole world embraced Zen, everyone would be happy. Another woman told me that Ronald Reagan had foiled the greatest Communist conspiracy in history by defeating Jimmy Carter. "Jimmy Carter was a Communist," she said. "He was the most clever Communist yet. His plan was to ruin America through ineptness." Another guy wore a T-shirt that said Pray for War. He told me that what the world really needed was a good war "to get our asses back in gear." Some of the causes were more mainstream. On a scenic overlook above the sea we met a boy with muscular dystrophy riding a special bicycle for Jerry Lewis's telethon. Near Santa

Barbara we met a man walking across the country to raise money for a hospital in Memphis.

In this cause-oriented atmosphere, we generated a lot of interest in HOPE. We raised several hundred dollars from people along the road. Yet all of these causes seemed slightly stilted in the context of California, where so many people were trying their hardest to impress each other. It was a society completely preoccupied with outward appearances. I enjoyed the people we met along Highway One. Their exuberance was refreshing after the world weariness prevalent in Asia. But as we proceeded down the coast, California began to bother me. People seemed to be so involved in themselves and their causes that they paid little attention to anything else. They devoted tremendous energy to selecting the proper pair of pants and the right shoes. They worked hard on tans. They owned expensive cars and bikes, and they talked a lot about their causes, as if having a cause was no different from owning a BMW.

As we got closer to Los Angeles, cities expanded and grew closer together. The cliffs smoothed out into low hills and beaches, and the local zoning laws protecting the shoreline grew lax. Strips of junk food jungles and discount plazas replaced ridges of conifers, and long shocks of asphalt replaced the open, grassy hills. We pedaled into Los Angeles during Southern California's brushfire season, when the grassy hills around the city become so dry that a carelessly tossed cigarette can end up burning thousands of acres. High banks of brown-black smoke rose over Highway One between Santa Barbara and Malibu. With a steady wind blowing south, the smoke joined with the orange-brown gauze of smog already hanging over L.A. We stopped to fish through our panniers for spare bandanas and goggles. As in the Third World, we would need some protection if we were going to see or breathe in this environment.

Our destination that morning was the Santa Monica pier, where we were holding a press conference for our arrival in Los Angeles. The local ABC and NBC affiliates, the *Los Angeles Times,* and three or four radio stations had confirmed that they were coming. After the press conference we were being met by a man named Vito Cetta. His family had seen us on "Good Morning, America" and had volunteered to put us up in their Santa Monica home while we were in L.A.

In Santa Monica we turned onto the pier, passing a beach

packed with scantily clad people who didn't seem to notice that the sun was just a scratch of light in the smog. On the pier a large man with a walrus mustache and a police radio told us to get off our bikes. "Get off 'em, or I'll fine yah," he shouted. We hopped off the bikes in the midst of a crowd eating burgers, snow cones, and potato chips. Everyone seemed to be eating something; no wonder there were so many fat people milling about on the pier. I was almost persuaded to give up my own gluttonous ways, although I still ordered a chili dog when Jim bought snacks at a grimy booth near the policeman.

After the Santa Monica press conference, we followed Vito's Porsche up a steep ridge, past apartment complexes, and up into a neighborhood of elegant, Spanish-style homes surrounded by fences, trees, and flowering bushes. On the way we saw posters and stickers everywhere for Tom Hayden, who was running for the state assembly spot from Santa Monica.

Vito was a small man with an athletic body, bushy mustache, and round glasses. His license plate said SIAMO! His house was at the end of a long ridge overlooking the ocean. He talked a lot about the view, although we could see little through the drape of smog hanging over the city. In the Cettas' yard a blue and gold flag flew from a tall pole. Yes on 12, it said, referring to the nuclear freeze proposition.

Bevin, Vito's wife, met us inside an elegant house full of natural fibers, polished wood floors, and contemporary art. The immaculately clean kitchen was covered with Mexican tiles and matching appliances, including a Cuisinart, blender, mixer, toaster oven, microwave, and trash compactor. Bevin, who was about to leave for a party, was tanned and as athletic as her husband. She wore a purple outfit of gauzy muslin with harem pants. "You guys make yourselves at home," she said, taking a couple of matching bowls out of the refrigerator. "I'm putting out some chicken salad. We have this great gourmet shop here. They make the *best* chicken salad." Rushing about the kitchen, she pointed out a cookie bin, a bread bin, and the corner in the refrigerator where they kept their beer and Chablis. "I'm going to a party for Tom Hayden," she said. "I'm on a committee of women taking him on a round of coffees. Jane Fonda is coming to this one," she said, still rushing around. "She's Tom's wife, you know."

After Bevin left, Vito appeared in his jogging clothes and showed us the Jacuzzi in their backyard. "I hooked up the Jacuzzi to a couple of solar panels," Vito explained, pointing to a set of black and silver panels on the roof. "Enjoy yourselves," he said, taking off for a run. After a few minutes in the hot water, our eyes started to burn in the smog, so we went back inside and took naps.

Vito Cetta was a second-generation Italian who ran a small architectural firm in Santa Monica. He was a quiet, confident man who worked hard, enjoyed his success, and talked a lot about his family. He was particularly proud of his Italian background. While we were in L.A., he was designing a Christmas card for his parents that patched together photos of his family's village in Italy. He had taken the pictures during a summer trip to Europe.

On our last night with the Cettas, Vito and Bevin invited us to a neighborhood meeting at a friend's house. They were showing a film about the nuclear freeze and trying to raise money for the Vote Yes on 12 campaign. At the meeting, about thirty people, mostly middle-aged and elegantly dressed, sipped herbal tea and talked about Jacuzzis, Tom Hayden, the smog, the World Bike for HOPE, and nuclear war. A table full of Proposition 12 bumper stickers, buttons, flags, and pamphlets were stacked next to baskets for contributions.

After a while we sat down in folding chairs to watch a nuclear freeze film called *No Frames, No Boundaries*. The title referred to a quote by astronaut Buzz Aldrin, who began the film by telling us that the earth as viewed from a spacecraft was one world without lines marking countries, race, or conflict. It was a world with "no frames and no boundaries." The movie then quickly ran through a history of war, starting with conflicts between animals and leading up to a long, dramatic view of a thermonuclear blast slowly mushrooming into a cloud of fire and dust. The gist of the film was that if we can knock down all of the "artificial" boundaries of politics and cultures, all the peoples of the world can join together to rid the planet of the nuclear curse. Peace, prosperity, and happiness will surely follow.

Up until the film, I was having a nice time at the party, chatting and telling stories about the trip. But watching *No Frames, No Boundaries* stirred something inside of me. It was a ridiculous movie. Here were all of these wealthy people talking about grand solutions to problems they didn't understand. I thought of our long trip around the world and began to feel the misery of Pakistan and India wash over me. It was like having a dream while I was awake. In my mind I felt the heat, the drenching sweat, the flies, the stench, and the naked, filthy children pressing in around me and shouting "Baksheesh!" I saw the squalid huts, the vultures, and the poverty. The tragedy of what we had seen overwhelmed me with anger. I suddenly wanted to grab these elegant, well-meaning people and tell them that this lofty talk about no frames and no boundaries was absurd. Had they *seen* India? Did they realize the horror and misery of a place like Uttar Pradesh?

Sitting in that living room in Southern California, I suddenly felt old. I had seen so much more than these people twice my age. I also felt sad, because so few of these people or of the well-meaning people we had met on the road had any idea about what was happening in the rest of the world. They blithely believed that their goodwill could wipe away any evil in the world. I understood this sort of thinking, because I had been raised to believe in it myself. But after all I had seen, I knew it was a lie.

The distance between Uttar Pradesh and upper-class Los Angeles was too great. They were two different planets, and I felt torn apart trying to straddle them. I was happy to be home, but I was no longer comfortable. It was as though I had discovered a horrible, tragic secret that made me a stranger in my own country.

12. Across America: Friend

After two weeks in America, the initial joy I had felt at being home was wearing thin. I couldn't identify what exactly was bothering me. Part of it was Los Angeles. Lost in a haze of smog, it seemed the epitome of an overindustrialized, overindulgent city. Television stations spent hours every day talking about celebrities and how to look more beautiful. Billboards advertised sheer panty hose, cheese-flavored dog food, and movies about beautiful women in bathing suits and men who could single-handedly subdue thousands of bad guys with their trusty magnums.

Leaving the elegant neighborhood of the Cettas, we pedaled around the base of the Santa Monica Mountains on Wilshire Boulevard. Our eyes burned in the thick smog as we passed endless strips of junky hotels, tiny tract houses, convenience stores, car dealers, and greasy gas stations. Broken bottles and squashed cans clogged the gutters. People haunted the smoky, concrete streets like ghosts in polyester and blue jeans. They ran from car to car and hung out on corners. This netherworld looked like an intentional perversion of the America we had dreamed about overseas. It seemed like a joke played on the mostly Asian and Mexican emigrant populations who had struggled to reach the golden shores of California.

After about six miles the strips broke up into parks, rows of palms, and tall buildings marking the edges of Beverly Hills and Hollywood. We got a glimpse of the 20th Century-Fox studios and the file cabinet architecture of Century City as we steered east onto Sunset Boulevard. Like so much of Southern California, Sunset Boulevard did not live up to its TV image. The Sunset we saw was an older, more dilapidated version of Wilshire. It had more adult bookstores, peep shows, and sinister men grasping bottles and smoking cigarettes. We turned left and picked up Hollywood Boulevard, running parallel with Sunset. A mile or two later, we passed the Capitol Records building, CBS records, and more adult bookstores. We were now in Hollywood, the center of glitz and fantasy in America. Could this netherworld of smog and delapidation really be the place where the romance and adventure of my childhood were created?

By four o'clock that afternoon, we were weary and our eyes ached from the smog. We began looking for a decent hotel, but we had to settle for a place called the Hollywood Inn, a motor inn whose sign had the stains of an AAA rating that had been removed. Inside the office we were surprised to find a familiar smell—curry. Visions of a large steel pot bubbling with gooey gruel flashed through my memory. An Indian manager in a bright yellow sari greeted us, took eighteen dollars, and gave us a room key. In the room I immediately turned on the television. Almost as quickly Jim turned it off. "I'm not going to tolerate that fucking television," he said irritably. "It's bad enough that I have to bicycle through the backlots of L.A. Do I have to watch them on TV, too?"

It was mid-morning two days later before we climbed out of the smoke cloud in the valley. Blue sky and sunshine appeared for the first time in six days. Fields of dry grass and wild trees stretched across low, scrappy hills. Later in the day we looked down into the valley and saw the light brown cloud of smog slithering between the ridges like heavy fog. "That stuff'll blow up here by four," said a cowboy in a felt hat. "The wind, she starts blowin' off the ocean 'bout noon. Blows that shit up 'ere. At night, the wind turns round and blows it back out to sea."

Finally free of the pollution of L.A., we pedaled under a hot sun into a land of bare mountains and ridges with rust-colored skin wrinkled by centuries of wind and erosion. The desert in Southern California is a land of rolling, scrubby chaparral occasionally broken by rocky ridges that hang forever on the horizon. Like Sudan or the Sinai, it is a desolate, virtually uninhabited land where the sun has scorched the flat stretches to a tawny brown. Sudden rainstorms have created the dry, eroded channels the Arabs in the Middle East call wadis.

Taking off my shirt and helmet, I wrapped a bandana around my head to soak up sweat. Pedaling fast, I breathed in the fresh air and felt the sun beating down from the clear sky. This was the sort of ride that usually buoyed my mood, filling me with exhilaration. But the sour taste of Los Angeles lingered no matter how hard I tried to shake it. I was facing our 3,000-mile journey across America in a dark, angry mood that seemed to make even the stunning, empty stretches of desert seem ugly. As I raced across the desert, images of the Third World continued to dominate my thoughts. I felt confused and disillusioned about my homeland. Even the people here who made an effort to understand the world were unable really to comprehend the plight of people we had met overseas. War, disease, death, starvation—I had taken this long, grueling trip to discover what these things meant. But what good was the understanding I had gained? Now that I was home, my experiences merely served to magnify the insanity of a world where privilege and suffering coexist, seemingly without design or reason.

It took four days to cross the deserts of California and western Arizona toward Phoenix. As in Southeast Asia, we rode fast, covering close to ninety miles a day. The scenery passed in a rush of scrub, outcrops of rock, and giant, balloonlike hills. We met only a handful of people on the desert. Living in ramshackle ranch houses and frontier towns, they appeared among the labyrinth of rocks and scraggly bushes like visions from movies and television. In Vidal Junction, California, we met a cowboy wearing spurs and a creased felt hat. Sitting on a tall horse, he warned us to watch out for rattlesnakes in our tents. "I had a friend crippled by one a them snakes," he said. "This guy gets in his bag, feels a pinprick, and pretty soon his leg don't move no more." In Rice, California, we met two local high school seniors who told us they were enlisting in the Marines. "I'm gonna learn how to work on cars in the service," one of them said, "you know, in one of those technical training programs. One day I'll open a garage."

In Parker, Arizona, near the Colorado River, we met a group of local citizens running for county offices in a town of clapboard buildings and trailer homes. In the parking lot of a hardware store in town, Louise F. Brock, a candidate for county assessor, was Scotch-taping her campaign poster among a half-dozen others on the hardware store door. Inside, a candidate for county supervisor, Frank G. Lee, sold us Mountain Dews and packets of M & M's while Patti Silvestri, a candidate for county treasurer, arranged stacks of "dollar bill" campaign flyers on a table brimming with campaign materials. On each oversized bill, Patti had substituted her face for George Washington's. Frank G. Lee told us that the people of Parker were really excited about the coming election, because the state legislature had just voted to create a new county with Parker as the county seat. "We're so new, we don't even have a name yet," said Louise F. Brock. "We call ourselves 'County Number Fifteen.' "

"From all the signs, it looks like everyone in town is running for something," I said.

"It's good to see folks so excited about an election," said Frank G. Lee. "It makes us proud to have a new county and to be Americans."

At a gas station near Parker, we met a man with a faded Soldier of Fortune T-shirt, a Colt .45 pistol in a holster, and two large knives hanging from his belt in leather sheaths. He looked like a cross between John Wayne and Meatloaf, with a macho swagger, long, stringy hair, and a stomach hanging two inches over a silver and turquoise belt. His girlfriend weighed at least four hundred pounds. I started to open my handlebar bag to grab my camera, but this was a scary-looking couple, so I just smiled and said hello. The man grunted, and he and his girl walked over to a Toyota Celica. Incredibly, they both fit into the small car. As they drove away I decided that it was time to remove the nuclear freeze button from my handlebar bag.

On October 28, Phoenix appeared suddenly like a white, clean, modern mirage in the middle of the desert. Our stay there was limited to a couple of interviews and a meeting with the local bicycle club. As quickly as we arrived, we were gone and back on the desert. But the desert to the east of Phoenix was different. Gradually, as the scrub country became rockier and the ridges more abrupt, the highway began to pitch almost imperceptibly upward. After two more days our pace began to slow and our breathing became more labored. Breaks became more frequent, and we drank more water. We were entering the foothills of the Rocky Mountains.

Two days out of Phoenix we began to climb the first major ripple in the Rockies, called the Mazatzal Mountains. For the next several days we would be biking up and down over scattered ranges, mesas, and plateaus. From the town of Superior, Arizona, we started our first real climb, pumping up through a weird, windblown canyon of rocks and bramble called Devil's Canyon. At dark we camped under a full moon casting spooky shadows across the boulders. It was November 1, Jim's thirty-third birthday. We celebrated with a bottle of Wild Turkey, a large campfire, and Hostess Twinkies with little birthday candles. Feeling buzzed, we walked among the rocks in the moonlight, shouting words that bounced across ridges and echoed through the canyon.

The next day, November 2, was election day in America. Jim, Don, and I rode fast down the far side of the Mazatzals into the town of Globe, Arizona, for breakfast at Cobb's Family Diner. The talk in the diner was about "Mr. Reagan's recession" and the coming winter, which a waitress with wavy, heavily sprayed hair told us would be a mild one. "It ain't near cold yet," she said. "That's a good thing for you boys." In town, posters made with construction paper and magic markers urged Globites to vote, which they were doing down the street at the city hall.

From Globe we pumped up another steep incline, heading toward the Fort Apache Indian Reservation. Relegated to this land were a people that once dominated most of the territory between central California and Texas. Cochise and Geronimo had once fought bluecoats in these rocky highlands. Only a hundred years ago this land had been as wild and unsettled as any land we had biked through overseas. I could imagine ragged Indian scouts toting long rifles up on the stony ridges, and could see their smoky camps of tepees pitched under tall cottonwoods lining valley streams. As we approached the reservation, I remembered that the Indians had been the bad guys when I played cowboys and Indians as a child. That was before my mother discovered *Black Elk Speaks*, and before I saw Dustin Hoffman in *Little Big Man*.

The faces of the Indians were round and dark. They stared at us with impassive eyes. Their enclaves were poor and ramshackle, the houses made of planks and crumbling adobe. Comparisons with the Third World were inevitable, although these buildings all had electricity, running water, televisions, and the other bare necessities for an American. Yet the poverty was real, especially because it was in America.

We were only halfway through the reservation at dusk. In the tiny Indian town of Carrizo, we bought a permit to camp on the reservation and had hot dogs microwaved by a drunken Indian who kept speaking menacingly at us in the Apache language, the first "foreign" language we had heard since returning to the States.

It was ironic that we heard the national returns of the white man's election on the Apache reservation. We were camped far off the road along one of those peaceful streams where the Apaches might have once pitched their tepees. It was a spot that spoke of history, of a forgotten way of life. No ruins existed here, but the sadness of loss was profound in the cold mountain air.

The night was dark and heavy with quiet as the returns came in on our shortwave receiver. My former boss on Capitol Hill, Senator John Danforth, won reelection in Missouri by a very close margin. Jerry Brown was trounced in California. The nuclear freeze referendum won in every state it was offered, except Arizona. The handgun restriction proposition in California failed. In Santa Monica, Tom Hayden was the new state assemblyman. Unfortunately the radio stations we could get on our Walkman radios didn't carry the election returns for Arizona's "County Number Fifteen."

From the reservation, we continued to pump hard through the mountains, camping at night and buying food in shacks selling the staples of the high country—bread, canned goods, junk food, cream, milk, butter, and whiskey. At night, after a supper of canned stew or spaghetti with Ragú sauce, when the cold winds blew across the mountains, we mixed a finger or two of Wild Turkey into our coffee. Then we would fall asleep, exhausted by the rough terrain and the thin air.

Now that it was November, we woke up most mornings to a thin layer of frosty dew over our gear. The cold made it difficult to pull out of our warm mummy bags. It was also turning our ride through the mountains into a series of clothing changes. If we were climbing and began to heat up, we stripped off our layers of sweats and windbreakers. If we were going downhill, we kept them on. It was an annoying alteration of hot and cold flashes that reminded me of biking in Europe a year earlier.

The three of us were spending most of our time riding alone. Each of us felt like keeping our thoughts to ourselves in the bleak beauty of the high country. Sometimes we spoke with each other only to agree on a place to meet at the end of the day. I often rode as fast as I could, far ahead of the others so that I could stop to write. In my journal, I was trying to sort out my thoughts about the trip. Slowly, almost imperceptibly, my attitudes about America were shifting from confusion and anger to something a bit more settled. I was seeing a country of staggering beauty: vistas of ragged ridges, mesas, and quiet meadows of dry grass and flowers. I was also meeting the people of the high country. They were scrappy individualists who took great pride in living on this bleak land. They were honest, nononsense folks who could shoot, cuss, and drink like any cowboy in a Zane Grey novel. They respected the land while claiming and protecting their worthless pieces of it with the wrath of God. "My gran'pa was killed by Induns defending my land," an old guy told us near Omega, New Mexico. "I'll be damned if I'll ever give it up." They were hicks and rednecks, but they were also good, basic people whom I was proud to call my countrymen.

In Red Hill we met an old man in a crumpled straw hat driving a pickup. "How fer yah ride on them things?" he asked. I told him, and he asked me why we'd want to go biking "all over hell." Then he asked me what my work was. "I'm a writer," I said.

He shook his head. "That ain't man's work," he said. "When I was your age, I was herdin' cattle out on this range. Now son, that's man's work."

In Datil we met a seventy-nine-year-old cowboy named Joe who owned the Navajo Lounge with his middle-aged daughter. When we came into the Navajo out of a freezing wind, Joe was eased back in a tilted chair, one pointed boot kicked up on a table. The other boot was on the hardwood floor next to a fat, sleeping German shepherd. Joe eyed three bikers in leg tights, fluorescent vests and helmets. "You boys from outer space?" he drawled, grinning. His daughter looked over from a big iron stove in the back of the small place.

"Looks more like they come from Frederick's of Hollywood," she said. Joe laughed at that, and I smiled, telling them that we were riding our bikes around the world.

"I'd have believed in outer space before that," Joe grinned. "But you boys look cold. Daughter, why don't you get these boys some hot coffee."

Our sojourn through the high country was interrupted nine days out of Phoenix when we pulled into Socorro, New Mexico, for a HOPE publicity stop. Socorro is one of a long string of retirement towns running south of Albuquerque along Interstate 25. A group of Rotarians in their sixties met us in a large Winnebago on the edge of town, in front of a U.S. National Guard Armory. The group was led by Art Stanton, the Rotary President, and Floyd Turpin, the chairman of the club's Events Committee. A photographer from the *Socorro Democrat-Defender* took our photos riding in front of a Welcome to Socorro billboard. Inside the Winnebago the men poured drinks over a portable sink as we pulled the bikes inside to ride into town.

The three of us took showers at Floyd Turpin's small house in the retirement area of Socorro. Floyd's wife, Ronny, served roast beef sandwiches on white bread. In the living room, next to a pool table, Floyd pulled Pearl Lights out of a special refrigerator. With the smell of apple pie in the air, we watched the end of a football game with Floyd on a remote control TV. I sat back on a deep, plush couch, feeling very relaxed and at ease.

Floyd was a stocky, powerful-looking man with tattoos, snow-white sideburns, a beer belly, and a generous smile. He had served thirty-six years as a first sergeant in the U.S. army and was full of stories about the service. "I started with the army in World War Two," he told us over more Pearls. "I was a truck driver on the European front. It was my job to take our boys out alive and bring 'em back dead." He had landed in Normandy soon after D-Day, fought in the Battle of the Bulge, and helped liberate Paris and Nice with Patton's Third Army.

Floyd had also served in Vietnam, where he was nearly killed when a supply column he was leading was ambushed by the Viet Cong. "My driver, my gunner, and most of the men around me was killed," he said. It shook him up so much that he had a stroke a couple of days later and took three years to recover.

In Socorro, Floyd and Ronny lived off his army pension, social security, and his earnings from working part-time as a handyman at the New Mexico Institute of Mining and Technology in Socorro. "It's a great life to be retired," he told us. "This country here is the greatest in the world. And I love bein' down here in Socorro. It's warm most of the time, and it never rains, so I can play golf almost every day." I asked him if he was any good at golf.

"Hell yes," he said, grinning, "you ask Art. He'll tell yah. I beat him all the time."

The next night, Jim, Don, and I gave our slideshow at the Socorro Rotary meeting. It was a fun, casual meeting where all the members were good friends. They wore club buttons and fined each other twenty-five cents for having ruffled hair or untied shoes. A cherubic priest played songs on an upright piano as everyone belted out "America the Beautiful." After our slideshow they gave us framed awards, and we chatted about our journey. The priest was moved by our photos of the Afghani mujahadeen and asked us to tell everyone about their "gallant efforts against Communism."

Another former army man asked us what we had taken for "the runs." "Hell, in the Big War, the runs was worse than getting shot at," he said.

"That depended on if yah got hit or not," said someone else.

Leaving Socorro, we once again pedaled into the high country east of the Rio Grande. The beauty of the land and the tough, sincere people continued to defy our expectations. A month earlier I had been ready to quit the trip, lost in a dark mass of confusion. Now I felt revitalized. Meeting people like Floyd Turpin and the people of the high country had taught me that there was more to America than dog food advertisements, television, and Hollywood. These were people I had never believed existed beyond the stereotypes assigned them by the image-makers of America. They were cowboys, miners, ranchers, and squatters, each with his own history and way of life.

That first day we stopped for lunch at the town of Bingham, a cluster of shacks belonging to a grizzled, tough old man with deep wrinkles from squinting in the sun. A thick cigar hung out of his mouth. Another was tucked into his cowboy shirt. The locals around Bingham called this fellow the Snake Man because he raised rattlers and copperheads in a deep pit on his property. But that wasn't all he had lying around his land. The Snake Man had old wagons, rusty mine cars, a complete mine drill circa 1880, motor parts, a refrigerator painted with a smiley face, a couple of rusty air conditioners, dozens of old canisters and barrels, several tables of rocks, and piles of bleached cow skulls. Like many other desert people, he seemed to enjoy collecting and arranging pieces of the outside world. In a cage out back were two mature bobcats that the Snake Man had captured and raised. "The government is tryin' to take those cats away from me," he said. "They'll be lookin' into the business end of my shotgun if they try."

That night we slept in a barn near the White Sands Missile Range, a military reserve about half the size of the Apache reservation in Arizona. The barn was owned by a middle-aged woman who ran the Bootlegger Saloon, a place serving drinks and victuals to the soldiers from White Sands. "All of that land you see across the highway belongs to the army," she told us. "They run the strangest tests over there, real star wars stuff. They had me leave for a few days one time for secret tests. When I came home a Pershing missile was lying on my front yard out there. Another time they killed one of my cows with a laser." She told us that the army had been trying to buy her land for years. "They are never going to get it," she said. "My grandfather homesteaded this land; he dug the well outside, one of the deepest you'll find around here."

As we biked across the Rockies, the land seemed to reverberate with history. Besides the living stories of the people we met, we also glimpsed the ruins of homes and shops abandoned by the people of the past. They appeared everywhere: low clusters of crumbling adobe structures and shacks bleached gray like driftwood. Occasionally we would pass through an entire street of old stores boarded up and abandoned. The bleached letters of B&B GEN MDSE were painted on a crumbling adobe building surrounded by tall weeds. An old-fashioned gas pump had been stripped and lay in pieces, its Phillip's 66 emblem almost faded away.

One afternoon, we stopped at a roofless, ruined gas station. Tumbleweeds clogged the boarded doors and windows. In front were two Depression-era gas pumps, lean towers of rust and broken glass. On the doorjamb of the station was a rusted Pepsi thermometer. Even with the rust, that old thermometer would have sold for thirty dollars in a New York antique store. If someone repaired the gas pumps, he could sell each of them for a couple of hundred dollars. But out here these artifacts were just worthless pieces of metal and broken glass crumbling into the desolation. Yet I could feel the history. Someone had worked and sweated for this place. They had bought that thermometer and tacked it up to their new gas station. Motorists in the curvy Fords and heavy, chugging trucks of that era had shouted "Fill 'er up!" under this big sky. Pieces of their lives were still scattered on the floor of the station—a boot, a table, a torn, yellowed, illegible newspaper, and some empty cans. The history here was close, and it was linked with the desolation of the high country. It was an example of the struggle to survive in this harsh land, and its ruin seemed as profound as the decaying castles in Spain, the bleached-white columns of Greece, the dissolving palaces of Suakin, or the dilapidated Moghul towns of northern India.

On November 9, we rode uphill into the Capitan Mountains, the last major ripple of rock in the Rockies. We climbed and climbed, through green forest land and into a dark storm that steadily dropped the temperature all day. When we reached the city of Capitan, a rustic tourist town, snow flurries were dancing in the streets. As the snow began to blow harder, we checked into the Smokey the Bear Motel, just down the street from the Smokey the Bear memorial. It was here in the Capitan forest that the original Smokey was found as a cub clinging to a charred tree after a forest fire. For fifty cents I bought a button saying I'd been there.

That afternoon I caught up on some HOPE business we had been neglecting since Phoenix. On a pay phone in the motel parking lot I called Scott Patton in Washington, talked to the Washington homecoming organizer and a couple of sponsors. When I was through with business, I called Laura. We had been talking every two or three days since California. It was a curious juxtaposition to be biking through the cold bareness of the high country by day and plugging into doses of Laura's New York lifestyle by night. Laura talked about negotiations with corporate finance clients, closing dinners at the 21 Club, jazz at Greenwich Village clubs, and jogs in Central Park. She also talked about that nagging question called the future. But things were starting to work themselves out. We had almost decided to live together, mainly because we couldn't conceive of *not* living together. But making the actual commitment was difficult. Both of us were feeling independent. I wanted time by myself to rest and figure out what to do after the trip. She was worried about losing the self-reliance she felt comfortable with after a year on her own.

The next morning we reached the crest of the Capitan mountains and began our plummet toward the plains. It was a wild, exhilarating downhill that eventually dropped us three thousand feet in only ten miles. We stopped halfway down in the town of Lincoln, where Billy the Kid once shot and killed the local judge. That same day, Pat Garrett began following the Kid with a posse that eventually caught him and had him hanged. The whole town of Lincoln seemed devoted to this single day and night in its history.

Just a few miles from Lincoln we left the mountains and began a new phase of our American journey. Biking out of the mountains and onto the southern edge of the Great Plains, we entered the state of Texas. Jim, Don, and I each had strong impressions about Texas, although none of us had spent much time there. Jim knew it from living in the bordering state of Oklahoma. Don and I knew it from two sources. First, we knew about Texas from our trips to Colorado ski country, where vacationing Texans had a reputation for whooping it up, spending lots of money, driving big cars, wearing big cowboy hats, and acting like fraternity boys in a campus bar. Our second source about Texas was our grandmother DuBose, who had been raised on a poor West Texas farm around the time of the First World War. My grandmother, nicknamed DeeDee, was the thirteenth child of Rachel Caledonia Stanfield, a formidable woman born in Arkansas during the last year of the Civil War. At age fifteen, she ran off and got married, traveled west in a wagon train, homesteaded one hundred acres of dry land in west Texas, outlived two husbands, ran another one off with a shotgun, and raised almost twenty children—thirteen were hers, the rest stepchildren—during the pioneer era of the Texas frontier.

The Texas that greeted us on the border with New Mexico was the proud, boastful Texas. Mounted on a stand of concrete and limestone was a huge piece of granite cut in the shape of the state. *Texas* was carved in large letters into the stone. It didn't say Welcome to Texas or You Have Just Entered Texas. It said only *Texas*, as if that were all that needed to be said.

But the Texas that followed the sign was nothing to brag about. Like the prairies in western Kansas, this land was flat and absolutely empty as it stretched for miles and miles under a giant sky. On this parched land only the heartiest of short grasses and weeds survived the intense heat of the summer and the frigid days of the winter. My grandmother used to tell me that one hundred acres of this land equals a single acre of land in a place like Ohio or eastern Kansas. "It was practically worthless land," she told me. A few miles from the border, we picked up cotton country. The rows of low, white cotton balls spread out against the brown-red earth looked like a million tons of paper that had been blown into fields of weeds and left to rot in the sun.

It was 350 miles from the border to Dallas, our next major publicity stop. For the first half of this journey, we passed through another string of mostly bleak towns composed of decaying shacks and overgrown streets. We could usually see these cities far in advance by their water towers rising over the flatlands. It was a miserable ride, a series of hard, frustrating days fighting cold headwinds and nights spent in cheap hotels with foam mattresses, stained shades, asbestos brick walls, and bad cable television movies. Our meals were in rustic diners and Dairy Queens, which were everywhere in west Texas. The diners disappointed us. We had dreamed of them overseas, imagining juicy fried chicken, home-whipped mashed potatoes, and pan-stirred gravy. But most diners in west Texas served frozen fried chicken, powdered mashed potatoes, and powdered gravy.

The people we met were friendly and, considering our view of Texans, humble. A motel owner in Tahoka, Texas, loaned us his battered Cadillac so we could drive to the local Dairy Queen for supper. In Clairmont, Texas, we were given free reign to eat all we could at the local café's smorgasbord. In a Dairy Queen in Post, Texas, a manager with an ear-to-ear grin told us that Jesus wanted him to give us free burgers. But these people *were* Texans. Most of them, even in the poorest towns, walked with a certain swagger and seemed unnaturally confident. It was the same sort of pioneer confidence that we had seen in the high country, a sense that a person could determine his own destiny if he worked hard, believed in God, and was man enough to fight for what he believed. The Texans we met got a strange thrill out of ribbing three weary bikers about their funny-looking riding clothes. "You boys ain't fairies, are yah?" asked an old cowboy in a gas station. In one diner we had the distinction of causing every head in the crowded place to turn and stare at our leg tights. We were like a group of longhairs walking into a John Birch meeting. "Don't worry," Jim announced, "we're bicyclists. These are our riding outfits." With a sigh of relief, everyone turned back to their coffee, sandwiches, and conversation.

The wind continued to slow us down as we pedaled across Texas. By the time we reached Haskell, Texas, my grandmother's hometown, we were four days behind schedule. Checking into another cheap hotel, we bought a six-pack of Lone Star beer and turned on the TV to watch *Halloween II* on cable. It is a remarkably stupid, pointless movie in which several promiscuous seventeen-year-old girls with big breasts get carved up by a maniac in a ski mask.

We had planned to take the next day off so Don and I could pedal nine miles north to the site of my grandmother's ranch. Rachel Caledonia Stanfield and some of her children are buried in the nearby town of Rochester, Texas. But we were way behind schedule. The strong headwinds had reduced our speed to about three-quarters our usual pace. In one of the most stupid acquiescences to our almighty schedule, we did not visit the grave of our great-grandmother. But I did call my grandmother who, at seventy-four, lived in Atlanta (we were hoping to make Atlanta in time for Thanksgiving). "DeeDee, I'm in your hometown," I told her on the phone at breakfast.

"You're in Haskell? Did you see Mama's grave?" I lied and told her we would try to. Then I asked her what she remembered about Haskell.

"I was just a little girl," she said. "I remember we were poor, but we never really knew it. It was an awfully hard life, but we didn't really know that either. We got our water from a well and had no electricity or even radio until I was about ten. We played a lot of games, and I had a doll. Since I was the youngest, everyone spoiled me. I still have a picture of that doll." She told me about a trip she took in 1916 by covered wagon train to Oklahoma. She was eight, and America was worried about the Great War dragging on in Europe. As they slowly rode north with their mule train, DeeDee heard explosions of artillery and gunfire as local militias trained for the war. "I heard talk about the war and the Germans," she said, "and I was convinced that the Germans were making all of the explosions and that they were going to get us."

"What happened to the farm?" I asked DeeDee.

"We sold it for almost nothing in the 1950s, after Mama died," she said. "Right after that they discovered oil. I still own a teensy percentage of the mineral rights, I'm not sure why. Some oil company sends me a fifty-dollar check every month."

After breakfast we pedaled into the Haskell town square. My grandmother had lived for a time in a little house on the square by the train depot. The house no longer existed among the neat stone shops and buildings. I tried to imagine my grandmother here as a little girl carrying a big floppy doll. In the old browned photos she is a round-faced girl with waist-length hair pressed in hot irons to make it wavy. I also tried to imagine my great-grandmother Rachel walking these streets in the severe black, high-collared dresses she wore in family photos.

A woman in the Haskell post office told me that she didn't recognize the name Stanfield but that she did know of several Crumps living north of Haskell. Crump was the name of DeeDee's father, the husband Rachel ran off with a shotgun. "She just didn't like him," said DeeDee, "so she pulled out a shotgun one day and told him to never come back." But her father did come back. He tried to kidnap DeeDee when she was eighteen months old. Apparently he grabbed her and took off running but tripped over a clothesline while trying to escape. This gave Rachel time to grab her gun, cock it, and fire a blast of shot into the air. DeeDee's father dropped the baby, ran away, and was never seen around Haskell again. We only have one photo of my great-grandfather Crump. He was a handsome, graying man who looked comfortable in a waistcoat and stiff tie. DeeDee thinks he was a businessman, but she doesn't know for sure. Rachel would never talk about him.

Pedaling east out of Haskell, I slipped a Billy Joel tape into my Aiwa, but I immediately turned it off. I was thinking about my grandmother and Rachel and Haskell and wasn't in the mood to hear rock and roll. Instead, I turned on my radio. Running through the dial, I came to a man shouting fire and brimstone. "Turn your eyes on the *Lord*," he screamed. "Give up your *evil, sinful* ways and *beg* God for forgiveness. Get down on your *knees* and pray." He went on, quoting scripture and comparing Jesus to the working man. "*Jesus* was a *working man*," he said. "He worked for your *salvation*, just like you *hoe* your fields, or you *drive* your truck, or you *dig* that well, or you *build* that house."

I pedaled on, listening to the preacher rave. He fit into my mood, filling me with history and religion and memories. The man's words seemed to echo across the flatlands, picking up the souls of the people who had struggled to live here. It occurred to me that their struggles to survive were no less than those we had seen around the world. But there was a difference, the difference that has always set America apart from most other countries. My great-grandmother may have lived in poverty, but she had hope and she had dreams. She had dreams that life would improve for my grandmother and her other children, for their children, and on and on. The people who settled this land were not content with their poverty. They came here, lived, and died for the success of future generations that they would never know. For most of my life, as a child of suburbia, I had considered this history irrelevant to me. But I was wrong. This was my heritage and my spirit, the soul behind my own dreams, hopes, and determination.

As these thoughts ran through my head, the preacher finally handed his microphone to his revved-up congregation to begin singing. They bellowed out boisterous, traditional hymns about carrying the light of Jesus, about going to the river to pray, and about crossing oceans wide and mountains high to spread the word of God. These were the sort of hymns that Rachel, my great-grandmother, sang and believed in long ago on these prairies. They were the hymns that DeeDee still sings every Sunday morning in her church in Atlanta. That morning I wished I knew the words, because I felt like singing along.

13. Across America: Homecoming

Texas is split into at least two distinct domains—the West and the Deep South. The city of Dallas is on the border between the two regions. After a quick publicity layover in Dallas, we pedaled due east, finding ourselves in the wooded, hilly region of the South, a land filled with lakes, trailer courts, old shacks, and yards full of plastic birdbaths and junked autos.

We all had firm impressions about the South, images and ideas collected since we were very young. Our deepest impression was that the South was a racist, sometimes violent region where a few mansions were sprinkled among many shacks; where bigoted Ku Klux Klan gangs constantly tormented blacks behind cotton fields; where fat county sheriffs harassed city slickers and hippies; and where slightly demented hillbillies carried shotguns, talked in primitive dialects, and hated strangers. These impressions had been fed to us on television shows and the news, in movies ranging from *To Kill a Mockingbird* to *Texas Chainsaw Massacre*, and in literature, which has an entire genre about the dark and demented soul of the South. Co-existing with images of racism and fear were images of the lazy, slow, good ole boy lifestyle of Andy Griffith and Opie going fishing, where Huey Long wore a white Panama hat and took care of his own, and where Southern belles sipped lemonade on the porch with callers in white linen suits.

As in Texas, Don and I also had a set of more personal images about the Deep South. Our grandfather, Robert DuBose, grew up in Monroe, Louisiana, a railroad town in the swampy bayou country east of Shreveport. His father, Walter Winston DuBose, was an engineer for the Southern Pacific Railroad for most of the first three decades of this century. Robert, our grandfather, attended high school at Monroe High, graduated from Louisiana Tech in nearby Ruston, Louisiana, and first met and courted DeeDee on a sunny porch in Monroe. That was in the summer of 1930, when she had come from Texas to take a job as director of a Camp Fire Girl camp on the Ouachita River north of Monroe. Robert was working as a Boy Scout leader in the same camp. DeeDee remembers Louisiana as a poor, quiet land of long evenings, conversation, lots of lemonade, and lots of sunshine. "Your grandfather used to visit my little house in a white linen suit and straw bowler," she told me. "He was handsome, blond, and real thin. He used to take Mama and me on rides in his daddy's Model A. We'd drive out in the swampy country for hours and then have picnics. It was a comfortable time, even if it was the Depression and we didn't have much money."

Pedaling across east Texas and northern Louisiana, we passed through a poor land of cracked, worn roads and junky rural communities appearing between the swampy bayous. No one seemed abjectly poor here, and no one seemed outrageously wealthy. The houses had running water, electricity, and all of the basics an American expects. The people, both black and white, wore blue jeans, T-shirts, and tennis shoes, just like they do in other parts of the country. But it was easy to see that poverty had existed here in recent history. Behind the comfortable, lower-middle-class homes along U.S. Highway 80 were often small, battered shacks, old cars, and pieces of wagons, discarded and left over from a previous era.

In Mound, Louisiana, we saw another remnant of a previous era when we stopped for a break at a decaying plantation. Mound Plantation General Store said a sign on a large, gray, bleached structure. The ruins of buildings and the twisted tracks of an old rail line were scattered across the fields near the store. "This place used to be a full-fledged Southern plantation," said an old man sitting on the porch of the general store. Leaning on a carved cane, he wore thick spectacles that magnified his blue eyes. As we drank sodas, he pointed to a hill across the highway. "Up there's where the big house was," he said. "It's burnt down now." Pointing to an old building beside the general store, he said, "That's the old Mound Hotel, where folks visiting the plantation stayed." He paused to scratch the ground below the porch with his cane. "Fifty years ago, this was like a small city. We had a railroad depot, an opera house, and a hundred people workin' in the fields. Everythin' was right here. Even had an undertaker."

"What happened to the plantation?" I asked.

"Lots of things." He shrugged. "The Depression hurt it, and then one of the boys who owned the place started gamblin'." He shrugged again. "Yah know, though, I think it was mostly time. I seen a lot of time go by here and seen a lot of changes." He looked up and stared at me with his lively, magnified eyes. "Time. That's what really happened here," he repeated. "Nothin' nowhere stays the same. Everythin' passes away."

Racing across the Deep South, we quickly clicked into a routine designed to get us to Washington as quickly as possible. We lived to bike. All our meals were bought in restaurants to save time, and every night was spent in a cheap hotel so that we could ride until dark and not waste time setting up camp. Even our diversions were minimalized. I did almost no writing, Jim did no birding, and Don took few photographs. Our breaks were kept to fifteen minutes, which was just enough time to drink a soda, buy a fresh supply of M & M's, and play two games of Centipede or Pac Man. Don almost always won these games. His initials were recorded as top scorer on machines all over the South. Jim only occasionally played video. He spent most of his time off the bike working voraciously on crossword puzzles, a pastime that could absorb a detail-oriented person like him for hours. At night we shut each other out with our Walkman's, read, or watched B-movies on television.

We covered the 175 miles across Louisiana to the Mississippi border in only two days. In our rush to cross the state, we didn't even stop in Monroe, my grandfather's home town. Thanksgiving dinner was Fritos and tuna fish on Wonder bread in a Rayville, Louisiana, hotel room. On the day after Thanksgiving we left Louisiana, pedaling across the wide, muddy banks of the Mississippi River. Jim was hurrying us along because he wanted to watch the Oklahoma-Nebraska football game on TV.

"*You* want to watch TV?" I kidded him.

"Dave, no one raised in Oklahoma would ever miss the Oklahoma-Nebraska game, unless he was dead."

In a heavy rain we bicycled across the river into Vicksburg, Mississippi, on a bridge crowded with speeding trucks and cars spewing water and mud. On a bluff on the Mississippi side, we stopped at a state tourist information area to inquire about hotels. "Let's check into any hotel," "Jim was saying as he glanced at his watch. "The game starts in twenty minutes."

"I'm real sorry, y'all," said a rotund woman behind the tourist services desk. "With Thanksgivin' weekend, there aren't too many hotels with vacancies." She tried calling two or three hotels for us, and then suggested we spend the night in one of the pre–Civil War mansions along the Mississippi. It sounded intriguing. She handed me the brochure for a mansion called Cedar Grove. The brochure said that the mansion had been featured on the "P.M. Magazine" television show, and was listed in the *National Register of Historic Places*. The brochure also listed several features:

> Union cannonball remains lodged in parlor wall.
> Jefferson Davis danced in the ballroom.
> Ulysses S. Grant slept in the master bedroom.
> Beautifully furnished with priceless period antiques including many of the original pieces.

Jim and Don were dubious about spending the night in an antebellum mansion. Jim mentioned money, and Don mentioned that we were already behind schedule. I reminded them that we were here in the middle of the South and had not yet stopped to see any of it. I also pointed out that the mansion was reasonably priced. "It's less than the Raffles," I told Jim. The tourist office woman added that it was going to be difficult to find a regular hotel this weekend. Jim frowned and said he didn't care what we did as long as he got to watch his game.

When we arrived at Cedar Grove, a thin, elegant man answered the door. "Of course we do not have a television," he said. "This is an *Antebellum mansion*, not a motel." Jim assumed an attitude of silent fury as he stalked into our antebellum room, put on his Walkman headphones, and spent the afternoon searching for scores in the Oklahoma-Nebraska game. Meanwhile Don and I showered, donned our khakis, and explored the house. It was filled with nineteenth-century opulence—crystal chandeliers, marble foyers, heavy velvet drapes, tall portraits in carved frames, lace doilies on mahogany tables, and ornate clocks. A plantation owner had built the mansion for his daughter, a woman I pictured in my mind as looking like Scarlett O'Hara in wide hoops and delicate curls. Elegant balls had been held here, even as the Civil War raged in the early days when the power and privilege of the South seemed supreme. But power and privilege can be fleeting. During the siege of Vicksburg, which lasted for six weeks, the house became a repository for starving, desperate graycoats trying to fend off a fleet of Union gunboats bombing the city from the river. When they finally gave up, more soldiers bivouacked in the mansion, but these had on blue coats and were led by General Ulysses Grant, who commandeered the downstairs bedroom for his own use.

I ended up in the mansion's library that evening, searching through leather-bound volumes collected over a hundred years. I found an encyclopedia published in the 1880s. Looking up India, I read about the glories of the British raj and the Maharajas. One smudgy photo showed Englishmen in white suits and waxed mustaches being toted about in a litter carried by turbaned Indian servants. Another shot showed a troop on safari being carried by elephants. It seemed appropriate to be studying these photographs in the Cedar Grove library. The faces of the English were proud and confident of their supremacy, a pride and confidence replicated in the painted faces hanging in this mansion. Like the Old South, the raj had been built on a system of privilege and arrogance that seemed invincible, yet both had fallen. In a sense, this was a major lesson of the trip—that history, or fate, is ultimately the great equalizer. We had seen a dozen civilizations lying in ruins. "Nothin' nowhere stays the same," said the old man at the Mound plantation. "Everthin' passes away."

The next morning an intense rainstorm began falling just outside of Vicksburg. A steady stream of traffic kicked up muck for hours as we pedaled up and down gradual hills and tried to navigate the crumbling, cracked edge of the highway's shoulder. Several times it deteriorated into gravel. We each had a flat, which we had to repair in the cold rain. After a few miles of this, we were all furious at the rain, the traffic, and the road.

As lightning and thunder cracked across the sky, we finally stopped at a run-down Stuckey's near Edwards, Mississippi. The owner, knowing that we were in a bind, charged us twenty-five dollars for a room with a rain-soaked carpet and roaches crawling around the bathroom. We bought canned pork and beans, eggs, bread, and beer at a convenience store across the street. Firing up the stoves in our room, we cooked dinner and watched an early *Dirty Harry* movie on TV. "Die, punk," Harry kept telling the sleazy guys he blew away with his .44.

This became a typical day as we sped across the South toward Atlanta. Following U.S. 80, we passed through cities like Jackson and Meridian in Mississippi and Selma and Montgomery in Alabama. Some of these cities had special meaning for us. My great-great-grandfather had been the first mayor of Meridian in the early 1800s, and Selma and Montgomery were cities we had read about in textbooks describing the civil rights battles of the 1960s. The smaller cities and towns had a mixture of Indian, Spanish, and English names—Pelahatchte, Morton, Kalem, Forest, Toomsuba, Cuba, Demopolis, Prairieville, Uniontown, Short, and Tuskogee.

The landscape was mostly rolling countryside that shifted back and forth between fields and forestland. On breaks we continued to play video games and drink can after can of Mountain Dew. In Selma I had my best game of Centipede—78,543. After Selma I stopped playing Centipede for a while, because hitting the "fire" button was starting to hurt my left hand. As Don said, this was an injury I could only have gotten in America.

In Atlanta, Welcome World Bikers posters hung on the front door, over the garage, and across the living room in my grandmother DeeDee's house. Spread out across her dining room table were silver trays brimming with roast turkey, sweet potatoes, cranberry jam, and stuffing. Cool glasses of wine glistened in the soft candlelight. As we ate, DeeDee beamed. "It's so wonderful to have you boys here!" she said. "This is the best Thanksgivin' I've ever had." She held our hands and bowed her head. "Dear Lord," she said, "it's just past Thanksgivin', but I don't think You'll mind if I offer You thanks for everything we've got here. Delivering these fine boys to my home has been the greatest blessing an old grandmother could ask for. You watched and protected them around the world, and for that we're all as grateful as we can be. Amen."

"Amen," we said as DeeDee squeezed our hands and smiled, her eyes full of happiness.

After supper we set up a slide projector and loaded Don's slides in a tray. Wrapped in an old quilt, DeeDee watched with a wide grin that bunched up a face full of wrinkles she calls "character lines." ("I feel so sorry for you folks with smooth faces," she says. "You've got no character!") Don started the show with slides introducing each of us—Jim was looking through his binoculars for birds in Malaysia, I was typing in a straw Philippine hut on Cebu Island, and Don was snapping photos of a Moslem cemetery in Pakistan. Other slides showed campsites on the Sinai and in Nepal, cooking gruel in Egypt, sipping tea on the Lake Nasser boat, visiting with the Afghan *mujahadeen* on Munir Shah's estate in Punjab, and on and on.

"I just can't believe it," DeeDee said. "Did you boys really bicycle in those places?"

"We sure did," I said, putting my arm around her frail shoulders. I noticed that a tear was running down her wrinkled cheek. "What's wrong, Deed?" I asked.

"I just wish your granddad was here to see this," she said. "He'd be so doggone proud of you, he'd be bustin'."

We took two days off in Atlanta, enjoying DeeDee's food, stories, and attention. "You boys really need to be spoiled by a grandmother," she said, and she was right. It was a loving, refreshing two days. We didn't try to get much publicity, although the *Atlanta Constitution* and a couple of radio stations interviewed us at a local Rotary meeting. I worked a little bit on fine-tuning a couple of my articles and made a few calls, but most of the time we rested. DeeDee told us bedtime stories about her childhood in Texas and about my mother when she was a little girl. She tucked us in at night and made tea and biscuits in the morning. She even made Jim feel like part of the family, which he greatly appreciated. "I'll be your grandma, too," said DeeDee, "since you don't have one here right now."

"You can be my grandmother any time," Jim told her, turning on his charm, which I hadn't seen in weeks.

On our last day in Atlanta, a card arrived at DeeDee's from

Laura. On the phone we had been seesawing back and forth for days about living together. I had decided that if it were up to me, we should live together, but she was still hesitant. I tore open the card and found Laura's final decision enclosed. It was a little children's book called *Monster, Will You Come Live with Me?* I immediately called her. "I love you," I said, feeling a tremendous sense of relief. After all of my worrying, I had not lost Laura. We were going to be together after the trip!

Blasting out of Atlanta on a warm, clear morning, we felt a sudden enthusiasm for biking. It seemed incredible that we were almost finished with our long ordeal. We were about 650 miles from Washington. For the first time in weeks the three of us felt like a team again. We sang songs, told jokes, and had long discussions on the bikes. In Athens, Georgia, home of the University of Georgia, we drank cappuccinos at the bar where the B-52's got started. In Elberton, Georgia—"where everyone is someone"—we stopped to have Cokes with some guys who cut and carved tombstones for the Boyd Granite Company. "That looks like hard work," I said to a big black man named Ricky Hamm. He was cutting huge slabs of blue bird granite into squares.

"Sure, it's damn hard work," said Ricky. "But it's a good job."

Near Elberton we stopped to help a black man and a white man chasing an old cow. "She cain't see," said the white man, "so when she gets away from the barn, she spooks." The cow was wailing and jerking to the left and right between a large barn and a stretch of woods. Jim and I hopped a fence yelling "Over there, Bossy," trying to force the cow toward the men. When they finally lassoed the poor beast, they came up and shook our hands with rugged, sweaty palms. "You sho' enough came along at the right time," said the black man.

In Calhoun Falls, South Carolina, we met a wrinkled man in a straw hat selling fireworks. Buying a dozen bottle rockets and smoke bombs, we shot them at each other at quiet spots on U.S. 72. Other roadside stands sold fruit and junk ranging from car parts to old clothes. For some reason nearly every town had a trampoline for sale. It was usually in the middle of a vacant lot with a big sign on it: For Sale, Good Price.

Everything seemed to be going better than it had for weeks. It was sunny, and we were making more than our scheduled mileage. Every flat tire or equipment breakdown was repaired quickly with all hands helping. I don't know why we had this second wind so late in the trip. It felt like the first days in Europe, when everything was fresh. But this harmony was short-lived. In fact, it ended abruptly just after breakfast one morning in Greenwood, South Carolina, about 180 miles northeast of Atlanta.

The temperature was dropping quickly that morning, so we spent extra time at a Greenwood diner while the sun heated things up. After eating eggs and bacon, we slowly donned our cold weather clothes, climbed onto the bikes, and began pedaling single file out of town. Don, in the lead, shouted "Slowing!" as he slipped a cassette tape into his Walkman. I pulled back on my brakes as a school bus rushed by just inches away. Then, suddenly, Don's front wheel fell into a rain grate in the road. As if in slow motion, his bike flipped high above the road, throwing my brother against the pavement as the bike reeled around to clatter down on top of him. I slammed on my brakes as the bus veered to the left to avoid crushing Don. I felt Jim crash into my rear, and then I was in the air, rolling with my bike onto the sidewalk.

I quickly jumped up and ran to Don, lying still under his bike. Jim and I pulled the bike away. "Did you break anything?" I asked anxiously. He was breathing heavily and holding his side. Blood dripped down his arm.

"Don't know," he gasped. "My side is killing me, and my arm."

"Can you move?"

He struggled to get up, with Jim and me helping. "Yow!" he screamed. "Watch the arm." Jim helped him off the street, and I ran over to a gas station to call an ambulance. A dispatcher asked me how serious the injuries were.

"He's walking around," I said. "I think he hurt his side and his arm." The dispatcher suggested that I call a taxi. Leaving the bikes at the gas station, we took a cab over to the Greenwood hospital and checked Don into the emergency room.

"He's broken his elbow and badly bruised some ribs," a bald doctor with square glasses told me an hour later in an examination room. Don lay back on a table with a large foam cast on his arm and bandages strapped around his chest. "We've got him in a temporary cast until the swelling goes down," the doctor said, adding that it would be several weeks before Don could bicycle or even use his left arm.

"I'm sorry," Don said to me from the table. "I guess I did it again." He smiled weakly.

"Don, it's okay," I said. "As I said in Bangkok, we're just lucky it didn't happen out in the middle of Sudan."

"But Dave," he said, smiling, "they don't *have* rain grates in Sudan."

Later that day we put Don and his smashed bike onto a bus to Columbia, South Carolina, where we had reserved a flight to Washington, D.C. Scott Patton would be there to pick him up.

"Can I trust you guys to behave?" Don asked us while the Greyhound people loaded his bike into the storage compartment of the bus.

"It'll be hard," I said, "but we've only got seven days to go."

Jim and I pedaled almost ninety miles the next day, traveling back roads to Chester, South Carolina. In the sunshine we split apart and enjoyed a ride through the quiet, rolling forestland of the Sumter National Forest. Despite Don's accident, we remained in high spirits. We were almost finished!

Much of the land in this part of South Carolina was covered by a thick leafy fern called kudzu. The stuff grew everywhere, engulfing abandoned houses, yards full of junk, and car lots. "They brought this ole kudzu stuff in durin' the Depression," a gas station man told us in Catawba Lake, South Carolina. "It was brung in from Japan to keep the ground from blowin' away." He chuckled, looking at a building across the road buried in mats of kudzu. "It sure as hell done its job," he said.

With Don's Nikons, I bugged Jim all day by stopping to take photos of anything I could find that was interesting. But he didn't mind. We were in great moods, and it gave him time to sneak in a few bird sightings. At one point, I think it was in Carlisle, South Carolina, I stopped to take photos of a pre–Civil War mansion. A historic marker told us that Jefferson Davis had slept in this house. Later I took photos of Christmas decorations in Chester and of big signs that said: No Trespassing, Property of R. J. Reynolds. It wasn't until I opened my camera to change film that I realized I had no film in either of Don's Nikons. Jim thought this was so funny he called Don in Washington to tell him.

From Chester, Jim and I flew across North Carolina, covering the 132 miles from border to border in just a day and morning of riding. It seemed like nothing could stop us, until the weather started turning bad near the Virginia border. The sun and warmth began fading as clouds and scattered drizzle moved over the Middle Atlantic seaboard. As the sunshine disappeared, so did our high spirits. In a sudden shift of moods, the anxiety we had sometimes felt before Atlanta swept over us with the suddenness of an ocean squall. As the winds gathered and the rain soaked into our clothes, five days started to look like forever.

We crossed the Virginia border at dusk on December 11, biking into the gray, industrial city of Danville in a freezing rain. It was a depressing ride. The first two hotels we tried were filled up. Riding a couple miles out of our way, we finally found a hotel called the Red Carpet. The Arab manager was friendly, especially when we greeted him with "Asalame." But when we asked him about taking the bikes into our room, he said, "No way! You are not taking those filthy bicycles into my room!" We told him that every hotel in the world had let us keep our bikes in our room. "I do not care! You will not put them in my room!"

It took a half hour in the freezing rain to find another hotel, an expensive place with a facade of flagstone and colored lights, a pool, and a small disco. They didn't mind if we took our bikes in our room, as long as we put down newspapers. That night, we took long, hot showers and tried to squeeze ourselves into the miniature tub to take baths. "I'd give a million yen for a Japanese bath right now," said Jim.

From Danville we had four days to bike 269 miles through the Blue Ridge Mountains to Washington, where project HOPE was planning a large homecoming ceremony on Capitol Hill. Even with perfect weather this distance was a challenge for two weary bikers. It was critical that we have no headwinds or cold weather, and only minimal rain or moisture. When we woke up at dawn on December 12 in Danville, all our worst fears were materializing outside our motel window. Snow blew hard through the parking lot, piling up in foot-high drifts against walls, cars, and bushes. When I turned on the TV, a local newscaster told us a large front of snow and heavy winds had been passing through southern Virginia since midnight. To top it off, Jim and I both woke up with clogged sinuses, runny noses, and headaches. Switching off the TV, we set our Casio alarms for nine A.M., slipped back into our warm beds, and went back to sleep.

At ten A.M. the snow slowed down. We took several Halls

Mentholyptus tablets, bundled up in every piece of clothing we owned, and tried to pedal through the snow. Fortunately, the snow was wet and slushy, not icy. A biker can pedal in almost any weather but ice. Tractors had cleared most of the roads, but not the shoulders. We were forced to ride in the narrow, wet, slippery lane next to trucks and cars flinging mist and filth against us. After a couple of miles, we decided it was suicide to keep biking. Stopping in a Sirloin Stockade Steak House, we drank coffee and had a second breakfast, hoping that the road conditions would improve. Near the Sirloin Stockade was a Big Ben discount store, where Jim bought a box of large Baggies for our feet.

By one o'clock the storm was clearing. The sun began shining in patches against the snowy white world. Reluctantly we put back on our layers of clothes, including three Baggies on each foot. Looking like blimps, we turned into a strong, freezing head wind. A bank thermometer read twenty-nine degrees. As trucks scattered flares of slush, we pedaled along the shoulderless highway. It was dangerous, if not stupid, to be riding under these conditions, but we had to make some distance if we were ever going to make Washington on time.

We could only bear to ride for twenty-five minutes at a stretch that afternoon. The bone-deep cold began by numbing our feet and hands and then quickly moved into arms and shoulders. When our legs became heavy and stiff with cold, we stopped in diners to drink steamy cups of coffee and hot chocolate. "You boys are just plain loco to be out in this weather," was a typical comment at these diners. When we told them why we were out, we almost always got our coffee free.

Our pace in the cold was so slow that we covered only twenty-five miles before nightfall. The sun set golden and orange over the white world, reflecting in bright, fiery colors off the snow outlining tree limbs, power lines and rooftops. Warm smoke poured out of chimneys in the Virginia countryside, scenting the air with burning cedar. Black horses behind picket fences snorted white steam and raced back and forth to keep warm. Almost like a miracle, we discovered a small motor lodge in the middle of rural Virginia. The hotel manager was so surprised to see us she provided a room free of charge. She also volunteered to toss our wet clothes into her drier. That night I called Scott.

"Are you guys gonna make it?" he asked nervously. "We've

got everything set for the sixteenth. We've even got Tip O'Neill to meet you and most of the sponsors are flying people in for the ceremony. What if you don't make it?"

"As long as we don't hit serious ice, we can bike in this stuff," I said, "but it'll be close."

As if on cue, when we woke up the next morning, the wet slush on the road had hardened into long patches of black ice. A thermometer outside our room said seventeen degrees. We got dressed in our fluffy, dry clothes and pushed the bikes across the street to a little diner for breakfast. It was ten A.M. before the sun had melted the ice enough for us to bike. As it was, we each slipped several times, tumbling off our bikes into the crusty snow piled along the highway. But we were too bundled up to get hurt.

The foothills of the Blue Ridge Mountains spread out around us, a dazzling world of white, but the biking was miserable. As the day progressed, the frequent rest stops got longer and longer. As we bundled up after one long stop, Jim started laughing.

"What's so funny?" I asked.

"I was thinking about Sudan. Remember how hot it was? We prayed for cold." I smiled too, recalling the baking, debilitating heat. I remembered my burned skin, my parched tongue, and the flash-dried carcasses of dead animals along the road.

Somehow we managed to bike fifty-eight miles that day, to Amherst, Virginia. When I called Scott, he was frantic. "There's no way in hell you guys are gonna make it," he said. "I've got press releases out, parties planned, entertainment lined up. . . . How could you do this to me?"

"Scott," I said, "put Don on." My brother was with him at the HOPE headquarters in Washington. "Don, tell Scott that we've got two days to bike 156 miles. It can be done."

"In the snow?" asked Don.

"As long as we don't get any more ice, we will make it," I said. He asked me if Jim agreed with my assessment.

"As usual, Don, I don't share your brother's optimism," Jim told him, "but you know how stubborn we midwesterners are when we put our minds to it. Barring any further catastrophes, we should make it."

The next morning, December 14, the thermometer outside our motel said seven degrees. We waited until the temperature rose to fourteen before starting. After a couple of rest stops, I scrawled a note into my journal. "Bitterly cold," I wrote. "Faces and any exposed flesh in pain. Using bandanas for facemasks. Feet nearly frostbitten. I seriously doubt that we can go on much longer."

In the town of Covesville, Virginia, we decided to stop for the day. It seemed pointless to go on. Jim was losing the feeling in his feet and hands, and my stuffed-up head felt like someone had grabbed it in both hands and was squeezing as hard as he could. I called Scott to tell him that we couldn't bike anymore unless it warmed up some. He said to keep him posted.

Then something strange happened. The temperature started rising. As we slowly downed hot coffee and ate a round of greasy burgers and fries, a thermometer outside the Covesville diner slowly rose. When it hit thirty-two degrees, we decided to try biking again. I called back Scott. "We're going to go for it," I said. "It seems to be getting warmer."

"How far do you have to go?" asked Don, also on the line.

"About 130 miles," I said. "If we can do another 30 today, that'll leave 100 for tomorrow. We've done that before."

"Yeah, when it was warm and flat and there was no traffic," said Don.

"We'll do it," I said, "if it kills us, which it probably will."

We got back on the bikes. The temperature kept rising as the sun dried the slush off the roads. In Charlottesville, Virginia, we stripped off our Gore-Tex shells and removed the Baggies from our feet. It was still cold, but the sun was warm and the roads were drying out. We rushed north, riding as far as we could until darkness forced us to stop in a shabby truck stop near Ruckersville, Virginia. Still ninety-four miles short of Washington, we lay back in our room as semis roared below. Before falling asleep, I called Laura to tell her it was almost over. "If everything goes right tomorrow," I told her, "this will be my last night on the road."

"Could it really be finished?" she asked.

After talking to Laura, I made what I hoped would be the last journal entry of the trip. *"Our last night on the road!!!!"* I wrote. "I can't believe it. Neither can Jim. We're ninety-four miles from D.C., but we'll make it. I feel an overwhelming happiness. In three or four days, I can relax. *No more biking.*" I turned the page and stared at the white, empty space. Then I wrote the last words in my World Bike for HOPE journal.

"In a few days, my life begins again . . ."

The next morning, we left the truck stop at dawn, determined to make it to Washington or die trying. The temperature rose to fifty degrees as we sped across the rolling hills of northern Virginia, but it began dropping again toward noon. By three it was down to thirty-five degrees as another rainstorm moved in. But nothing was going to stop us. We passed through Warrenton, New Baltimore, Gainesville, the Manassas National Battlefield, and Fairfax in a steady drizzle. Toward the middle of Fairfax, a suburb of Washington, the sun set as we pedaled in a steady spray of water and muck through the heavy traffic. It was a harrowing ride. We had no lights, and our reflector vests were covered with mud. But we kept on, finally pedaling into the quiet residential area of Arlington, Virginia, where Laura Schultz, our homecoming organizer, was putting us up for the night. Tomorrow we would pedal the few miles left to the U.S. Capitol for our homecoming ceremony. As we turned in to Laura's driveway, Don, Laura, and Scott dashed outside into the rain to greet us. Don gave me a big hug, wincing as I squeezed his ribs. Laura, a big, vivacious woman, gave us each a kiss. Then I turned around to face Jim. We were both filthy with mud and grime.

"We made it, you jerk," I said. He grinned and held out his hand. I took it firmly in my gloved palm and shook it hard.

"Welcome home, Dave," he said. We stood there, our arms interlocked for almost a minute before Laura interrupted us.

"I've got to tell you all about the publicity tomorrow. . . ."

The next morning Jim and I slipped into brand-new World Bike for HOPE T-shirts, strapped on our helmets, adjusted our rearview mirrors, and took off on our battered bikes for the last time on this long journey. Don, Scott, and Laura followed us in a HOPE van. It had looked like rain that morning, but as we pulled away from Arlington toward the Potomac, the clouds suddenly blew away. Sunshine illuminated the streets of Washington as we biked to the Lincoln Memorial. Almost forty bikers were waiting to escort us down Constitution Avenue, including Dave French. He was riding his Fuji from the trip and wearing his World Bike for HOPE T-shirt. "I never thought I'd see this day," he said. "You guys actually made it!" We shook his hand, talked to a few reporters, and then took off toward the Capitol, back to where it had all begun so long ago.

In the bright sunshine we took over a whole lane of traffic on Constitution Avenue. The ride was like a dream. Blood roared through my head as I turned my pedals and watched the grand, gleaming monuments of America's capital city pass by. The Washington Monument, the Jefferson Memorial in the distance, the White House, and the museums of the Smithsonian. Passing down the mall, I saw the great dome of the United States Capitol and the huge American flag waving high above it. Even in my most cynical moments, these sights had always seemed a bit larger than life. Now, after being away for so long, I was almost moved to tears.

Many friends were waiting for us on the Hill. My uncle Bob, who had first shared this dream with me; my mother and father, who had suffered with us over these past months; and John Walsh of Project HOPE, who had made the expedition possible. The only person missing was Laura. She was waiting for me in New York. I would join her in our apartment in two days, after all of the hoopla of our homecoming had died down, so that we could begin our new life together.

Our new life together. Those were frightening words, because I had no idea what was coming next. But I was finished. Finished! I was poised at one of those moments in life when a chapter closes in a story that does not yet have an ending, and another chapter is about to begin. I felt the immense satisfaction of having initiated a grand design and finished it; of having crafted something and shaped it, although I had no idea what I had shaped. I knew that the man standing under the Capitol on that sunny December day was a different person from the twenty-three-year-old kid who had left those steps 380 days earlier. But it would be months, maybe years before I would understand what it had meant to pedal the ends of the earth.

Afterword:
A Small Planet

Sometimes I dream about India. Flies buzz in oppressive clouds. The heat is drenching and filthy. Faces brush past, lost souls fed by TV images of starving children and raving mobs. I cry out.

"Dave," comes a voice incongruous with nightmares. "Dave, it's a dream." My eyes pop open. My wife is silhouetted in the pale light of our bedroom. One of the dogs groans, still asleep beside the bed. Outside the stars pierce brilliant holes in the sub-zero skies of Vermont. These are the same stars, sprayed across the night since Eden, that watch Indian holy men chant Vedas half a world away.

I resist overly romantic recollections about my year abroad, although these memories long ago crowded out the nightmares. I remember the sun shimmering in watery waves above the Sahara. Butterflies glow phosphorescent in the dusky jungles of Borneo. The characters in the book have taken on a larger than life dimension, frozen in time. Khalil, the Palestinian, stands proudly in his *kaffiyeh* headgear and his dreams of college in America. Bedja tribesmen from Sudan ride giant camels and raise curved swords. Abdul, the self-proclaimed sexiest man in the world, remains an obnoxious boy begging me for

267

the contraband centerfold of a *Playboy* magazine.

It takes a nightmare for me to remember the misery. Not my own misery. That was at best temporary and only worth recalling because it begins to describe the suffering I observed among those who have no house in Vermont, no Cuisinart, no rock albums. It seems absurdly lucky to have been born in America during the twentieth century. My friends and I are pursuing careers in business, law, medicine, writing, and music, largely oblivious to the fluke in history that has created our tiny, precarious niche on this small planet.

I have settled into the comforts of rural Vermont. Laura is training to be a doctor. We live near an Ivy League campus where friends occasionally discuss India, Egypt, or the Philippines. They debate issues of rebellion, Marxism, and warfare. Somehow, because I was there, they think I can make sense out of a sudden headline. I mention the misery. They nod their heads in sympathy, but most of them do not understand. How can they? The suffering is too remote. I mention that Khalil, a beautiful, statuesque Arab, wants only peace. And Saer, the quiet, thoughtful Israeli. He wants only peace. Both fear a second Holocaust.

"Holocaust?" say my friends. "Isn't that too strong a word?"

I wrestle with the problem. Jim Logan has married and lives in a cabin deep in the interior of Maine. He and his wife met while tramping the forests in search of herons, warblers and marsh ducks. My brother Don, too, has married and lives in a cabin. His is near the shore of Maine, on a marshy cove covered in the winter with pancake slabs of ice that buckle daily with the tide.

In just two weeks I'm off on another adventure, this time in Africa. Jim Logan and I will cycle from Cape Town to Cairo in a meandering line from south to north. Jim seeks colorful plumage and midnight bird calls on the bush. In his gear is a telescope the size and shape of a bull rifle to gaze at stars and comets. I plan to collect tales for children yet to be born. We will pedal slowly on faraway highways, colleagues in an ancient search for explanations.

David Duncan
Norwich, Vermont
February 1986

Acknowledgments

This is a book with a cast of thousands. Top on the list are Don Duncan and Jim Logan, my compatriots for 380 days. It seems almost trivial to say that they made the trip and the book possible, because they did much more. They encouraged me, supported me, and put up with me. The three of us have shared moments of suffering and frustration, and moments of happiness and fulfillment. I have missed them since we finished the trip and went our separate ways. Dave French was also a great companion, especially in those long days preparing for the trip in Washington, D.C.

I would like to thank my family for their endless support and understanding. My mother and father lived through the fear of losing both their sons yet never stopped encouraging us to finish this journey and many others, past and future. Mr. and Mrs. Logan also deserve special mention for their support and encouragement. My grandparents gave us material and spiritual support. Without Grandfather Brown and his Kansas City friends, who raised money for us at a critical moment, the trip might have been aborted in Egypt.

I thank the newest member of our family, Laura, who recently became my wife. She not only put up with the trip, but also lived through it a second time as I wrote this book.

I thank the folks at Project HOPE: John Walsh and the Walsh family, the HOPE staffs in Millwood, Virginia, and in Cairo. I am grateful to my friends in Washington—Bud Litton, Kris Horne, Jim Craig, Mathew Murray, John and Lou Ellicott, Dick and Jane, Laura Schultz—and to the office of Senator John Danforth. Thanks also to Carol Massman and friends in Kansas City. Special thanks to Paul Zevnick (and to the firm of Paul, Hastings, Janofsky and Walker), Bob Hunter (of the National Insurance Consumer Organization), Michelle Lavine, and Scott Patton.

Thanks also go to Bob DuBose, my fellow dreamer; Dr. Burris Duncan, who made the dream possible; John Wallace, my Scottish mentor; Sandy and Jeanne Robertson, who provided support when we most needed it; Margi and Courtney Catron, who came to our aide in San Francisco and around the world; and Atsuko Sugahara, who made Japan a special place. For more recent help, I thank Pam Bernstein, Morgan Entrekin, John Herman, Jennifer Reich, Jim Stein, and Jacquie Saul, who made this book possible.

Another round of special thanks to our sponsors: Ken Moriya at Fuji Bicycles, Mark Graff at Eclipse, Dana Anderson at Eddie Bauer, Don Dougherty at Rotary International, Tom Todd and Beverly at American Express in Washington, D.C., Kate Burns at Miller Beer in Washington, D.C., Felicity Bliss at Hallmark, the Potomac Pedalers in Washington, the other sponsors and volunteers of the Washington Bike for HOPE and the Kansas City Bike for HOPE, and all the rest of the people who made the trip financially possible.

Finally, I am grateful to the world of people we met on the road—all the people who put us up, gave us directions, told us stories, and filled these pages with color and drama. I wish I could mention all of you by name, but you number in the hundreds. Many of you were nameless to us, contributing just a wave or a nod on a lonely road. A few people deserving special mention are the officers and staff of the U.S. embassies (especially the U.S. International Communications Agency) in France, Italy, Greece, Israel, Egypt, Sudan, Pakistan, India, Nepal, Thailand, Malaysia, Singapore, the Philippines, and Japan.

I also thank all the following: In Israel and the Occupied Territories, Khalil, the Ezyon Kibbutz, the Israeli army, and the Bedouins of the Sinai. In Egypt, Colonel Sukker of El Kantara and Achmed in Alexandria. In Sudan, Monsder, Gassame, Kirsi Gandhi, Peter of SUDAN NOW, the UN High Commission for Refugees in Gedaref, Lalamba (Gruffy, Megan, and Tweldeber-hum) in Showak, and the Red Sea Club in Port Sudan. In Paki-stan, the Karachi Press Club, the YMCA, the Faisibads in Hyderabad, the Sukker Rotoract Club, the Pakistani police, Abdul, Munir Shah Khan, Aurang, and the Lahore Hilton. In India, Nick Hanks, Beldev, and the Indian police. In Nepal, the Butwal Industrial Institute, the Slovicks, Shining Hospital, and Drona Shumshere Rana, Minister of Tourism. In Thailand, the British Hospital. In Malaysia, Doris Wong and the Malaysian police. In Singapore, Tom Tao at the Raffles. In Borneo, Francis Kong. In the Philippines, Dr. Anthony Riviera. In Japan, At-suko Sugahara and friends, Fuji Bicycle, Sony, SunTour, the Osaka Mayor's Office, the Tokyo Governor's Office, Motoharu Morishita, Minister of Health and Welfare, and the Japanese Diet. In America, the Houghtons, the Cettas, the Krugers, the Turpins and the Socorro Rotary Club, the Shreveport Rotary Club, the Atlanta Rotary Club, and everyone else along the way. Thanks!